The Human Firm

T0330702

The Human Firm challenges mainstream neoclassical perspectives on the firm. John F. Tomer argues that in an age of globalization and rapid technological change, understanding business behavior and government policy toward business requires an appreciation of the firm's human dimension. This book integrates economic analysis with sociological, psychological, managerial, ethical and other non-economic dimensions, enabling the reader to appreciate broad aspects of business behavior which are critical to understanding the new economic age in which we live.

John F. Tomer's socio-economic theory of the firm explains why some firms are adapting well to new economic realities and some are not. He explains why some firms adopt socially responsible ways and high performance organization, and some do not. This book focuses on what it means for firms to achieve their full contribution to society, and the typical gap between actual and potential performance. The neoclassical theory of the firm, while useful for understanding markets and allocative efficiency, largely ignores the human dimension. *The Human Firm* provides a fuller picture, integrating the concepts of organizational capital and human capital with the theory of the firm.

The Human Firm is very much in the socio-economic tradition, viewing economic actors as partially embedded in society. In this book, firms and other actors who are rationally striving to achieve their ends respond in part to economic incentives and in part to social influences. *The Human Firm* bridges the gap between classical theories of the firm and purely sociological approaches. It is written for socio-economists, particularly heterodox economists, economic sociologists or psychologists, and organizational behavior specialists.

John F. Tomer is Professor of Economics and Chairperson of the Department of Economics and Finance at Manhattan College, New York. He is the author of *Organizational Capital: The Path to Higher Productivity and Well-Being*. He is president and a founding member of the Society for the Advancement of Behavioral Economics.

Advances in Social Economics
Edited by John B. Davis
Marquette University

This series presents new advances and developments in social economics thinking on a variety of subjects that concern the link between social values and economics. Need, justice and equity, gender, cooperation, work, poverty, the environment, class, institutions, public policy, and methodology are some of the most important themes. Among the orientations of the authors are social economist, institutionalist, humanist, solidarist, cooperatist, radical and Marxist, feminist, post-Keynesian, behavioralist, and environmentalist. The series offers new contributions from today's most foremost thinkers on the social character of the economy.

Published in conjunction with the Association of Social Economics.

Books published in the series include:

Social Economics
Premises, Findings and Policies
Edited by Edward J. O'Boyle

The Environmental Consequences of Growth
Steady State Economics as an Alternative to
Ecological Decline
Douglas Booth

Economics for the Common Good
Two Centuries of Economic Thought in the
Humanist Tradition
M. Lutz

The Human Firm

A socio-economic analysis of its behavior and potential in a new economic age

John F. Tomer

Routledge
Taylor & Francis Group

LONDON AND NEW YORK

First published 1999
by Routledge

Simultaneously published in the USA and Canada
by Routledge

Published 2014 by Routledge

2 Park Square, Milton Park, Abingdon, Oxfordshire OX14 4RN

711 Third Avenue, New York, NY 10017

Routledge is an imprint of the Taylor and Francis Group, an informa business

First issued in paperback 2015

British Library Cataloguing in Publication Data
A catalogue record for this book is available from the British Library

Library of Congress Cataloging in Publication Data
The Human Firm: a socio-economic analysis of its behavior and
potential in a new economic age/John F. Tomer.
    Includes bibliographical references and index.
    1. Social responsibility of business. 2. Industries – Social aspects. 3.
    Industries – Environmental aspects. 4. Issues management. 5.
    Industrial sociology. 6. Human capital. I. Title.
HD60. T664   1999
98–35366
658.4'08–dc21
CIP

ISBN 978-0-415-19927-8 (hbk)
ISBN 978-1-138-86593-8 (pbk)
ISBN 978-0-230-45692-7 (eISBN)

Dedicated to
my two sons,
Russell
and
Jeffrey

Contents

Illustrations

Figures

About the author

John F. Tomer is currently Professor of Economics and Chairperson of the Department of Economics and Finance at Manhattan College, Riverdale, New York. He teaches introductory macroeconomics, public finance, a seminar on the Japanese economy, and a course on business, government, and society. His recent articles have appeared in the *Journal of Socio-Economics, Ecological Economics*, the *Review of Social Economy, Human Relations*, the *International Review of Applied Economics*, and a book entitled *Ethics and Economic Affairs* (Routledge 1994). His first book is *Organizational Capital: The Path to Higher Productivity and Well-being* (Praeger 1987).

Tomer is currently president and a founding member of the Society for the Advancement of Behavioral Economics. He is also an active member of the Society for the Advancement of Socio-Economics, the Association for Social Economics, and the Association for Evolutionary Economics. He believes that the discipline of economics can be improved greatly by integrating economic insights with the insights of other disciplines such as sociology, psychology, history, and philosophy. He also believes that the study of economics can benefit from incorporating humanistic and even spiritual perspectives (deriving from the religious and wisdom traditions of the East and West).

Tomer is very proud of his family of four including his wife, Doris, and sons, Russell and Jeffrey, now twenty-one and seventeen years old, who reside with him in Troy, New York. Tomer at age fifty-six is active in basketball, tennis, and skiing, among other sports, and still hopes to realize some of his unrealized potential in the latter two.

Preface

The Human Firm is intended to be a socio-economic theory of the business firm's behavior. It is economics, but not mainstream economics; it is economics that is integrated with the other social sciences. *The Human Firm* is very much in the socio-economic tradition because it views economic actors as partially embedded in society. This is in contrast to mainstream economists who tend to view actors as behaving independently, rationally, and entirely self-interestedly, i.e. unembedded in society. It is also in contrast to sociologists who tend to see actors as behaving entirely in accord with social norms, rules, and obligations, i.e. fully embedded in society. In this book, firms and other actors who are rationally striving to achieve their ends respond in part to economic incentives and in part to social influences. The concept of organizational capital is a key to understanding the firm's behavior. Using the organizational capital concept, one can understand (1) how social relationships influence actors and (2) how firms and other actors can utilize organization to attain their ends. Organizational capital will be familiar to many socio-economists as a type of social capital embodied in a variety of human relationships within and without the firm.

Sometimes, the behavior of the human firm reflects the higher side of human behavior including the ethical, moral, and spiritual aspects; at other times, it reflects the lower side. Human firms are potentially highly competitive and highly responsible. Unfortunately, as we know, it is rare for these potentials to be fully realized. This book will help us understand the nature of that human potential, why it is so often unrealized, and what can be done to raise the likelihood of that realization.

Acknowledgments

My research grows out of the heterodox economic tradition, a tradition that is very much alive and growing despite the current dominance of the main-stream economic orthodoxy. I feel very fortunate to have been encouraged and nourished by a great many behavioral economists, socio-economists, social economists, institutional economists, and others. These heterodox economists and I have similar visions of what economics could be if it were not dominated by the excessively mathematical mainstream that is so often divorced from economic reality and policy relevance. Intellectually, I continue to be indebted to and appreciate the intellectual foundation that Harvey Leibenstein built. For some time now, behavioral economics has been my professional home. Thus, it is important to recognize the help I have received from many of my fellow colleagues in the Society for the Advancement of Behavioral Economics (SABE). Shlomo Maital, SABE's founder, read a number of chapters and is a continuing source of encourage-ment and support. Morris Altman, who has worked closely with me on many SABE activities and has accompanied me on a fair number of European conference adventures, read the entire manuscript and has provided very helpful advice. As far back as I can remember, Dick Hattwick, a fellow founding member of SABE, has taken a special interest in my writ-ings. We seem to be on the same wavelength. Dick has published a significant number of my articles (before they became chapters) in his capacity as editor of the *Journal of Socio-Economics*. I especially appreciate the help he gave when I was first trying to publish this book. I also appre-ciate the support of Art Goldsmith who shares with me a strong interest in the connections between psychology and economics.

Romesh Diwan's good advice contributed greatly to the improvement of two chapters. His wife, Joyce Diwan, also helped by generously donating time to produce several figures with a computer graphics program. I value greatly the friendship and support that Romesh and Joyce have given me over the years. John Davis, who is editor of the *Review of Social Economy*, saw the value in an earlier version of Chapter 2 which was published in his journal. John also was particularly helpful in linking me up with Routledge and putting in a good word on my behalf at a critical time before I had a book contract. The attention and interest of Steve Piersanti, along with the comments of several readers he commissioned, led to a significant improvement in the manuscript. Mark Lutz, Ken Lux and I share an interest in the highest human potential and in developing a humanistic economics rather than an economics that is narrow and technical. I appreciate their past support and hope our paths continue to cross in the future. I have also benefited from the support and advice from Peter Boettke, Shoshana Grossbard-Shechtman, Roger McCain, Mark Pingle, and Rune Wigblad.

My greatest debt is to my wife, Doris. I appreciate greatly her love and the energy she devotes to holding our family together. She has shown great patience to stay with me despite my evolving enthusiasms, middle age, and occasional irritability. Lastly, I want to mention my two talented sons, Russell and Jeffrey. As far as I can tell, they have not yet discovered a strong interest in economics (not to mention behavioral economics), but I suspect that one day they will.

Credits

Chapter 2

John F. Tomer, "The Social Causes of Economic Decline: Organizational Failure and Redlining," *Review of Social Economy*, vol. 50, no. 1, 1992, pp. 61–81.

Chapter 3

John F. Tomer, "Organizational Capital and Joining Up: Linking the Individual to the Organization and to Society," *Human Relations*, vol. 51, no. 6, 1998, pp. 825–46.

Chapter 4

John F. Tomer, "Rational Organizational Decision Making in the Human Firm: A Socio-Economic Model," *Journal of Socio-Economics*, vol. 21, no. 2, 1992, pp. 85–107.

Chapter 5

John F. Tomer, "Strategy and Structure in the Human Firm: Beyond Hierarchy, Toward Flexibility and Integration," *Journal of Socio-Economics*, vol. 24, no. 3, 1995, pp. 411–31.

Chapter 6

John F. Tomer, "Beyond the Machine Model of the Firm, Toward a Holistic Human Model," *Journal of Socio-Economics*, vol. 27, no.3, 1998, pp. 323–40.

Chapter 7

John F. Tomer, "Social Responsibility in the Human Firm: Towards a New Theory of the Firm's External Relationships," in Alan Lewis and Karl-Erik Warneryd (eds), *Ethics and Economic Affairs* (London: Routledge, 1994), pp. 125–47.

Chapter 8

John F. Tomer, "The Human Firm in the Natural Environment: A Socio-Economic Analysis of its Behavior," *Ecological Economics*, vol. 6, 1992, pp. 119–38.

Chapter 9

John F. Tomer, "Beyond Transaction Markets, Toward Relationship Marketing in the Human Firm: A Socio-Economic Model," *Journal of Socio-Economics*, vol.27, no. 2, 1998, pp. 207–28.

Chapter 10

John F. Tomer, "A New Rationale for Industrial Policy: Developing the Capabilities of the Learning Firm," *International Review of Applied Economics*, vol. 7, no. 2, 1993, pp. 208–22. Published by Carfax (PO Box 25, Abingdon, Oxfordshire OX14 3UE, United Kingdom).

1 Introduction

Why a theory of the human firm is needed

In an age of global competition and rapidly changing technology and management, understanding business behavior and government policy toward business requires, more than ever, an appreciation of the firm's human dimensions, the dimensions left out of the neoclassical theory of the firm (and its extensions). *The Human Firm*, through its integration of economic analysis with sociological, psychological, managerial, ethical and other non-economic dimensions of firm behavior, will enable readers to understand aspects of business behavior that are critical to appreciating the new economic age in which we live.

Differences among firms abound. Some firms are adapting well to the new economic realities; in others, economic performance is suffering. Some firms have chosen socially responsible ways which are in harmony with their social and natural environments; others have not. Some firms have adopted strategies and structures allowing them to respond in an integrated, flexible way to change; others have not. Some firms deal with problems requiring decisions in a highly rational way; others do not. Some firms have developed long-lasting, authentic partnerships with their customers; others have not. Some firms, through leadership, create workplaces that elevate their members' lives; others do not. Why do some firms live up to their human potentials while other firms fail to do so? The neoclassical theory of the firm, while useful for understanding markets and allocative efficiency, allows us little insight into these matters. Thus, *The Human Firm* will focus on (1) what it means for firms to achieve their full potential contribution to society and (2) the typical gap between actual and potential performance. In doing so, this book will integrate the concepts of organizational capital and human capital with the theory of the firm more completely than has been done heretofore.

What do we mean by the word "human" in *The Human Firm*? First, we do not mean humane. The word humane connotes mankind's capacity to be kind, tender, merciful and sympathetic, and is far too limited for our purposes. The essence of what it is to be human has been considered by the philosopher Mortimer Adler (1985: 161–3). He finds that while actual human conditions and behavior vary greatly around the world, what is common to all humans are the qualities representing our highest human potential, not just our potential for humaneness. These qualities generally correspond to those of a person who could be described as fully human, self-actualized, or psychologically healthy, to use the words of Abraham Maslow (see, for example, Maslow 1971). On the other hand, another important aspect of human nature is fallibility, the propensity to fail to accomplish what could be accomplished and to fail to be what we could be. The analyses of the human firm in this book are designed to help us understand behaviors that represent the highest human potential in a business context as well as behaviors representing the all-too-human failure to realize that potential. In contrast, in neoclassical economics, human behavior in firms is depicted one-dimensionally as economically rational. There is little in the neoclassical literature that reflects the highest qualities of human nature or, for that matter, the lower ones.

Organizational capital

To understand more about the proposed theory of the human firm, it is necessary to explain about the essence of the organizational capital concept. Organizational capital is a kind of human capital in which productive capacity is embodied in the organizational relationships among people; it is not simply embodied in individuals, as in the case of human capital deriving from education. Investment in organizational capital means using up resources in order to bring about lasting improvement in organizational relationships, and thereby, improving productivity, worker well-being and social performance. The development of high-quality organizational relationships makes possible and brings out the best in human nature (Tomer 1987).

Precisely because it is embodied in social relationships, organizational capital is also a kind of social capital. Social capital is a term that has been used, typically by economic sociologists, not simply to refer to productive capacity but more generally to denote a resource that enables actors to accomplish their ends (see, for example, Coleman 1988). The firm's social or organizational capital formation reflects (1) the degree to which, and the manner in which, the firm's actors have become socially connected to each other and to the organization as a whole, and (2) the degree to which, and the manner in which, the firm has become connected to society. Emphasizing that organizational capital is a type of social capital helps us bear in mind that economic production processes are inherently social in nature and that the firm is at least partially embedded in society.

Organizational capital can be considered a factor in the production function. In the conventional production function, the potential or maximum output is determined by the endowments of inputs such as land, tangible capital, labor, human capital and the state of technological knowledge.

Typically, actual output is much less than potential output; that is, the gap between potential and actual output is typically positive and substantial. This output gap reflects internal inefficiency in firms, or what Harvey Leibenstein has called X-inefficiency. Internal inefficiency comes from slack in production, which reflects such things as low worker effort and best business practices not being used. Actual output can be explained by both the factor endowments and the degree of inefficiency. If it were not for the inefficiency, the actual output produced from these factors would have equaled the potential output.

An enterprise's X-inefficiency reflects the state of its organization and management, that is, the amount and appropriateness or quality of its investment in organizational capital. Thus, organizational capital, a factor heretofore missing, should be included in the corrected production function. A firm's organizational capital endowment is inversely related to its internal inefficiency. This follows from the presumption that firms devote time, energy and resources to changing their organizational relationships in order to decrease internal inefficiency, i.e. to reduce the output gap. The greater this investment in organizational capital, the less the inefficiency. Obviously, in some cases, it may not work out this way if the organizational innovation fails.

The organizational relationships in which businesses and governments invest, like other aspects of reality, are both hard and soft. Hard attributes are tangible, physical, measurable, capable of being expressed in mathematical relationships, visible and explicit. Soft attributes are the opposite to the above and involve less definite, immeasurable and holistic aspects of the world. The right hemisphere of the brain is said to be better at appreciating the softer aspects, and the left hemisphere is better equipped for dealing with the hard aspects. Financial relationships, ownership and organizational structure (hierarchy) are relatively hard; whereas enthusiasm, fairness, kindness, harmony and compassion are relatively soft.

To illustrate the hard and soft aspects of organizations, consider the organizational relationships that are part of the Mondragón producer cooperatives in the Basque region of Spain. A unique feature of Mondragón's organization is their legal structure involving workers' voting rights, their rights to the economic profit, and their rights to the net book value of the cooperative. These are relatively hard aspects. In contrast, Mondragón is also notable for some of its soft qualities such as the spirit of cooperation and solidarity that has been developed in these cooperatives.

To appreciate the nature of organizational capital, it should be noted that the flow of organizational capital investment adds to the stock of organizational capital. Flows, of course, are amounts per time period, whereas stocks are amounts that exist at one point in time. It is useful to distinguish between quantitative stocks and qualitative stocks. Economists have largely concerned themselves with quantitative stocks such as the money supply or tangible capital goods. When, for example, there is a change in the money supply during the year (flow), the money supply at the end of the year (stock) differs from what it was at the beginning. Similarly, annual investment (flow) changes the stock of tangible capital goods (technology given). In the case of quantitative stocks, the flows can be positive or negative, and thus, the stocks can increase or decrease in a fully reversible way.

Similarly, flows change the value of qualitative stocks, but in this case the stocks correspond to human relationships and qualities that change in ways that are at least partially irreversible. When, for example, a person spends money on educational activity (flow), one's stock of human capital involving new human capacities is increased. To the extent that education changes the person's thinking, knowledge or appreciations, the qualitative character of this person has changed irreversibly, hopefully for the better. Whenever technological and organizational change occur, there is an investment (flow) process that changes irreversibly the qualitative stocks of tangible and intangible capital. For example, if the formal organizational structure along with established paths of communication were changed, it would be unlikely that the organization could ever return exactly to its original situation. Presumably, the intangible or human types of capital are less reversible than the tangible types. Economists, I believe, have paid too little attention to the qualitative nature of such stocks, which are important to the functioning of the economy. This is especially true for the soft aspects of these stocks. Because organizational capital is a qualitative stock which has as many or more soft qualities as hard ones, it is easy to see why economists have overlooked it.

From the above, one can begin to appreciate how in a human theory of the firm, the organizational capital concept plays a central role as a unifying concept. It allows us to link hard and soft aspects of organizational relationships to many aspects of the firm's economic and social performance. It allows us to think clearly about organizational innovation, what needs to be done to bring out the highest potential in people, and what role the government might play in this process. Simultaneously, it allows us to think systematically and clearly about organizations, and it fosters the compassionate and loving side of our nature with respect to our attitudes toward people at work. It helps erect a conceptual bridge between, on the one hand, humanistic, intuitive, even spiritual visions of what business firms could be and, on the other hand, the logical, left-brained theoretical apparatus of orthodox theory. Such bridges may make possible more coherent discussions between heterodox and orthodox economists about the nature of the firm.

Towards a new understanding of the firm's behavior

How does a firm behave when confronted with alternative courses of action? Will the firm pollute or engage in pollution prevention activity? Will the firm organize itself internally to meet its long-run competitive challenges, or not? Will the firm in its relationship to customers choose to be a long-term partner, or simply choose to be a short-term transactor, viewing each separate sale as the desired end? The models of firm behavior developed in this book provide answers that are in sharp contrast with those of neoclassical economic theory.

The neoclassical model

In the neoclassical model, the firm is assumed to have perfect knowledge of alternative courses of action and to choose the alternative that maximizes its current period profit. The neoclassical firm's decision makers are obligated only to the owners, the recipients of profit. External social influences or responsibilities are not a part of this model, nor are internal relationships or ethical considerations. Of course, if the firm fails to consider the external costs (costs imposed on others) of its actions in its decision making, leading to an inefficient resource allocation, the firm may be regulated by governmental entities. The latter may impose explicit regulatory incentives on the firm to counter the problematic market incentives. In this case, the neoclassical firm's behavior will be determined by the combination of market and regulatory incentives. Figure 1.1 depicts these determinants of the firm's behavior.

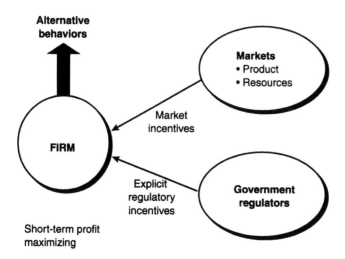

Figure 1.1   Neoclassical model of the firm's behavior

An overview of the socio-economic model

A general version of the model

This book develops a socio-economic model of the firm's behavior that is quite different from the neoclassical model. The socio-economic model's broad outlines in abbreviated form, i.e. a general version of the model, are considered in this chapter. Later chapters develop more specific, expanded versions of the model, applied to a variety of contexts.

The partially embedded firm

Both neoclassical and socio-economic firms are affected by the same market and regulatory incentives. An important difference between firms in the two models relates to the issue of the firm's embeddedness in society. In early pre-market societies, economic activity tended to be submerged in a particular society's web of social relationships. Here, the behavior of economic organizations was heavily embedded in society. For example, in medieval Europe, the economic exchange between lords and serfs was submerged in the social and political aspects of their situation. In dramatic contrast to this, the neoclassical (N-) firm is an isolated entity, motivated almost entirely by economic considerations. Because the N-firm is minimally influenced by social relationships, it is not embedded in society. N-firms are essentially abstractions in the minds of neoclassical economists; they are not real world firms. Between these extremes is the socio-economic (SE-) firm that is partially embedded in society (Granovetter 1985). SE-firms respond in part to economic incentives and in part to social influences. Such firms respond to the expectation of profit but also act in accord with moral values, commitments to community, and other social bonds and influences depending on the web of socio-economic-political relationships in which they are involved.

To improve their performance, SE-firms may invest in organizational capital, that is, create social relationships that better serve the firm's actors and the firm as a whole. Because of the improved intangible social connections, these actors, while still responding to economic incentives, can be expected to respond more favorably to social influences. These actors are not the detached economic maximizers of mainstream economic theory. Potentially, they are actors who are both constrained by social relationships and effective because of them. When firms invest wisely in organizational capital, they improve both their social responsibility and productivity.

Determinants of firm behavior

In the general version of the socio-economic model in this chapter, the focus is on the most important and general determinants of a firm's behavior.

First, as indicated earlier, the SE-firm is affected by market and regulatory incentives. The SE-firm's behavior is also determined by (1) the special opportunities available to it, (2) the "macro" social forces from society, public, and community, (3) the "micro" social forces from extra-firm institutions and infrastructures, and (4) the firm's internal organizational capabilities. In essence, the firm's internal organizational capabilities, i.e. its social and organizational capital, determine the firm's capacity for successfully taking advantage of opportunities for economic gain while honoring its social obligations. The two external social influences, macro and micro, are often crucial insofar as they either encourage or discourage the firm's efforts to achieve its potential performance. Figure 1.2 depicts these basic features of the general version of the socio-economic model. The model's determinants of firm behavior are considered in more detail below.

Special opportunities are known or knowable developments of which firms can take advantage to improve their economic, social or political situation. These could include new technologies, new managerial knowledge, new consumer behavior or attitudes, new government regulations and so on.

The *macro social forces*, the first of the two external social influences,

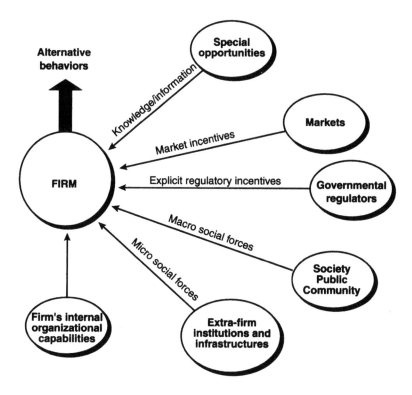

Figure 1.2 General version of the socio-economic model of the firm's behavior

reflect broad community and societal influences, and thus, high level norms and moral values. They also reflect the public's awareness, concerns, goals and demands. These macro social forces tend to encourage behavior and innovation in society's overall interest, but tend to be diffuse in their impact. One example in the U.S.A. is public attitudes in favor of environmental conservation and against industrial pollution. These have become a significant influence on businesses.

The *micro social forces*, on the other hand, are those that operate in the local environment of the firm and emanate from certain extra-firm institutions and infrastructures. Extra-firm institutions include educational institutions, trade associations, suppliers and consultants, and infrastructures include such things as standard industry and managerial practices. The micro social forces, in contrast to the macro ones, are direct, immediate and salient in their impact and may reflect fears, anxieties, prejudices and social self-interest. When members of firms conform to these influences, their inclinations toward positive change and innovation may be blocked. Thus, it is not uncommon for the macro and micro social forces to be in conflict with each other. For example, firms may experience generalized public pressure to lessen their pollution while encountering influences counter to this from standard industry practices and consultants. However, extra-firm institutions may, at other times, provide valuable encouragement, important knowledge, and other influences crucial to firms carrying out progressive innovation.

A variety of *internal organizational capabilities* are the key determinants of how a firm responds to the special opportunities and incentives confronting it. Among these are the firm's capability for (1) rational organizational decision making, (2) socially responsible behavior, (3) entrepreneurial behavior, and (4) organizational learning. These human capabilities derive to a considerable degree from the organizational capital investments the firm has made.

In the socio-economic model, the firm's decision makers are not assumed to be substantively rational, automatically and invariably selecting the optimum alternative, as is assumed in the neoclassical model. The SE-firm's decision makers are boundedly rational, intending to make the best possible decisions but frequently failing to do so because of the limitations of their mental abilities and knowledge. Nevertheless, the quality of their decision making can be significantly enhanced by improving the organization's decision-making processes, i.e. improving the procedural rationality of the organization. Improving these processes involves investment in organizational capital and can be expected to raise the firm's capability for *rational organizational decision making*.

Firms with a high capability for *socially responsible behavior* are able to voluntarily exercise self-control, aligning their efforts with the common good in the long term rather than simply allowing the market or government or even pressure groups to control them. A firm with this capability has developed the discipline to be in harmony with its internal and external stakeholders as well as society as a whole. The key to this discipline is decision making that reflects a highly ethical orientation, patience, and a willingness to be held accountable for one's actions. To a great extent, this is a capacity that inheres in the organization, one that can be improved through investment in organizational capital.

Firms vary in their capacity for *entrepreneurship*, their capability for envisioning and carrying out change. Entrepreneurship requires a substantial ability to deal with risk and uncertainty, and it thrives when there is an openness to new approaches and the time and opportunity to try them. To a significant degree, the capability for entrepreneurial behavior can be enhanced by improving organizational conditions, i.e. making the right kinds of investment in organizational capital.

The fourth important capability of firms is *organizational learning*. Following Argyris and Schon (1978), learning is not simply the acquisition of information. Learning starts when individuals discover that their mental models, which indicate the expected consequences of particular actions under a variety of assumed conditions, are in error. Because of the discrepancy between expected and actual outcomes, individuals learn; that is, they revise their models. In organizational learning, mismatches between expected and actual organizational outcomes reveal the error in individuals' shared mental models. Organizational learning involves a process of inquiry, reflection and evaluation in which the model is revised and becomes embedded in organizational memory as well as the regular practices of the organization. "Learning organizations" have developed in themselves through investment in organizational capital a very high capability for organizational learning. Learning organizations are organizations that continuously manifest high-quality, appropriate organizational learning, and thus are continuously expanding their capacity to create and deal with the future (Senge 1990).

The ideal (Z) firm

The ideal (or Z-) firm is the SE-firm that has developed all these internal organizational capabilities as much as possible, thereby reaching its highest human potential. The Z-firm is thus both highly competitive and highly responsible. It is not only outstanding in responding to competitive challenges related to its basic business activities, but it has also found fully responsible ways to deal with its external and internal stakeholders and society as a whole. To put this in perspective, the Z-firm is on the ideal end of a continuum of actual SE-firms. Actual firms rarely come very close to this ideal either because of insufficient human and organizational investments or because of discouragement from their external environments. Actual firms, therefore, ordinarily manifest some degree of inefficiency and irresponsibility.

To better understand the ideally responsible behavior of the Z-firm, let us contrast its behavior with that of the N-firm in the case where the activities of both firms are accompanied by a negative externality and there is no governmental regulation. The negative externality implies that a byproduct (for example, water pollution) of these firms' production inflicts damage on some people who did not consent to this impact and who do not receive compensation for it. First, consider the N-firm's behavior. Because it seeks to maximize short-term profit and is uninfluenced by external social influences, the N-firm's decision makers will not even consider the fact that its production victimizes a group of people. As long as the activity is profitable, the N-firm will undertake it, regardless of whether it produces damaging pollution. The N-firm clearly cannot be expected to behave in a socially responsible way.

The Z-firm's response to a negative externality situation is dramatically different. Unlike the N-firm, which is impervious to external social influences, the Z-firm, because of its partially embedded nature, is strongly affected by external social influences such as those from the local community which may strongly disapprove of the victimization of some of its members. Because the Z-firm has invested highly in its internal organizational capability, it differs from the N-firm with regard to four very important attributes or capacities: ethical orientation, patience, innovativeness and organizational learning. Due to its highly ethical orientation, the Z-firm will seek win–win relationships with its external stakeholders. Due to its patience, it will be willing to sacrifice current profit for the prospect of future gain, even if uncertain. Because of its innovativeness and ability to learn, it will be able to discover and take advantage of opportunities that enable it to gain economically while pursuing an ethical, socially harmonious course of action.

This socially responsible behavior of the Z-firm provides a solution to the negative externality problem. It is not that the Z-firm's behavior will be expected to have only positive impacts on others; it is that the Z-firm's self-regulated behavior will have no socially unacceptable negative impacts. The Z-firm will not, for example, engage in any behavior (water pollution) that the negatively affected parties cannot consent to. In order to achieve a solution in which both the firm and its stakeholders come out ahead, the Z-firm would have to learn from society what kinds of behavior are acceptable and unacceptable and use this knowledge to negotiate mutually acceptable behavioral alternatives. The negative externality problem would be eliminated because the only damage inflicted would be on people who had fully consented to the decision regarding the firm's behavior. (Recall that, by definition, a negative externality implies that the damage is imposed on people who have not consented to this impact.)

This idea that a firm's socially responsible behavior can ideally resolve negative externality problems is developed further in later chapters. One reason this idea is attractive is that if all firms behaved ideally, this would eliminate the need for government regulation of negative externality situations. But, alas, such visions of dismantling government regulation are premature at best, as actual firms generally fall far short of realizing their Z-potential. One important reason for this failure is analyzed below.

Failure of the firm

From the standpoint of neoclassical economic theory, firms, or more accurately markets, typically fail because of problematic economic incentives, ones that lead firms either to impose too much external cost on, or provide too little external benefit to, third parties. As analyzed above, SE-firms which had developed their internal organizational capabilities as much as possible would be capable of overcoming this type of market failure.

The *socio-economic failure of the firm* is an analysis of another important, newly recognized type of failure which is included in the socio-economic model. This failure occurs when micro social forces, because of the directness and salience of their impact, strongly influence firms' behavior in ways counter to society's best interests. Here, failure is not due to economic incentives; it is due to the unsatisfactory nature of the social influences (possibly reflecting fears, prejudices, vested interests, etc.) on the firm. As analyzed in later chapters, these micro social influences may be the critical reason why firms, for example, make too few home mortgage loans to certain older urban neighborhoods (the redlining problem); fail to adapt to the new realities of global competition (the problem of the decline of competitiveness); fail to behave responsibly with respect to the natural environment (the environmental problem); or fail to behave in a socially responsible manner in other contexts.

Implications for governmental policy

The socio-economic model has implications for governmental policy that differ greatly from those of the neoclassical model. Because in the neoclassical model, failures occur as a consequence of problematic market incentives, the heart of neoclassical policy recommendations are for government to provide incentives to firms that counter these market incentives. Neoclassical type market failure also can be an important problem in the socio-economic model, but it would not be a problem for firms whose capabilities were highly developed enough to enable them to resolve this failure.

Government policy recommendations in the socio-economic model follow directly from an understanding of the main determinants of the firm's behavior. To ameliorate societal problems such as the ones mentioned earlier requires government measures that influence favorably firms' behavioral determinants. That is, government could:

1) encourage development of firms' internal organizational capabilities;

2) provide firms with knowledge of special opportunities;
3) identify and reduce the undesirable micro social influences emanating from extra-firm institutions and infrastructures and strengthen their desirable influences;
4) strengthen desirable macro social influences.

When government does these types of things, the government behaves more like a *coach* than a regulator (Hampden-Turner 1988). Just as the athletics coach is needed to nurture and facilitate the development of both individual team members and the team as a whole, the governmental coach is needed to foster the development of the capabilities of both individual firms and the socio-economic systems in which they are embedded.

The Z-firm in a new economic age

There is another element that needs to be added to our conception of the Z-firm. This is something that more and more seems important as we move closer to the next millennium. To understand this extra ingredient, it is important to consider the nature of the dramatic underlying paradigm shift that is part and parcel of the emerging new economic age.

In the old scientific paradigm, the world is modeled as a machine, like a clock, which can be fully understood by comprehending the functioning of each part. In the new science, the emphasis is on holistic models in which the world is a whole system that is more than the straightforward sum of its parts (Wheatley 1992: 8–10). Increasingly, all of us, not just scientists, are coming to see the wholeness, the connectedness, the relationships and the dynamism in all things. Whereas economists, following the example of Sir Isaac Newton's physics, have focused on analyzing the hard, material components of the economy, it is time for economists to follow the lead of modern scientists and others who increasingly recognize that reality often cannot be reduced to simple cause and effect, that it often involves a constant flux of dynamic processes, and that connection, creativity, compassion and intuition are essential ingredients in the human economy.

Reflecting this paradigm shift, economists' machine model of the firm needs to give way to a holistic model. The needed holistic model, of course, includes conventional tangible inputs, but it also includes as inputs intangible soft ingredients, and it includes recognition of the social determinants of the firm's behavior. Further, the model includes certain "higher" aspects of human behavior which defy quantification or measurement along a monetary dimension. Without a holistic model, it is not possible to understand why given the same material resources a few companies achieve greatness, others fail miserably, and still others are mediocre. What is missing from the economists' machine model are such qualities as passion, inspiration, *esprit de corps*, enthusiasm, vigor, zest, vision, strongly held values, deep commitment, spirituality and highly ethical orientation. To understand the origin of these qualities, one must appreciate that not only people but business organizations have a deep inner truth, a higher reality, sometimes called *spirit* (Hawley 1993: 16–17). When people are able to be in unity with their own spirits and can also align with the spirit of their organization, the firm is capable of tapping tremendous energies in its members. It is only through great leadership that a firm can hope to come close to realizing this ideal state of balance that may enable the firm to achieve its highest possible socio-economic performance.

Organization of the book

In the chapters that follow, the basic ideas of the general socio-economic model of the firm are developed further and applied to a variety of contexts in order to understand the behavior, the potential and the failures of the firm. Each of the following chapters was originally written as a separate article containing a model that focuses on only one aspect of the human firm's behavior to the exclusion of other parts. These articles, many of which have been published in professional journals, were written over a period of about seven years. In the process of creating this book, the articles have been rewritten and in some cases updated. Inevitably, however, the chapters written earlier will reflect the references available at that time and may not reflect certain later developments. Despite this, each chapter makes an important application of the general theory of the socio-economic firm. It is felt that little would be gained by a wholesale effort to rewrite the chapters using fresher references and examples. Part of the rewriting task has been to integrate these separate pieces into a whole. This task involved determining how the chapters would be grouped, eliminating unnecessary duplication, and providing clear transitions from topic to topic. How well these efforts at integration have been accomplished, only the reader can judge.

The remainder of the book is organized into four parts. Part I consists of two chapters that focus, respectively, on the two key concepts of embeddedness and organizational capital. Chapter 2 examines (1) the idea that firms are partially embedded in society, (2) the nature of the external social influences on firms, and (3) why these may cause failures of the firm, failures that are different from the market failures typically analysed by economists. Two examples of the "socio-economic failure of the firm" are analysed. The first is an organizational failure associated with the decline of competitiveness of U.S. firms. The second example, the bias in mortgage loan-making known as redlining, is included in an appendix.

Chapter 3 applies and extends the concept of organizational capital. It concerns a central problem of organizations, i.e. why employees ordinarily make too few efforts on behalf of the interests of their organization and fellow employees. By drawing on organizational behavior literature relating to the joining-up process, organizational commitment and organizational citizenship behavior, and integrating these insights with economic theory, this chapter provides a new explanation of why employees' efforts are typically suboptimal and what organizational activities can resolve this problem. The key variable explaining whether organization members behave responsibly or not is the presence of organizational capital formed either during the joining-up process or in preparation for it.

Part II is focused on the internal functioning of the firm and how this affects the firm's competitiveness. Chapter 4 is concerned with the rationality of decision making in firms. It examines what rationality means, why departures from rationality are a common occurrence, and what can be done to improve the rationality of decision making. This chapter develops a socio-economic model of the rationality of organizational decision making that synthesizes the most important organizational insights concerning the making of large, complex, ill-structured decisions and links these to important economic concepts.

In response to global competition and a rapidly changing business environment, corporate strategies and structures are becoming more flexible and integrated. The purpose of Chapter 5 is to develop a model of the flexible, integrated (FI-) firm. To appreciate fully the FI-firm, it is necessary to contrast its operations with the hierarchical (H-) firm which incorporates strategy and structure in the mode typical of the large western corporation during much of the second half of the twentieth century. The analysis here focuses on the reasons for believing that the FI-firm is better adapted to current competitive realities than is the H-firm.

According to mainstream economic theory, businesses are essentially machines, vehicles for transforming inputs into outputs. An alternative model developed in Chapter 6 is a holistic one that understands the firm as a human entity in which the whole is more than the sum of the parts. It explains why peak performance can only be achieved in the presence of a critical combination of, or right balance between, the soft (leadership, spirit, etc.) and hard (management, organizational structure, financial structure, etc.) factors. Embodied in this model is the hypothesis that certain soft factors not included in mainstream economic models are essential to explaining the behavior and performance of the firm, especially its competitiveness.

Part III deals with how the firm exercises responsibility in its relationships with its stakeholders, its customers, affected communities, government and so on. Although employees are not included in this list of stakeholders, it should be noted that Chapter 3 (in Part I) explores an important aspect of the firm's relationship with its employees, i.e. the circumstances under which employees will behave in an organizationally responsible manner.

The purpose of Chapter 7, the first in Part III, is to understand the essence of socially responsible behavior. This chapter develops a socio-economic model dealing with the firm's external relationships, a model that integrates economic theory, especially theory concerning negative externalities, with noneconomic insights concerning the social responsibilities of businesses. The model explains when firms can be expected to behave in a socially responsible manner.

Chapter 8 applies and builds on the insights concerning social responsibility of Chapter 7. In contrast to short-term oriented, opportunistic approaches, managements are increasingly setting high environmental goals, integrating environmental management with other aspects of management, developing environmentally oriented strategies that harmonize economic and environmental interests, and utilizing sytem-wide approaches along with socially responsible decision making. This behavior cannot be explained by the neoclassical model. Thus, Chapter 8 develops a socio-economic model of the human firm's behavior with respect to the natural environment, a model incorporating social, environmental and ethical realities not found in the neoclassical model.

When economists think of product markets, they generally think of transaction markets, where the goal of sellers is, pure and simple, to make a sale. Although long-term buyer–seller relationships are not new, relationship marketing, where sellers aspire to develop long-term, symbiotic, learning partnerships with customers, is emerging as an important new phenomenon. Chapter 9 develops a socio-economic model designed to explain the human firm's choice of marketing orientation along the continuum from transaction to relationship marketing. The model includes important social and organizational factors normally left out of mainstream economic models.

With regard to the implications for government policy, a common theme emerges from the socio-economic models of the different chapters. This is that society can be made better off in a variety of ways by government "coaching" actions designed to bring about improved firm behavior. In other words, various kinds of government industrial policy have great promise. Chapter 10 attempts to answer in a careful and rigorous manner the key industrial policy question: is government intervention justified in order to raise national competitiveness? This chapter answers in the affirmative, and attempts to provide a more convincing rationale for industrial policy than economists and others have heretofore developed. The new rationale builds on the insight that firms are capable of both organizational learning and behaving economically responsibly to society. Government intervention makes sense when it can successfully influence the organizational learning of a nation's firms.

Part IV consists only of the concluding chapter. Chapter 11 starts by summarizing the human firm's important capacities and behaviors. Next, it develops in a broader fashion than in Chapter 10 the implications for an alternative approach to government policy; that is, it develops the view that the government coach ought to assist the human firm in realizing its true potential, thereby raising the competitiveness and responsibility of the socio-economy. Finally, based on our findings regarding the nature of the human firm, the last section is suggestive regarding the nature of "human capitalism" and how it differs from the neoclassical conception of capitalism.

Although the concept of organizational capital is a common thread running between them, the focus and substance of *Organizational Capital* (Tomer 1987), my first book, and *The Human Firm*, the present one, are substantially different. *Organizational Capital* focused largely on explaining worker effort, cooperation, productivity, worker well-being and economic growth. *The Human Firm*'s focus is explicitly on the theory of the firm, particularly explaining the firm's rationality, its social responsibility, its failure to adopt state of the art management methods, its strategies and structures, its leadership and so on. In other words, *The Human Firm* represents an effort to develop the kind of socio-economic (or behavioral economic) theory of the firm needed given the nature of today's social and economic problems.

It is time to go beyond the orthodox economic theory of the firm and recognize the human dimensions of the firm which orthodox theory omits. In the new economic age we have entered, economic development will increasingly depend on developing the intangible human qualities of our firms. To think clearly about this and to formulate policies that support economic development, we need to understand the firm as a human institution. That is what the *The Human Firm* is about.

Part I

Embeddedness and organizational capital

Applying two key concepts

Part I develops the view that the human firm is a socio-economic entity partially embedded in society. Because of the social influences on the firm, its performance can be either impeded or fostered. Its performance is also very much determined by the organizational relationships developed in it, that is, by its investment in organizational capital. Chapters 2 and 3 apply these two key concepts, embeddedness and organizational capital.

2 The human firm in the socio-economy

Embeddedness and socio-economic failure

The human firm is a social as well as an economic entity. Its behavior is determined not only by market forces but by societal ones. As economic sociologists put it, the firm, along with other elements of the economy, is embedded or encapsulated in society. On the one hand, this understanding of the socio-economic nature of the firm allows us to appreciate how firms can realize their highest potential by choosing behavior that is in harmony with its social environment and responsible to society's highest expectations. On the other hand, it enables us to appreciate how firms can fail to perform well precisely because they accommodate to retrogressive social influences. This chapter starts by further elaborating the idea of the firm's embeddedness. This provides a foundation for later chapters that deal with the issue of responsibility. It also provides the foundation for this chapter's explanation of the concept of socio-economic failure of the firm.

An important purpose of this chapter is to help the reader gain an appreciation of the power of the social forces acting on the firm. This is done through an examination of the hypothesis that a socio-economic failure of the firm has occurred in the case of (1) U.S. firms' failure to adapt their management to important new competitive realities and (2) mortgage redlining in urban areas. The chapter is organized as follows. Section 1 argues that it makes sense to view firms as socio-economic entities that are partially embedded in society. Section 2 focuses on the concept of market failure as orthodox economists use the term, and defines a new type of market failure known as development failure. Section 3 defines and explains about the concept of the socio-economic failure of the firm, which derives from the idea that the economy, and its firms, are partially embedded in the society. Section 4 defines the concept of organizational failure and explains how it is a type of socio-economic failure of the firm. Organizational failure is viewed as a situation where learning fails to take place. Section 5 develops in detail the hypothesis that U.S. management has not adapted to the new competitive realities of the 1970s and 1980s, i.e. managerial learning has been too slow. The social forces holding back the needed organizational innovation, in spite of sufficient market incentives, are the essence of the hypothesized socio-economic failure of the firm. In this chapter's appendix, the mortgage redlining example is analyzed.

The embeddedness of the firm

The firm is partially embedded in society

Do social structure and relations impact on the operation of the economy? This, in the jargon of sociologists, is the question of the embeddedness of the economy in society. Relying on anthropological research relating to early-pre-market societies, Polanyi (1957: 46) concluded that in these societies "man's economy...is submerged in his social relationships." He does not act on behalf of his individual economic interests; "he [only] acts so as to safeguard his social standing, his social claims, his social assets." This is the view of the economy as heavily embedded in society and man as "oversocialized." Recall the lords and serfs of medieval Europe, whose economic exchange was generally guided by traditional social roles, not by narrow self-interest. Very few, if any, believe that the modern economy is embedded in this way. Most non-economist social scientists believe that with modernization, the economy has become an "increasingly separate, differentiated sphere in modern society" (Granovetter 1985: 482).

Neoclassical economics assumes that economic actors are self-interested, rational, and minimally affected by social relations. In other words, "neoclassical economics operates...with an atomized, undersocialized conception of human action" (Granovetter 1985: 481–3). Here there is little trace of the economy being embedded in society.

In contrast to the extremes of under- and oversocialized man, a more fruitful view of the economy–society relationship is the partially embedded conception developed by Granovetter:

> Actors do not behave or decide as atoms outside a social context, nor do they adhere slavishly to a script written for them by the particular intersection of social categories that they happen to occupy. Their attempts at purposive action are instead embedded in concrete, ongoing systems of social relations (1985: 487).

If the economy is partially embedded, this means that economic actors such as firms respond in part to economic incentives and in part to social influences. According to Granovetter (1985: 490, 506), individual decision makers in firms operate in the context of personal relations and networks of personal relations in which they seek sociability, approval, status and power. Etzioni (1988: ch. 12) emphasizes the role of moral values, commitments to a community, and social bonds as factors that "encapsulate" competitive markets, and thus firms.

The social forces on firms

The social forces that influence firms at times constrain and discourage, and at other times encourage, support and legitimize their behavior. These forces may be external to the firm, or internal if they have been internalized. Further, it is useful to distinguish between micro and macro social forces.

Micro social forces are ones operating in the local environment of the firm. They may originate from extra-firm institutions such as suppliers, consultants, creditors and trade associations, or from the standards associated with typical industry practices. Thus, their effects are direct, immediate and salient. Frequently, they reflect the human needs relatively low on Maslow's hierarchy of needs. Therefore, they are likely to reflect fears, anxieties, prejudices and social self-interests. People impacted by these forces tend to conform to them, thereby blocking their inclinations toward change, innovation and satisfaction of their higher needs. At other times, the micro social forces are progressive, providing the social encouragement firms need in order to raise the level of their performance.

Macro social forces reflect broader community and societal influences, and thus high-level norms and moral values. They are more diffuse in their impact, and their relevance for business behavior is typically not as obvious. They tend to reflect the higher human needs, including even aesthetic and spiritual considerations. Macro social forces tend to encourage behavior and innovation in society's overall interest.

Micro and macro social forces can be in conflict with each other or with market forces (pursuit of economic gain), and these social forces can be very strong. As Etzioni (1988: 93–108) points out, normative and affective social forces influence people's thinking and decision making such that they frequently do not make the kind of choices they would have made if they had used all their logical abilities in pursuit of their economic self-interest.[1]

Market failure

When analyzing the reasons for an economy's deficient performance, economists usually point to economic factors, especially to the insufficiency of economic incentives. In contrast, this chapter will argue that in some important situations, it is the social influences on firms that cause the problem. First, let's consider the orthodox view of market failure.

The orthodox view

The term, market failure, as used by many orthodox economists, is a microeconomic phenomenon whose presence implies less than optimal allocative efficiency. In these situations, the independent, maximizing behavior of agents in a static context does not lead to an efficient outcome. Among the reasons for such market failures are:

1) the imperfect flow of information;
2) transactions costs;
3) the nonexistence of markets for some goods;
4) market power;
5) externalities;
6) public goods (Stokey and Zeckhauser 1978: 297ff).

The term "market failure" is increasingly being used more broadly as a rationale for government intervention in the economy in situations where the market does not perform up to society's objectives. Two examples well recognized by economists are the failure of the market, by itself, to achieve a satisfactory distribution of welfare, or to maintain full employment of resources. The list of types of market failure is apparently still growing; for example, see the list compiled by Baumol and Blinder (1988: ch. 29).

Development failure

Datta-Chaudhuri (1990) has used the term "market failure" in connection with an economy's failure to achieve its potential rate of development. For example, his research indicates that India and the Philippines grew at a much slower rate than South Korea because the former countries' institutions (their soft infrastructure) inhibited certain types of private sector learning and adjustment necessary for more rapid development. South Korea, on the other hand, with considerable assistance from its government did a better job of creating the institutional forms and environment necessary for rapid industrial learning.[2]

It is useful to recognize explicitly that the type of market failure referred to above is a *development failure*. Development failure involves the failure of the market by itself to achieve a rate of growth of output and well-being deemed satisfactory by the society. Development failure is dynamic in nature; it is not simply a static failure to achieve allocative efficiency. Development failure implies a dysfunction in the processes necessary for the achievement of ongoing economic development. It implies a failure of the economy's institutions to adapt and to develop new competencies appropriate to new situations. Thus, the existence of development failure provides the rationale for government actions to discover the nature of the dysfunction and to correct it. In the absence of corrective action and in the presence of significant foreign competition, de-industrialization is likely to occur at least in advanced economies, if not in developing ones.

The types of development failure correspond to the main types of processes necessary for economic development to occur. These include financial, entrepreneurial, educational and organizational failures. First, financial failure occurs to the extent that financial institutions fail to channel funds to those activities that are most important for the society's continuing economic development. For example, one suspects financial failure when large amounts of U.S. funds were channeled, especially in the 1980s, into hostile takeovers and leveraged buyouts and too little money went to activities with higher prospective economic development payoffs. Second, entrepreneurial failure occurs when an economy's economic development suffers from insufficient innovative activity. Perhaps the society is doing too little to encourage and develop entrepreneurial talents, or perhaps there are institutional features that discourage would-be entrepreneurs. Third, educational failure involves the failure of educational and training institutions to impart the kind of skills, appreciations and knowledge necessary for the society's current stage of economic development. The fourth type, organizational failure, involves a dysfunction in the organization or management of economic enterprises. The latter would be classified as a market failure if the failure of organizational adaptation were merely a matter of insufficient market incentives. However, as indicated below, the failure may be caused by the social influences on firms.

Socio-economic failure of the firm

The term "socio-economic failure of the firm" is a sub-class of a more general category, *socio-economic failure*, which applies to all economic actors, not just firms. While the focus here is only on the firm, it is presumed that the analysis could be generalized in order to apply it to other economic actors.

A *socio-economic failure of the firm* occurs when micro and macro social forces conflict and firms act in conformity with the micro forces because of the directness and salience of their impact. Note that failure here means the lack of a satisfactory economic outcome from the standpoint of society as a whole; in other words, an outcome not conforming with macro social forces. Let us consider two cases. In the first or "pure" case, firms also experience a conflict between the micro social forces and market incentives. The socio-economic failure occurs because social forces or influences (the micro ones), not an insufficiency of economic incentives, are instrumental in firms choosing to do too much or too little of the activity in question. One example is when a high status, influential consultant's advice is decisive in discouraging a client firm from using progressive new methods that are likely to be profitable for the firm and approved by society.

The other, "impure" case occurs when micro social forces and market incentives are in accord but in conflict with macro social forces. Here, both a socio-economic failure of the firm and conventional market failure occur as the failure is caused jointly by social and market forces. To illustrate, suppose in the consultant example above that the financial returns to the firm would be insufficient to justify the firm's adoption of the new methods, but because of significant positive external benefits spilling over to society, doing so makes sense from a societal standpoint. Here the consultant's advice is part of the socio-economic failure of the firm, and the positive externality is the market failure.

Organizational failure

The purpose of this section is to develop the hypothesis that an organizational failure has occurred in the U.S.A. and that this is an example of a socio-economic failure of the firm.

Defining organizational failure

An *organizational failure* is a development failure that involves dysfunctioning in the organization or management of economic enterprises. Organizational failure may occur when the organization or management of enterprises fails to change in appropriate ways in response to new competitive situations. For example, it is alleged that U.S. management has failed to adapt to important new features of the global competition that emerged in the 1970s and 1980s.

It is useful to view organizational failure as a failure to invest in appropriate organizational capital or as a failure to prevent disinvestment in organizational capital (Tomer 1987). The result of the failure is that the economy's output growth is lower than desired, either because in the former situation the production possibility frontier does not shift out as fast as desired, or because in the latter situation it shifts inward.

To my knowledge, the concept of organizational failure as a kind of market failure first appears in the writings of Michael Best. Best (1982) first uses the notion of organizational failure to characterize the "modern politicized market" and its "socially irrational production and consumption patterns." Later, Best (1986) uses the term organizational failure in a much more specific way with a meaning close to the way the term is defined above. The organizational failure that Best analyzes is the lack of strategic planning on the part of business enterprises in the UK, a lack which has left the UK at a competitive disadvantage *vis-à-vis* the enterprises of countries that have successfully evolved institutional relationships supplying the necessary strategic planning. In his earlier writings, Oliver Williamson (see for example 1971: 383–4) uses the term "organizational failure" to refer to situations in which the failure of a business to adopt a preferred organizational form leads to impaired economic performance.

The hypothesis of socio-economic failure of the firm

It is hypothesized that the failure of U.S. management to adapt organizationally to the new realities of global competition in the 1970s and 1980s is a socio-economic failure of the firm. (It is widely believed, although not well established, that U.S. firms are adapting more successfully in the 1990s.) This failure is believed to have led to decreased competitiveness of U.S. firms, a declining market share for U.S. firms in many significant industries, low productivity and economic growth, and a host of other economic symptoms. These results certainly represent a development failure, as they are far from satisfactory from the standpoint of American society; that is, this outcome is out of line with the macro social forces that reflect the desire of U.S. people for moderate or higher rates of economic growth accompanied by rising standards of living. Furthermore, there is plenty of evidence that market incentives are not the problem as particular foreign and domestic firms have profited greatly from their well-adapted organizational innovations. Thus, to demonstrate that this organizational failure is a socio-economic failure of the firm, it is necessary to explain about the particular micro social forces that were keeping U.S. firms from adapting successfully to the new realities, i.e. keeping them from successful learning.

Organizational failure as learning failure

Organizational failure may be analysed as a failure in a firm's process of learning about managing itself. The relevant learning occurs when members of the organization become more knowledgeable and competent about managing and organizing the enterprise. The competence so developed becomes embodied in individuals or groups of individuals collectively. Conventional learning involves the acquisition and application of managerial knowledge in situations where the firm is making relatively minor adjustments in its mode of operating. This can result from production experience (as in learning by doing) or from extra-organizational sources including training sessions, book learning and so on. In contrast to this conventional learning, organizational learning is not simply information absorption; it generally involves situations where creative change central to the way the firm operates is occurring.

Conventional learning is essentially the same as the learning analyzed by the learning curve, which shows decreases in average total cost with increases in cumulative total output of a good. With the adoption of a major new non-managerial technology, the experience gained from the use of the technology should allow opportunities for learning about needed organizational adjustments as well as other well-known forms of learning by doing (McCain 1988: 37). This conventional learning could involve improvements in organizational structure and communication patterns necessary to take best advantage of the new technology.

On the other hand, organizational learning is a process that begins when individuals discover that their mental models, which indicate the expected consequences of particular actions under a variety of assumed conditions, are in error (Argyris and Schon 1978). Because of the discrepancy between expected and actual outcomes, individuals learn; i.e. they revise their models. Thus, organizational learning involves a process of inquiry, reflection and evaluation in which the model is revised and becomes embedded in organizational memory as well as the regular practices of the organization. It is very much a creative process that expands the organization's capacity. Organizational learning cannot simply be depicted as a movement down a learning curve; it involves a discontinuity or break in the learning curve. The major change resulting from organizational learning may or may not initially result in lower average cost or higher quality output but presumably would do so as experience with the new mode of operating accumulates.

Any failure of learning in an enterprise would mean a decline in its economic performance (e.g., higher average cost or lower product quality) relative to what it would have been had the learning occurred. In the absence of a similar learning failure on the part of its competitors, this would lower the firm's competitiveness, likely causing a decline in its share of the industry's activity. Failure of the breakthrough type of organizational learning would be of especially great significance for an enterprise, as it would allow its competitors not only the initial performance advantage resulting from the breakthrough but a subsequent advantage as they moved down the new learning curve.

Should such a major organizational failure occur, the accompanying decline in the competitiveness of many of a nation's firms *vis-à-vis* foreign competitors (assuming they are not experiencing organizational failure) could result in a decline of a significant number of the country's high-productivity industries. Thus, organizational failure could be an important cause of deindustrialization. Organizational failure does not necessarily mean a total absence of firm learning. If the learning is too slow or too little to avoid a decrease in competitiveness, an organizational failure occurs. This raises still other questions. What is the nature of the "learning disability"? What micro social forces contribute to this disability? How can this social incompetence be remedied?

Organizational failure in the U.S.A.

The purpose of this section is to apply the hypothesis of organizational failure as socio-economic failure of the firm to the U.S.A. during the 1970s and 1980s. In developing this hypothesis, careful consideration will be given to the arguments of writers who believe an organizational failure has occurred and is continuing. First, we must consider the nature of the new realities which have been the stimulus for many firms to change.

The new realities

Is, as Alvin Toffler (1980) believes, a new civilization (the third wave) emerging from the dying industrial civilization? Or, as W. Edwards Deming suggests, are we in a "new economic age"? Whether or not we interpret current change as a grand societal break with the past, it is clear that U.S. firms face important new realities. First, according to Gunn:

At no time in history has the rate of change been greater in technology than since the 1960s. In manufacturing, technological change has occurred primarily in three areas: information technology, materials technology, and manufacturing process technology.

(Gunn 1987: 3–4)

Computer-aided design, computer-aided manufacturing, computer-aided engineering, flexible manufacturing systems, robotics and computer-integrated manufacturing are among the most important of these technologies. These make possible smaller, faster, more flexible operations.

The second important new reality is the character of the increasingly global competition. Regardless of the nature of their product, U.S. companies can increasingly expect competition from foreign companies in domestic markets; U.S. firms also intend to compete and/or produce in foreign markets. The stiffest competition has come from the Far Eastern countries, particularly Japan:

Not only have Far Eastern manufacturers virtually taken over many industries…, but they have demonstrated a zeal for improving manufacturing effectiveness and product quality, and for totally satisfying their customers, that has been astonishing.

(Gunn 1987: 3)

The third new reality is the changing tastes of consumers. Consumers are demanding higher quality and more diverse goods faster than ever before. Product life cycles are shorter, and markets are fragmenting. Fourth, there are a variety of other factors causing uncertainty in world markets. These include large variations in energy prices, gyrating exchange rates, financial and other business restructuring, and the record rate of business and bank start-ups and failures (see Peters 1988: 36–7).

The management problem

An increasing number of leading business thinkers agree with Deming's view that "Management has failed in this country."[3] According to *Business Week* (1989), "there's no escaping one fundamental fact: U.S. companies are being outmanaged by their toughest competitors." According to Tom Peters (1988: 42), the necessary management changes "are not being made fast enough." Thomas Gunn's (1987: xv) assessment is less reserved: "The management of these companies [mostly U.S. manufacturing companies] are paralyzed, either unable or unwilling to act."

What is it about U.S. management that is not well adapted to the new realities? There are two main views on this subject. One is that American management is obsolete: the other is that a number of new, but maladaptive, principles guide U.S. management.

The obsolescence of management

In the view of Robert Reich (1983), Frank Hearn (1988) and others, the management model that emerged around 1920 and was dominant until at least 1970 is now obsolete and is the major source of the decline of American industry. This management model is associated with the bureaucratically structured, large-scale organization that has accompanied high-volume standardized production. Among the key features of the management model are production jobs characterized by routinization and specialization (Hearn 1988: 4). Routinized jobs are simplified ones with a small range of tasks and low skill requirements, enabling low labor costs using unskilled or semi-skilled laborers. To achieve their goals efficiently, organizations using the management model formalize their operations, increasing "their reliance on clearly specified, explicitly formulated, and rigidly prescribed rules of conduct, task definitions, and job responsibilities so that behavior within the organization is made more predictable and more impersonal" (Hearn 1988: 4). This reduces organizations' dependence on individual discretion, initiative and personal qualities, but increases the number of managers needed in the hierarchy to coordinate and control the operations.

There are several reasons why the management model is obsolete. The first is that it lacks the flexibility of response necessary in the face of constantly changing markets. Because it was designed for stability, the management model lacks the ability to adapt quickly to altered circumstances such as demand shifts. Because workers in the management model are only prepared to solve old, routine problems, they are unprepared to solve new problems and to innovate in the face of new situations. In sum, the management model's rigid delineated relationship between management and labor, its strict separation of the thinkers from the doers, and its reliance on narrowly programmed responses from workers makes it unable to offer the kind of timely, motivated responses needed given the new realities (see Hearn 1988: 103–6; Reich 1983: 127–34).

The second reason for the obsolescence of the management model is that it is ill-suited to getting the best results from the new manufacturing technologies. According to Shoshana Zuboff (1985) and Richard Walton (1985b), when information technology is used in such a way that worker efforts are eliminated or made more routine and less skilled (consistent with the management model), it is not possible to achieve fully effective utilization of the new technology. Utilized in this way, workers are likely to resist the new technology. Moreover, there is little possibility for workers to experiment, learn, be creative and work cooperatively with others toward joint goals, all of which are necessary to get the maximum economic performance from this technology.

The message of Hayes and Jaikumar (1988) is similar. The real impediment to achieving the promise of the new technology—improved cost, quality, flexibility, delivery speed and design—is the U.S. managerial infras-tructure. In other words, it is the attitudes, policies, systems and habits associated with the management model that "are incompatible with the requirements and unique capabilities of advanced manufacturing systems" (1988: 79). Other elements of current managerial practice associated with the managerial model that are inadequate in this regard are cost accounting, capital budgeting, organizational structures, top officer skills and manage-rial styles, and the lack of people with a generalist as opposed to specialist outlook (1988: 79–85; see also Gunn 1987).

The third reason for the obsolescence of the management model stems from the system of industrial relations that has coexisted with the manage-ment model starting from the late 1930s. This system:

> offered a kind of crude social contract in which government guaranteed workers' rights to bargain collectively for wages and working conditions. Most large companies reluctantly tolerated unions. The unions refrained from challenging management prerogatives. Employees sought security in industry-wide master contracts and in an elaborate set of job classifi-cations and work rules. The old industrial relations system was a kind of armed truce, balanced and undergirded by labor's ability to inflict damage, by industry's ability to live in a predictable competitive environ-ment, and by government's willingness to enforce the ground rules.
>
> (Kuttner 1988: 6)

This system is widely acknowledged to have broken down by the late 1970s (Kuttner 1988). The reason for the breakdown of the system is that:

> all the major preconditions of the old social contract have dissolved. Global competition and deregulation have ended oligopoly; the strike no longer has the force that it once did; many companies are much more anti-union; and, if one more assault were required, the National Labor Relations Board is no longer impartial.
>
> (Kuttner 1988: 6)

What is left of the old industrial relations system is simply incompatible with the economic performance required because of global competition and the new manufacturing technologies.

New managerial principles

According to Robert Hayes and William Abernathy (1980), it is not the obsolescence of U.S. management but the new managerial principles that U.S. managers have increasingly subscribed to during the 1960s and 1970s that are the cause of U.S. management failure. In this view, U.S. businesses are failing "to compete over the long run by offering superior products"

(1980: 68): "These new principles, despite their sophistication and widespread usefulness, encourage a preference for (1) analytic detachment rather than the insight that comes from "hands on" experience and (2) short-term cost reduction rather than long-term development of technological competitiveness" (1980: 68). The overriding criterion for companies using these principles is "maximum short-term financial return." In seeking this, companies use three important practices: financial control, corporate portfolio management, and market-driven behavior (1980: 70–2).

Financial control uses short-term financial measurements to evaluate the performance of individual managers and management groups. In corporate portfolio management, financial risk and return analysis is used to guide decision making with respect to acquiring and divesting business units in the attempt to achieve the optimum portfolio of businesses. In market-driven behavior, the emphasis is on using consumer analyses and formal market surveys as the dominant guide to new product decisions rather than relying on the development of new products through technological innovation. In the final analysis, according to Hayes and Abernathy (1980: 68), the management failure is "a failure of both vision and leadership—that over time has eroded both the inclination and the capacity of U.S. companies to innovate." Hayes and Abernathy believe that the needed leadership requires much more than controllers, market analysts and portfolio managers. For a similar analysis of management failure due to new principles, see Harrison and Bluestone (1987) on the "new managerialism."

In conclusion, the U.S. organizational failure is believed to stem from businesses' adherence to (1) the management model and (2) new management principles, both of which are ill-adapted to the new realities.

World class management

What type of management is well-adapted to the new realities? An increasing number of authors believe they see the shape of the winning management of the future. According to Peters (1988: xiii), a revolution in American management practices, which "challenges everything we thought we knew about managing," is necessary. The successful firm in the 1990s will be:

- flatter (have fewer layers of organization structure)
- populated by more autonomous units (have fewer central-staff second-guessers, more local authority to introduce and price products)
- oriented toward differentiation, producing high value-added goods and services, creating niche markets
- quality-conscious
- service-conscious
- more responsive
- much faster at innovation

- a user of highly trained, flexible people as the principal means of adding value
- a user of gain sharing
- smaller
- highly participative (Peters 1988: 34–7).

Peters has developed in detail forty-five prescriptions to guide managers desiring to transform their company's management. Grayson and O'Dell (1988: 237–44) believe that the most successfully adjusted companies will feature (1) drive, (2) flexibility, (3) continuous improvement, (4) continuous learning and (5) a shared sense of purpose.

It is clear that to a considerable degree these visions of the management future owe much to the current state of Japanese management. Japanese companies have demonstrated that they are considerably more flexible than American companies in the sense of offering a broader choice of products, changing their products more frequently and being faster to respond to market demands and changing opportunities (Friedman 1988; Peters 1988: 61). Key features of the Japanese management approach are indicated in the formal guiding philosophy of NUMMI, General Motors and Toyota's joint venture in California. Among its elements are:

1) *kaizen*, the never-ending quest for perfection;
2) the development of full human potential;
3) *jidoka*, the pursuit of superior quality;
4) build mutual trust;
5) develop team performance;
6) every employee as a manager; and
7) provide a stable livelihood for all employees (Peters 1988: 341).

For an economic analysis of the superior internal efficiency (X-efficiency) of Japanese management, see Tomer (1987: ch. 7). A full consideration of the features of Japanese management is beyond the scope of this chapter.

The organizational ideal according to Robert Reich (1983) is flexible-system production which is fundamentally different from the old management model. Organizations with flexible-system production have flat organization structures, provide workers with employment security and treat them fairly, require a high degree of worker participation, place a premium on teamwork and cooperation, require the integration of traditionally separate business functions and require a "less rigidly delineated relationship between management and labor and a new relationship with government" (Reich 1983: 129–30, 134, 257–9, 278). A somewhat similar ideal called "flexible specialization" has been expounded by Piore and Sabel (1984).

From the standpoint of the relationship between the individual and the organization, the ultimate participative ideal is Theory Z management or simply Z-management (see Tomer 1987: ch. 8, especially 92–6), the type of management in a Z-firm. Among the characteristics of Z-management are: "lifetime" employment, workers as members of a community, workers with high, varying responsibilities with emotional, spiritual commitment expected, implicit control of workers through internalized goals, clear goals and strong humanistic values predominate, and workers have rights to all economic profits (94–95). In Z-management, the ideal is not only flexibility and efficiency but democracy and community. It should be noted that producer cooperatives such as the Mondragón cooperatives in the Basque region of Spain have been widely cited as embodying the ideal of democracy and community as well as having high economic performance. All in all, it is clear that the new managerial ideal represents a paradigm shift from the old management model.

Barriers to change

Why do not managerial practices which are well adapted to the new realities diffuse faster? If some firms in the U.S. have adjusted well and have adopted flexible, participative management, if not Z-management, why are not other U.S. firms quickly following? What is the reason for this failure of organizational learning? As might be expected, there are micro social forces at work.

The first answer has to do with the idea that management is "deeply embedded in culture" (Drucker 1988b: 75). This means that how we manage is linked inextricably with what we believe and the way we perceive and behave. It follows that it is more difficult to change a society's management than to change technology or technique because managerial change requires changing "who we *are*, as well as what we do" (Pascale and Athos 1981: 27). Pascale and Athos believe that managers' "blind spots related to American culture and society" contribute to these managers' difficulties with managerial innovations that break with the established Western mold (1981: 24–5). The micro social forces, in this view, are the internalized social values of managers. Thus, any manager desiring to undertake major managerial innovation is likely to experience significant opposition from other managers who feel threatened by changes that do not jibe with accustomed values.

A second, related answer is that the character and thinking of U.S. manufacturing managers is an impediment to change. According to Wickham Skinner (1988: 276–8), these managers, due to the nurturing and hardening of manufacturing history, "are typically conservative, risk-aversive people who prefer sequential to parallel uncertainties, with a low tolerance for ambiguity, and a strong distaste for any prospect of wholesale changes"; "They are often seen by human resource managers as authoritative, dominating, and mechanistic in their personal management styles" (1988: 280). Skinner contrasts the knowledge, skills, attitudes, thinking style and assumptions of the manufacturing manager needed in the future with the typical present-day manager and finds the contrast to be striking (1988: 280–1). The tendency of these manufacturing managers to discourage managerial change initiatives is a significant micro social force.[4,5]

Third, following Mancur Olson (1982), Kuran (1988: 162) argues that "in *stable* societies established groups block efficiency enhancing changes that run counter to their interests, and that, as a result, economic growth slows down." Such groups have typically taken a long time to organize and are unlikely to change their goals or preferences. Which groups have vested interests in blocking an industry move away from the management model, and which have an interest in slowing or not being helpful to such a move? Among the possible groups are educational institutions, management consultants, organized labor and the business media. Due to their accumulated knowledge and skills related to the old management model, these groups have a large stake in existing management methods. Consider one aspect of education:

> Even if America were to devote more resources to education, simply more of the same would not prepare its youth for roles in flexible-system enterprises. At best, the current system of education prepares young people for preexisting jobs in high-volume, standardized production.... Few students are taught how to work collaboratively to solve novel real-world problems—the essence of flexible-system production.
>
> (Reich 1983: 215)

Thus, the social influences and pressures from these different groups with vested interests in the managerial status quo are an important component of the micro social forces inhibiting change.

Fourth, new organization of work must ultimately rest on a new organization of society involving changed ideology and a new consensus about national directions:

> But ideologies resist change, particularly when change seems to threaten people's economic security. The process of long-term decline once under way, has a self-perpetuating quality. It rigidifies old ideologies and engenders a widespread conservatism.
>
> (Reich 1983: 238)[6]

In a related manner, the Cuomo Commission on Trade and Competitiveness (1988: 99–103) believes that the U.S. needs a new national consensus as part of the process of implementing a competitiveness strategy.[7] Thus, the existing ideology and consensus are micro social forces supporting the prevailing managerial order.

In sum, to support industry adjustment to better adapted management, what is needed are fundamental changes in the nation's economic institutions, values, ideology and consensus. Currently these are lacking, though there are increasing signs of change. Without such change, the micro social forces collectively can be expected to be an effective barrier to needed managerial change.

In order to get a better perspective on the hypothesis developed here, Figure 2.1 applies the general version of the socio-economic model of the firm's behavior of the introductory chapter to understanding organizational failure as socio-economic failure of the firm. The firm is depicted as having two alternative behaviors with respect to adapting to the new competitive realities. Either it can choose to continue with its maladaptive management, or adopt well-adapted forms of management. The socio-economic failure of firms occurs because the kinds of micro social forces described above are collectively the critical reason why far too many firms continue with maladaptive management.

Two other reasons should be mentioned briefly. First, the turbulent financial climate indicated by the prevalence of hostile takeovers, leveraged buyouts and the like provides a disincentive to thinking about the long term and carrying out beneficial organizational innovations (Kuttner 1988: 7). Second, significant change may not occur until a critical mass of expected change is achieved and then change is likely to come quickly and thoroughly (Kuran 1988: 163–7).

There is one other significant possibility. Maybe America is simply aging.

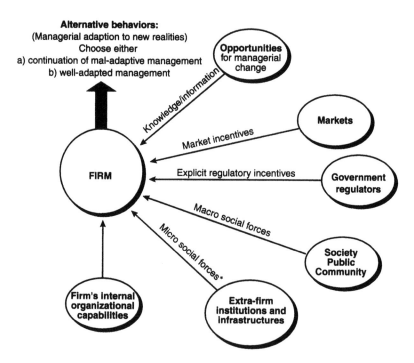

Figure 2.1 Application of the socio-economic model of firm's behavior to organizational failure

In Kindleberger's (1974) view, the U.S.A. seems to be experiencing a period of declining vigor (a climacteric) such as Great Britain started to experience around the turn of the century. According to this hypothesis, there is an "S" curve reflecting three stages in the life of an economy: a slow start, then rapid growth, and ultimately a slowdown. "After a certain point in economic aging or slowdown, the economy is unable effectively to adapt to economic stimuli" (1974: 43). Kindleberger (1980: 48) believes the U.S. economy has "lost the capacity to adapt to a changing economic environment, and to give birth to new economic ideas, institutions, goods." In this condition (also called "social arteriosclerosis"), the economy still has capacity but drive, vigor and adaptability have faded (Norton 1986: 19; Kindleberger 1974: 44). Whereas in the vigorous middle stage, the country's manufacturers develop new goods for export as fast or faster than old goods come to be imported, in the aging stage this is not so. The U.S. appears to be in this latter stage of the product cycle because its imports are increasing and it "continues to lose...export markets in old goods, but replacements of new goods do not emerge" (Kindleberger 1980: 48). For other symptoms of aging, see Grayson and O'Dell (1988: 73–5). Is such decline inevitable as it is with organisms? After all, societies are not organisms. Can youthful adaptive capacity be restored? Can it be restored without shock therapy or the "sociological equivalent of defeat" (Norton 1986: 19)? Or is the apparent decrepitude mainly a product of the constraining influence of the micro social forces?

Conclusion

There is considerable evidence to support the hypothesis that in the U.S. firms' failure to adapt organizationally to the competitive realities of the 1970s and 1980s is due in large part to the kind of micro social influences analysed above, not to insufficient market incentives, lack of knowledge, economic aging and so on. In other words, a socio-economic failure of the firm involving insufficient investment in organizational capital has occurred. Perhaps greater understanding of many other economic problems can be attained by analyzing similarly the social forces that impact on economic actors, not just the market forces.

An important issue is whether this socio-economic failure is continuing in the 1990s. On the one hand, the U.S. economy seems to have regained some of its former vigor, especially when compared to Japan and Western industrial nations. There is evidence of increased efforts at learning new managerial methods, and a lessening of the influence of some of the micro social forces that have been holding back change. However, despite the breakthroughs and inspiring performances by some firms and some sectors, there seems to be considerable persistence in old maladaptive forms of management. There is little evidence of a wholesale revitalization through investment in high quality organizational capital.

Developing the policy implications of this analysis is an obvious next step, one that is beyond the scope of this chapter. However, it should be noted that to the extent that the hypothesis of socio-economic failure is correct, policy recommendations based only on a conventional market failure analysis will be flawed (see Chapters 10 and 11 for the implications for government policies).

While the hypothesis of organizational failure as socio-economic failure requires much more research, a definitive acceptance or rejection of this hypothesis may not be possible. This raises the question of whether the U.S. can afford the luxury of a lot more research before acting? The risks to inaction, many more years of deficient growth, are obviously high. The U.S. and other Western countries need leadership on this question, and they need leaders who perceive the need to act before economists have analyzed all the data.

Appendix: the redlining example of socio-economic failure

Mortgage lenders, it is frequently alleged, are biased with respect to their loan making in older "declining" urban areas. In this example of the socio-economic failure of the firm, let us assume that in the urban area under consideration, lenders could make a satisfactory rate of profit on loans given the risk and other factors involved. Therefore, if lenders decide to put, in effect, a red line around this area and not make any loans there, it is hypothesized that micro social forces are the reason.

The micro social forces are reflected in a predominate housing market ideology widely shared by housing market participants such as real estate brokers, appraisers, home builders, life and fire insurance companies, governmental housing-related agencies, mortgage lenders and others (Tomer 1984: 12). This ideology reflects prevailing prejudices about what types of neighborhoods, housing and socio-economic groups are desirable and where decline is likely to take place. Micro forces are also reflected in the policies and practices of these housing market participants, practices that put pressure on mortgage lenders to adopt lending practices that conform to the prevailing pattern (1984: 12–14; see also Tomer 1980: 201–4).

These micro social forces are in clear conflict with the macro social forces. The macro social forces reflect society's concern for preventing the decline and impoverishment of particular areas as well as entire cities. They also reflect a concern for the well-being of the residents of such areas. If lenders accommodate to the micro forces and refuse loans to the area, this will, by denying funds necessary for the purchase and maintenance of the area's housing, contribute to the deterioration of housing and other conditions in the area. The prophecy of decline reflected in the housing market ideology and practices will have become the reality. In this example, the micro social forces impacting on mortgage lenders have overwhelmed both the macro social forces and market forces.

3 Organizational capital and joining-up

Linking the individual to the organization and to society*

Introduction

Organizational capital is the product of the firm's investment of time and energy into creating and modifying its organizational relationships. There are many types of organizational capital and many reasons for investing in organizational capital. This chapter is concerned with the type of organizational capital that results when firms endeavor to create a bond between their members and the organization in the joining-up process. In other words, this chapter concerns the organizational capital formed in the process of selecting and socializing new members. The motivation for forming this kind of organizational capital is to overcome the tendency for employees to devote too little effort on behalf of the organization.

Do employees ever make efforts on behalf of their employing organization's interests or fellow employees' interests when it is not in their direct self-interest to do so? If so, when? Although the existing organizational economics literature has attempted in a variety of ways to address this question, these efforts have not been altogether successful. Therefore, by drawing on the organizational behavior literature relating to the nature of the joining-up process, organizational commitment and organizational citizenship behavior, and, integrating these insights with economic theory, this chapter (1) provides a new explanation of why employees' efforts are typically suboptimal, and (2) suggests organizational activities that can help resolve the problem.

The chapter is organized as follows. The first section examines the problem of inadequate organizational citizen efforts. Section 2 provides an economic analysis of the problem which indicates that employees' utility-maximizing efforts are likely to be suboptimal from the organization's standpoint. Section 3 summarizes several types of economic analysis that offer "solutions" to the suboptimal effort problem. The fourth section brings

* This chapter has benefited from comments made by Shoshana Grossbard-Shechtman, Roger McCain, Hugh Schwartz, and Shoshana Neuman.

to bear organizational behavior insights regarding the joining-up process, the process by which an individual and organization form a mutual commitment. Section 5 explains how the process that creates organizational commitment forms organizational capital, an investment which can payoff by raising employees' citizenship efforts. The sixth section defines two new types of organizational capital and explains their relevance. Section 7 develops a socio-economic model explaining organizationally responsible behavior. This model indicates that the organizational capital formed in the joining-up process is crucial to overcoming the suboptimal effort problem. In Section 8, the model's implications for economic theory are examined. The ninth section explains how the joining-up process can also create the kind of organizational capital that links the individual to society, thereby making possible a solution to suboptimal societal efforts. Conclusions are provided in the final section.

The organizational problem

The problem addressed here is that employees typically devote less effort to their work activities than would be optimal from the standpoint of their organization. First, employees devote insufficient effort to discretionary activities, not directly or explicitly recognized by the formal reward system, but which promote the efficient and effective functioning of the organization in general. Second, employees devote insufficient effort to "behaviors that immediately benefit specific individuals and indirectly through this means contribute to the organization" (Williams and Anderson 1991: 602). These two have been called *organizational citizenship behaviors* (1991: 601; Organ 1988: 4–6). Third, employees devote insufficient effort to avoiding behaviors that impose costs on the organization in general and/or specific employees.[1]

The following are examples of employees making insufficient citizenship efforts of these three types. First, employees might fail to conserve and protect organizational property, fail to volunteer for difficult or potentially problematic committee assignments, fail to observe informal rules devised to maintain order, fail to give advance notice when unable to come to work, and so on (see Williams and Anderson 1991: 606). Second, employees might fail to help others who have been absent, fail to help others with heavy work loads, fail to go out of their way to help new employees, fail to pass along information to co-workers, and so on. Third, employee actions might directly or indirectly lead to the destruction of organizational property, the creation of unsafe or unhealthy conditions, the undermining of employee morale and others' work motivation, opportunistic advancement of themselves at the expense of others, and so on. All of the above either reduce organizational efficiency and effectiveness or fail to take advantage of opportunities to improve it.

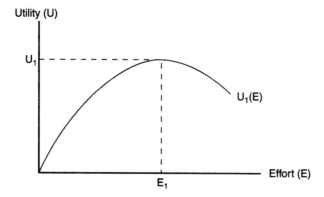

Figure 3.1 The individual's utility–effort relation

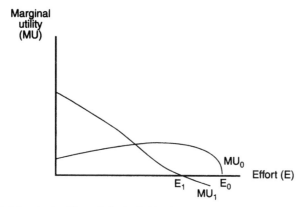

Figure 3.2 Marginal utility of the individual and the external marginal utility (or benefit) to the organization

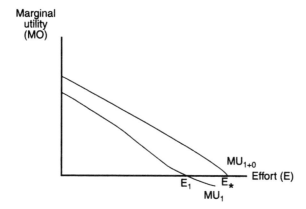

Figure 3.3 Optimal effort levels

An economic analysis of the problem

Because the problem is suboptimal employee effort, it is useful to begin with Harvey Leibenstein's utility-effort analysis. In Leibenstein's view (see, for example, 1976: ch. 6), employees choose the effort level that maximizes their utility. As shown in Figure 3.1, the individual employee's utility (net of any disutility) function ($U_I(E)$) is hump shaped, and an employee will choose effort level, E_1, to achieve the maximum utility, U_1. The chosen level, E_1, is what is best for the individual, but it is not necessarily best for the organization. Another way to view the same situation is depicted in Figure 3.2. Here, the MU_I curve shows how the individual employee's marginal utility varies with effort. The utility maximizing individual will choose effort level E_1 where MU_I is equal to zero. (Please note that the assumption of maximizing behavior is used here in order to obtain a clear, definite result, not because people are believed to behave precisely in this way.)

In this analysis, the employee is a recent hiree whose status is specified in an employment contract. This employee's values and other attributes are not well matched to the organization, and the individual has not been socialized or trained by the organization. Thus, this employee cannot be said to have a psychological attachment or bond to the organization. From this follows the hypothesis that employees such as this one will in choosing an effort level only consider the "private" returns, the utility realized by themselves; they will not consider the "social" returns, the benefits (or utility) to the organization in general and/or to other employees. It should be noted that it is assumed for now that the organization has not created any special arrangements for economic incentives that would cause the utility maximizing individual to take the social/organizational returns into account.

The MU_O curve in Figure 3.2 shows the marginal utility (or benefit) to the organization from a typical employee's effort. The benefits included in MU_O are only the external social benefits received by the organization, the ones for which the employee receives no direct formal or explicit organizational rewards. That MU_O is positive at low levels of effort indicates that even at these low effort levels, some of an employee's efforts will typically be directed to satisfying the organization and/or other employees. Psychologically unattached employees will not consider these in choosing their effort levels, but they will direct their efforts to providing at least a minimal amount of these organizational benefits because of societal and organizational conventions. That MU_O is larger at high effort levels where MU_I has become small indicates the substantial opportunity for organizations to benefit from extra (perhaps unconventional) efforts of employees. For more on the role of conventions with respect to employee effort, see Leibenstein (1987: chaps 6–7).

The MU_{I+O} curve in Figure 3.3 indicates the vertical summation of the marginal benefits (or utility) to the individual and the organization, i.e. MU_I + MU_O. As indicated earlier, the psychologically unattached, utility-maximizing employee will choose effort level E_1, because only the private returns which MU_I reflects are considered. If, however, the employee considered the benefits realized by the organization as well as the individual benefits, the employee would choose effort level, E_*, at the point where MU_{I+O} equals zero. This is the optimal effort from the organization's standpoint. It should be noted that this analysis bears a strong resemblance to the way economists analyze a positive externality. In the latter, a firm's output is shown to be too low from society's standpoint because the firm has not considered the external benefits deriving from its output.

In sum, the explicit organizational incentives brought to bear on employees lacking psychological attachment to their organization are expected to lead them to choose only those efforts for which they are rewarded. Although this is individually rational, it is far from optimal for the organization because these employees are refraining from (1) expending extra effort in the organization's best interests, (2) efforts in co-workers' best interests, and (3) the extra efforts necessary to avoid incurring costs to the organization. If these employees were to expend the extra efforts, internal efficiency (X-efficiency) would be substantially higher.

The above analysis applies with particular force in the presence of team-work when it is difficult or impossible to determine precisely the separate contributions of the individual members of the team and when monitoring and other related supervisory actions are costly.

The psychologically unattached employee will typically free ride for the following reasons. First, this employee is likely to have no qualms about receiving from the organization certain "public good" type benefits, from which employees cannot be easily excluded. Second, this employee will be unwilling to pay the price (for the benefits received) in the sense of making extra efforts that reciprocate them.[2]

A slightly different way of looking at the problem is that employees typically experience a variety of economic incentives some of which are functional from the organization's standpoint, others of which are dysfunctional. When employees respond to the functional incentives, this benefits both the employee and the organization. However, when employees respond to dysfunctional incentives, it benefits the employee at the expense of the organization. Thus, a key question at the heart of organizational economics is: what can the organization do to get its employees to respond to functional incentives but not to respond to the dysfunctional incentives? Still another way to put the question is: how can the interests of the individual and organization be aligned?

Other economic analyses of the problem

The prisoner's dilemma

Leibenstein (1987: chaps 5–7) and others (for example, Tomer 1987: ch. 6) have used a number of variants of the prisoner's dilemma game to show why employees typically choose suboptimal effort from the organization's standpoint. Essentially, employees and another party each have two choices: (1) cooperation with high effort, and (2) non-cooperation with low effort. Regardless of what the other party (management, other employees, etc.) does, employees who attempt to maximize their payoff (and who lack trust and a long-term outlook) will choose non-cooperation. As a result, the expected outcome of the game is joint non-cooperation with suboptimal employee effort, an outcome whose individual and organizational payoff is far lower than that for joint cooperation. In Leibenstein's (1987: 97) view, however, this outcome is typically circumvented because "the pressures on employees and managers to conform to conventions will help *to counter* manifest or latent incentives that tend toward..." joint non-cooperation. Although conventions "solve" the prisoner's dilemma in the sense that joint non-cooperation is avoided, the outcome, according to Leibenstein, is still likely to be suboptimal from the viewpoint of both the individual and organization.[3]

Moral hazard

To explain suboptimal employee effort, mainstream organizational economists have found the moral hazard concept to be particularly useful. For example, according to Milgrom and Roberts (1992: ch. 6), moral hazard involves postcontractual opportunism on the part of the agent in a principal–agent relationship. It can occur when the employee's (or agent's) interests are not aligned with those of the employer (principal) and the employer cannot easily determine whether the employee is behaving in accord with the principal's goals or opportunistically in accord with the employee's self-interests.

The new economics of personnel

The "new economics of personnel" (for a useful review, see Main 1990) is a term that has been used to describe three major developments in economic theory that focus on "organizational arrangements which align the employee's interests with those of the employer to produce a self-policing incentive scheme" (Main 1990: 93). These are: efficiency wage theory, deferred compensation theory, and the theory of hierarchies. Each proposes a financial incentive scheme designed to raise employees' effort levels.

First, efficiency wage theory argues that employers may find it in their interest to set wage rates above the level necessary to recruit sufficient employees. This is because there are a number of reasons why labor productivity is believed to depend directly on the real wage paid by the firm (Yellen 1984). Paying a wage premium is expected to raise the productivity of workers who are concerned with the prospect of dismissal and unemployment, because these employees now experience a higher cost of job loss which leads them to shirk less. For related reasons, the wage premium is expected to lower turnover, reduce worker malfeasance, improve the quality of job applicants, improve morale and cooperation, reduce unionization (and thereby make work practices more flexible), and increase effort through higher group work norms (Main 1990: 93–5; Akerlof 1984).

Second, in a deferred compensation payment scheme, a worker in the early stages of an employer–employee relationship accepts wages lower than could be earned elsewhere (especially during a training period) with the expectation that eventually, as the employee's productivity rises, higher than market wages will be paid (Lazear 1981). In effect, the worker is making a financial commitment to the firm somewhat like posting a bond, a bond that would be forfeited upon unsatisfactory performance. It is argued that "the bonding activity provides a self-selection mechanism in attracting only those who are prepared to work hard, and so acts to screen out malingerers" (Main 1990: 97). Moreover, if dismissal and unemployment are the penalties for shirking, the incentive not to shirk is strong because shirking workers could not only lose current income but the "bond" as well.

Third, hierarchical organizational structure can be utilized to provide incentives similar to deferred compensation (Main 1990: 99–101). Promotional ladders used in hierarchies offer the prospect of increasingly well-paid jobs that may stimulate an increase in overall productivity even if the pay of promoted individuals far exceeds the value of their marginal product:

> Far from suggesting organizational inefficiency, high ranking individuals earning vast salaries may be the very device required to stimulate junior employees to greater efficiency. It is also clear that restricting certain jobs to internal promotions, with open competition limited to defined ports of entry, can be interpreted as a method of delivering prizes to tournament winners.
>
> (Main 1990: 101)

The literature on the new economics of personnel provides other examples of such incentive schemes, but it is beyond the scope of this chapter to consider them. For a detailed theory of the nature and form of efficient incentive contracts in the presence of moral hazard, see Milgrom and Roberts (1992: ch. 7).

Moral commitment and leadership

Because it is difficult to create foolproof incentive schemes, employers need alternative ways to try to align the interests of employees and employers. Mark Casson (1991: ch. 1–2) explains how leadership which draws on people's capacity for moral commitment can provide such an alternative. Employees who act out of moral commitment are acting ethically rather than simply responding to economic incentives. When acting in this way, these employees become self-monitoring agents who avoid imposing costs on the organization in order to avoid the guilt they would feel if they were to violate their moral commitments. The organization's leader is the one who is instrumental in developing the common understandings that employees are expected to commit themselves to. Further, the leader may optimize how he or she "manipulates" the messages that are sent to followers in order to get their desired adherence.

The joining-up process: an organizational behavior perspective

Joining-up refers to a process by which two distinctly separate entities, an individual and an organization, form a relationship that shapes their future interactions. How well the joining-up process is managed plays a critical role in determining the organizational productivity of the employee (Kotter 1973). If the process goes as well as possible and a strong mutual bond or commitment is created between the individual and the organization, employees will generally behave as organizational citizens and make correspondingly high effort choices. If, on the other hand, the process leaves employees psychologically unattached, there is no reason to believe that such employees will make the kind of efforts on behalf of the organization that an organizationally committed employee would.

The joining-up process consists of two stages: selection and socialization. Ideally, both stages are designed to produce a good fit between the person and organization. Selection processes not only assess job-related characteristics such as developed skills and abilities, intelligence, knowledge and experience, but may "serve the subtle function of selecting individuals whose values are compatible with organizational values and screening out those whose values are incompatible" (Chatman 1991: 461). Similarly, individuals select organizations perceived to match their values and needs.

Organizational socialization refers to the process by which a newly selected member of the organization comes to learn the values, norms, required behavior, expectations and social knowledge essential to participation in the organization (Chatman 1991: 462; Schein 1988: 54). Through socialization, the new employee comes to identify with the organization and internalize its values. Socialization occurs in firm-sponsored social activities, in training programs, in mentor programs and in a variety of other formal and informal work settings. Chatman (1991: 476) finds that socialization and selection make complementary contributions to improving the match between the values of the employee and the organization. Through the various socialization experiences, employees learn how they fit in the organization, and the organization learns what the employee can contribute. "Though the process is psychologically gradual, this mutual acceptance is organizationally symbolized by specific events such as a promotion, raise, new assignment, or formal performance appraisal. These events signify that a psychological contract has been negotiated," and that the new employee has been granted full membership in the organization (Schein 1978: 111).

If these two joining-up stages go very well, the result is organizational commitment, "an individual's psychological bond to the organization, including a sense of job involvement, loyalty, and a belief in the values of the organization" (O'Reilly 1989: 17). Strong culture organizations do much to develop this commitment and sense of ownership in their members. On the other hand, "in typical corporations, members comply with directions but may have little involvement with the firm beyond self-interest; that is, there is no commitment to the firm beyond that of a fair exchange of effort for money and, perhaps, status" (1989: 18).

The presence of organizational commitment is a stabilizing force indicating that the individual's purposes are to a great extent aligned with those of the organization. Organizational behavior models predict that committed employees will be willing to make personal sacrifices for the organization and do not depend primarily on external rewards or punishments (Williams and Anderson 1991: 604; Wiener 1982: 421, 426). It follows that such employees will act as organizational citizens in devoting efforts to organizational purposes much beyond what they can expect to be rewarded for. In such "high-commitment organizations" (Nota 1988), there is also reason to believe that there will be a "lack of politics" ("results are what count, not covert alliances" (Kotter 1988: 41)) and a lower degree of anxiety and confusion—a calming effect.

Organizational commitment, organizational capital and the suboptimal effort problem

Although suboptimal organizational effort, as analyzed earlier, is likely to be a problem in organizations where employees are psychologically unattached, in high commitment organizations where there is a strong employee-organization bond, things should be quite different. Because such bonded employees experience full membership or "ownership" in the organization, the external or social benefits to the organization should be largely internalized. When employees identify with the organization and share its goals and values, they will in a sense benefit, even if not directly, from their efforts that benefit the organization and/or other employees. As a result, they will not desire to be free riders. Naturally, few if any organizations will be able to realize fully this ideal, but the improvement of firms' joining-up processes will surely payoff in higher employee citizenship efforts and higher organizational productivity.

Developing the firm's joining-up process certainly requires a significant amount of time, attention and resources. Thus, it is useful to view this process as an investment in organizational capital. This organizational capital formation will be worthwhile for the firm to the extent that it fully or partially eliminates the externality that caused the suboptimal employee effort. To fully understand the nature of this organizational investment, it is necessary to analyze further and consider the types of organizational capital involved.

The varieties of organizational capital

Defining terms

Investment in organizational capital (a kind of human and social capital) refers to the using up of resources in order to bring about lasting improvement in productivity and/or worker well-being through changes in the functioning of the organization (Tomer 1987: 24). Unlike pure human capital that is embodied only in individuals, pure organizational capital is embodied only in the relationships among individuals. Thus, it can also be considered a type of social capital. There are two other kinds of organizational capital each of which are hybrids of the two pure varieties; these are called H-O and O-H capital. H-O capital relates to attributes embodied in individuals but which contribute in important ways to the functioning of the organization (Tomer 1987: 25-8). O-H capital derives from the firm's investment in information about the actual and desired characteristics of current and prospective employees, information which may be embodied in specific employees or the organization (e.g. its files).

Below, we focus on a new way of analyzing and classifying organizational capital, i.e. according to the role it plays in the process of joining the individual to the organization. From this perspective, there are two new types. The first, *pre-organizational capital*, comes before or is in preparation for the actual linking of the individual to the organization but is a necessary ingredient for the success of this process. The second, *linking organizational capital*, is what is formed during the joining-up process. These two types differ in the extent to which they are composed of the three basic types of organizational capital, pure, H-O, and O-H.

Pre-organizational capital

Pre-organizational capital refers to certain human qualities that provide productive capacity in that they are a necessary antecedent to successful joining-up. These qualities are nonoccupational attributes many of which are developed in the natural process of growing up. Some of them are acquired as part of family life, others through school experiences or other activities, and others seem to be an intrinsic part of the character or spirit of some people and not others. Pre-organizational capital is embodied in individuals, it is a type of H-O capital, and it is general in the sense that it is not firm-specific or organization-specific.

Among the pre-organizational capital qualities are those "virtues" analyzed by Amyra (now Shoshana) Grossbard-Shechtman (1988). These include loyalty, honesty, trust, a disciplined manner, an ethical orientation and cooperativeness. Workers possessing these virtues are believed to be more productive than those without them because, among other things, they have a lower probability of quitting, they shirk less, and they are less likely to misuse capital (1988: 200). It follows that firms will demand workers who have invested in or developed these virtues or at least "seemingly virtuous behavior," the observable behavior that is highly correlated with true virtue.

The model developed by Wiener (1982: 424) similarly "recognizes that some people are more likely to develop commitment toward a particular organization than other people." His model emphasizes two "personal predispositions," generalized loyalty and duty. These along with the congruency of a person's values with the organization determine organizational commitment.

In addition to the above, the following should be included on the list of pre-organizational capital qualities:

1) a person's appreciation of his/her life's main purpose;
2) the ability to adapt one's purposes to the life situations one encounters;
3) patience (the willingness and ability to sacrifice short-term gain for long-term gain);
4) the ability to see the big picture and take a long-term view;
5) lack of personal rigidities associated with earlier life experiences such as traumas (i.e. lack of tendency to respond to stressful situations in a way related to the emotions of an earlier situation);
6) social character (the values, appreciations, and attitudes common to the society).

An individual's endowment of all these pre-organizational capital qualities determines a person's generalized capability for being successfully joined to an organization. Individuals with a high endowment of these qualities are expected to develop a more effective psychological contract with the organization, develop more cooperative, trusting and efficacious relationships with other organization members, and make deeper commitments that integrate their own purposes with those of the organization than do others with comparatively low endowments. To the extent that developing strong individual–organization attachments is important for productivity, it follows that a society's endowment of this capital provides real economic capacity.

There are two important implications of the above for firm behavior.

First, firms will demand, and thus seek to select, recruits with the kind of endowments of pre-organizational capital that lead to successful joining-up. In part, this means selecting people with compatible purposes and values. In part too, it means selecting people who are most likely to be able to adapt to organizational requirements. It also means selecting people with the psychological qualities that enable them to forge viable relationships with others and make long-term commitments (assuming firms desire this). Second, firms will design their socialization processes in such a way as to take best advantage of the pre-organizational capital endowments of their selected workers.

Different societies invest in or develop different pre-organizational qualities. For example, in Japanese schools, in marked contrast to U.S. schools, janitors are not required because children clean and otherwise service their classrooms with relatively little overt supervision. From this experience, Japanese children acquire favorable attitudes regarding work cooperation, cleanliness and responsibility, attitudes which undoubtedly contribute to the productivity of their future workplaces. Similarly, many societies utilize sports activities to impart important cultural attitudes. Young athletes acquire a sense of disciplined intensity, teamwork and sportsmanship or ethics, among other things, that surely carries over to their work life. Although societies find many ways to socialize their youth, thereby investing in desired pre-organizational capital, people have a degree of choice about how they develop themselves, and thus, can decide to invest in and develop those qualities that they personally desire or those that will provide them with sought-after opportunities.

Linking organizational capital

Linking organizational capital is the organization-specific productive capacity formed during the two stages of the joining-up process, selection and socialization. During the selection process, O-H and H-O capital formation take place. First, organization members involved in selecting new employees not only draw on their existing stock of O-H capital involving knowledge of actual and desired characteristics of employees but they accumulate new knowledge (O-H capital) concerning prospective employees, some of whom become new members. Second, the selection process serves to inform, educate and orient prospective employees, thereby adding to their stock of H-O capital. The latter may be best utilized if these job candidates are hired by the organization undertaking the selection process, but this stock of H-O capital embodied in these prospective employees could wind up benefiting other organizations should these individuals be hired by similar employers.

During the socialization process, H-O, O-H and pure organizational capital formation takes place. First, H-O capital becomes embodied in new organization members as they learn the values, norms, required behavior, and expectations necessary for their full participation in the organization. Second, O-H capital accumulates to the extent that the organization acquires knowledge about what new employees can contribute and where they can function best. Third, to the extent that an important and desired end product of socialization is a lasting bond between the employee and the organization, pure organizational capital embodied in the newly created relationship is formed. In sum, the joining-up process when managed well is one that creates three valuable types of linking organizational capital which combine with new employees' stocks of pre-organizational capital to be an important determinant of employees' behavior and productivity.

A socio-economic model of individual behavior in the organization: the role of linking organizational capital

Organizationally responsible behavior

To understand better the role played by pre-organizational capital and linking organizational capital in overcoming the externality that causes suboptimal effort, we develop a socio-economic model of the individual employee's behavior within the organization. This model is focused on explaining the extent to which the individual behaves in an organizationally responsible manner. Ideal *organizationally responsible behavior* is in the organization's long-term best interests; it involves optimal effort choice from the standpoint of the organization, and it involves a high degree of organizational citizenship behavior. Responsible employees respond to economic incentives but do not respond to incentives that would lead them to behavior counter to the organization's best interests.

Note that employees acting in an organizationally responsible manner are at times acting out of commitment in the sense used by Sen, that is, they are "choosing an action that yields a lower expected welfare than an alternative available action" (Sen 1977: 328). From the standpoint of strict utility maximizing by individuals, it is counterpreferential choice. However, as Sen (1977: 334) points out, this is not unusual: "every economic system has...tended to rely on the existence of attitudes toward work which supersedes the calculation of net gain from each unit of exertion." Moreover, "to run an organization entirely on incentives to personal gain is pretty much a hopeless task" (1977: 335).

Other variables

For the purposes of this analysis, two human qualities, which are not pre-organizational capital qualities, are assumed to be possessed in some degree by all people. The first is economic striving, which includes the desire for consumer satisfactions, status, monetary rewards and distinction. The second is the desire to belong, be part of and identify with something larger such as an organization, community or society.

In this model, the extent to which individual behavior is organizationally responsible is explained by the following:

1) economic or "market" incentives stemming from circumstances within the organization;
2) organizational incentives;
3) macro social forces stemming from society, community or the public;
4) micro social forces stemming from extra-organizational institutions with a direct influence on the individual;
5) the stocks of pre-organizational capital and linking organizational capital that join the individual to the organization.

The organizational incentives referred to above are the explicit and implicit social influences and sanctions stemming from laws, rules, regulations and conventions, the purpose of which are generally to counter the negative organizational effects of certain of the economic incentives. The macro social forces are the broad community and societal influences reflecting the public's awareness and concerns, societal goals and demands, and society's generalized support for responsible behavior. Although these tend to encourage responsible behavior in society's overall interest, they are diffuse in their impact. The micro social forces emanate from extra-organizational institutions in which the individual has a significant involvement. These include his or her family, peer groups, professional associations, religious organizations and so on. Depending on the situation, these may have a direct, immediate and salient influence, encouraging or discouraging an individual's sense of organizational responsibility. Other factors including organizational climate, leadership behavior and external economic factors such as the firm's extent of competitive success could at times be a significant influence on individual behavior, but these are not emphasized here.

The essence of the model

The main elements of the model are shown in Figure 3.4. Although the individual's organizationally responsible behavior is affected by the economic incentives confronting the individual and the extent to which organizational incentives counter the negative influences of these, the key determinant of an individual's responsible behavior is the organizational capital that joins the individual to the organization. In addition, individual behavior will be more responsible when the macro and micro forces encourage it and will be less responsible when they discourage it.[4] Despite individual economic striving that could lead a person to make choices in their own short-term interests at the expense of the organization, an individual with a high endowment of important pre-organizational capital qualities and a solid

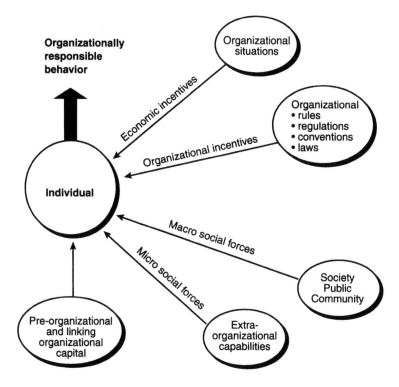

Figure 3.4 A socio-economic model of an individual's organizationally responsible behavior

link to the organization is likely to choose behavior in the long-term best interests of both the organization and his or her self.[5]

In this model (at least in its general case), individuals are partially embedded in the network of social relationships in the organization which means that individuals respond in part to economic incentives and in part to social influences (see Granovetter 1985). This is in contrast to neoclassical economics (in a sense a special case of this model) that assumes that individuals are self-interested, rational and minimally affected by social relations, i.e. that they are "undersocialized." Our model is also in contrast to the "heavily embedded" or "oversocialized" view that people's economic interests are almost entirely submerged in their social relationships.

Another way to look at the outcome of successfully linking the individual to the organization is that employees will have developed a new mode of behaving; they will have developed a kind of personal strategy integrating their individual purposes and competences with those of the organization. Analogous to a corporate strategy that bridges the gap between (1) the corporation's goals and distinctive competences and (2) the external threats and opportunities confronting it, the individual needs to develop a coherent behavior pattern that integrates his or her economic striving, need to belong, competences, and life purpose and focuses these on the organizational situation that he or she encounters. If, through joining-up activities, a critical mass of the organization's members successfully develops such personal strategies, we would expect this to make for a highly motivating organizational climate in which individuals are stimulated to realize their highest productive capabilities. Moreover, it is expected that individual behavior in such a situation will tend to be calm, focused, lacking political orientation, flexible and appropriate.

Examples

As a way to illustrate some of the above, let us first consider the simple example of littering. Individuals striving to achieve their personal and organizational productivity goals will probably experience an economic incentive to litter their workplaces. This is because satisfactorily disposing of accumulating trash requires scarce time, energy and attention that might alternatively be used to raise an individual's measured productivity. However, where the joining-up process has gone ideally, there should be no litter problem. The first reason is that the newly hired employees will have brought with them generous endowments of such pre-organizational capital qualities as a disciplined manner, an ethical orientation and cooperativeness. Second, we expect the newly hired organization members will have acquired a sense of ownership of the organization's purposes that is integrated with their own. Thus, these employees should not feel burdened with taking care of trash because they will not desire to gain at the organization's or other members' expense by not taking care of their share of trash disposal. On the other hand, it is easy to imagine that employees who are less deeply committed to the organization and lacking virtues such as cooperativeness may opportunistically take advantage of the fact that they can gain personally by shirking on their organizational trash responsibilities.

The work organization of the Israeli *kibbutz* is a suggestive second example. On the one hand, as Leibenstein points out, "there is almost a complete absence of differential economic incentives in the kibbutz" (1989: 233; see also Levi and Pellegrin-Rescia 1997). For example, there is a lack of differential pay for differential contributions, a lack of promotions or career structures, and a lack of ability to accumulate personal wealth. On the other hand, *kibbutzniks* work hard and the amount of free riding appears to be far below what would be expected given the incentives. In part this seems to be explained by nonmonetary incentives such as peer approval, general approval and the sense of belonging and common destiny of *kibbutz* members (1989: 234–5). Perhaps, however, there is another important reason which is suggested by our earlier analysis, namely, that *kibbutz* members are firmly bonded to their *kibbutz* and deeply committed to their way of life. No doubt this is in part a product of their selection (only one out of ten outside applicants are accepted for membership) and socialization processes, and thus, their organizational capital formation.

Some implications for economic theory

Economic theory regarding the agency problem is focused on (1) the conflict of interest between principals (say, owners) and agents (say, managers) and (2) the types of contracts that may serve to resolve this conflict by providing incentives for agents to act in the interests of the principals (see for example Jensen and Meckling (1976)). As agency theory is essentially a branch of neoclassical economics: it subscribes to the undersocialized view in which economic actors within organizations are assumed to be utility maximizing and unaffected by social relationships. In the special case of our model, where organization members are not bonded to the firm and not involved in social relationships that limit their responses to economic incentives, there may be little difference between our model and agency theory. However, in the more general case in which employees go through a joining-up process and are involved in significant social relationships, there is a great deal of difference. If the individual has become a full organization member and has a deep commitment to the organization, the employee can no longer be thought of as an agent because he or she will have acquired the outlook and behavior of a principal. Alternatively, if the joining-up is partial (as is more common), we would expect the member to behave partly as a principal and partly as an agent of the organization. In this case, a "contract" providing some economic incentives is needed to bring the individual's behavior more in line with that of the "principals." As Pascale observes, "the less we rely on informal social controls [especially socialization], the more we must inevitably turn to formal financial controls and bureaucratic procedures" (1985: 29).

The economic theories that come under the banner of the "new economics of personnel" assume that the employee is an agent of the organization. Realizing this helps us appreciate that these theories are oriented to discovering how certain patterns of economic incentives are able to align the employee-agent's interests with those of the employer in a relatively self-policing way. In contrast to these theories, the joining-up/high commitment solution to the suboptimal effort problem is not based on economic incentives, and thus is fundamentally different.

The joining-up/high commitment solution is also quite different from Leibenstein's prisoner dilemma solution, involving external pressure to conform to conventions.[6] When a person conforms to conventions, the individual is simply choosing alignment with an external cue. Thus, this behavior does not stem from within, that is, from internalized, strongly felt convictions or commitments, as is the case when an employee has become a full member of the organization through a successful joining-up process.

Linking the individual to society

An employee who is behaving in the organization's best interests may, of course, not be behaving in society's best interests. In other words, organizationally responsible behavior does not necessarily imply socially responsible behavior. To understand the latter, it is necessary to extend our model so that it includes the link between the individual and society.

Firms that behave in a socially responsible way are acting as societal citizens in the sense that they are conforming voluntarily to the norms and goals of society. There is reason to believe that the extent of a firm's socially responsible behavior is determined largely by the same kinds of factors that explained an employee's organizationally responsible behavior in our earlier model. First, an employee acting on behalf of a firm confronts economic or market incentives some of which are functional for society and others of which are dysfunctional in the sense that they involve externalities. Similar to the case for organizational responsibility, a decision maker, if acting in a socially responsible manner, will respond to the functional incentives but not respond to the dysfunctional ones that would lead to inoptimal societal outcomes.

The second factor explaining socially responsible behavior is the existence of societal incentives deriving from laws, regulations and conventions the purpose of which are generally to counter the negative effects of the market incentives (see Chapter 8). Third and fourth are the macro social forces and micro social forces of extra-firm institutions which encourage or discourage socially responsible behavior. Fifth is the key factor, the organizational capital that links the individual to society.

Two types of organizational capital are involved. The first is a type of pre-organizational capital; it corresponds to an individual's attitudes and understandings regarding what it means to be a good societal citizen. A person's endowment of this capacity determines that individual's generalized ability and desire to act in society's best interests. The second is a type of linking organizational capital in that it is formed during the joining-up process. An organization invests in this type of organizational capital when it makes efforts to orient its selection and socialization processes in such a way that its new members will be more likely to behave in socially responsible ways. Overall, the desired outcome is employees who are not only bonded or committed to the organization but committed to their society, thus behaving in ways best for society even when this may not be in the organization's best interests. Obviously, this is an ideal and a difficult state of affairs to achieve.

Conclusion

Economists generally recognize that employee-agents face a variety of incentives to free ride and, consequently, that these agents' utility-maximizing responses are at the expense of the organization's principals. Mainstream economists have, thus, sought insights into the ways in which principals structure their organizations in order to provide economic incentives that counter the tendency to suboptimal effort. While these writings have yielded some interesting and important theoretical results, they are ultimately unsatisfactory because they fail to utilize organizational behavior insights regarding the joining-up process and how an individual and organization can create a deep mutual commitment. Potentially, the joining-up process can solve the suboptimal effort problem by creating employees who are full organization members, and thus, principals in their outlook and behavior. The important contribution of this chapter is its integration of insights concerning the joining-up process with the insights of economic theory. In particular, this chapter has explained how in the joining-up process two new types of organizational capital, pre-organizational and linking, are formed.

Judging by the kind of selection and socialization processes generally used by Japanese companies, they have been more successful than Western companies at applying these organizational insights. All too often, Western firms have chosen over-reliance on financial incentives to motivate their employees. The result has typically been increasing inequality in the distribution of employee compensation and lackluster economic performance. Thus, understanding the role of the joining-up process in overcoming suboptimal effort would appear to be very important for creating "world class" companies that can compete successfully in the global economy. Further, modern economies should be able to gain from fostering the development of the kind of human qualities associated with both societal and organizational citizenship behavior.

In the chapters that follow in Part II, the organizational capital concept is applied in order to understand other aspects of the firm's behavior in relation to competitiveness.

Part II
Competitiveness
Rational decision making,
flexibility and integration, and
leadership

The three chapters of Part II are concerned with three aspects of the firm's internal functioning and how they contribute to its competitiveness. These chapters focus, respectively, on rational organizational decision making, flexibility and integration in strategy and structure, and leadership and spirit. Developing these different capabilities of the firm requires quite different kinds of investment in organizational capital.

4 Rational organizational decision making in the human firm

A socio-economic model

Contrary to what we learn from neoclassical economics, real firms are not simply and inevitably optimizing machines. Because they are human firms, they strive for rationality in their decision making but rarely come close to this ideal. Nevertheless, firms can raise their capacity for rational decision making through appropriate investments in organizational capital, thereby enhancing their competitiveness. To understand this possibility, it is necessary to develop a socio-economic model of rational organizational decision making in the firm.

There is no shortage of important insights concerning organizational decision making in the literatures of economics, management and psychology. The problem is that these insights are rarely brought together in an integrated way. Particularly lacking is the linking of management and psychological insight with economic theory. Thus, the purpose of this chapter is to synthesize the most important organizational insights concerning the making of large, complex, ill-structured decisions and to link these to important economic concepts. The concern here is with the rationality of this decision making, what rationality means, why departures from rationality are a common occurrence, and what can be done to improve the rationality of decision making. The result is a socio-economic model of the rationality of organizational decision making.

Some economists will object to this chapter on the grounds that it is insufficiently economic as conventionally defined. Nevertheless, this research ought to be of great interest to economists because the rationality of economic decision-making behavior is at the heart of economics. One example of the fruitfulness of working in the interdisciplinary territory of decision making is the work of Herbert Simon, the Nobel Prize-winning economist, psychologist and all-around extraordinary social scientist. Despite these efforts, Simon's contributions have been underappreciated by the economic profession and insufficiently integrated with economic theory. The present work in part attempts to remedy this latter deficiency.

The model developed here is not a political or conflict one; it is not concerned with the processes of high level conflict resolution, nor with the motivations or preferences of different organizational participants. The organization's goals (however ill-formed or implicit) and the processes by which these goals are determined are outside the scope of this research.[1] The focus here is on the organizational processes and influences that determine the expected quality of the resultant decisions. A higher quality decision is one that comes closer than another to the optimum, the one that does more than any other to advance the organization's goals. An important question is: how can the capacity of the organization be raised in order to generate decisions of the highest quality, that is, to make decision making as rational as it is possible for it to be? In essence, the intent is to develop a theory of not-so-bounded rationality, a theory of organizations as potential enhancers of human rationality and human potential more generally. Organizations devoting time to raising these capacities are investing in organizational capital and thereby raising their internal efficiency (X-efficiency).

A novel aspect of the model developed here is its consideration of the quality of mental activity. The quality of mental activity has to do with the role of emotions and the balance of left versus right brain hemisphere activity, especially the balance of intuitive ways of knowing with more conventional information processing ways. These factors, about which there is considerable disagreement and controversy, are rarely considered by economists and are not always included in managerial and psychological treatments of decision making.

The first section of the chapter considers the meaning of rationality and contrasts substantive rationality with procedural rationality. The next three sections each develop an important element of the decision making model. The second section considers the activities involved in information processing, especially the steps in decision making and decision strategies that may involve short cuts to the decision-making process. The third section deals with the structures and processes that bring to bear organizational influences that regularize decision-making behavior. The fourth section considers how the quality of mental activity relates to the quality of decision making. Finally, the fifth section provides perspective on the model and relates its elements to economic concepts such as X-efficiency and organizational capital.

The concept of rationality

Rational economic man

According to modern orthodox economists, rationality in decision making means "the logical application of means to attain particular ends" (Lutz and Lux 1988: 91). In this view, "rational economic man" chooses the one alternative that maximizes the value desired (typically his or her utility or profit). This rational decision maker single-mindedly and eagerly calculates until the optimum is determined (1988: 95). It is assumed that all relevant information can be reduced to a common measure of the desired value; there are no irreducible qualitative considerations.

It should be noted that in common usage, as reflected in dictionary definitions, rational behavior is behavior that is characterized by reason. Rationality as reasonable behavior is a much broader and less precise phenomenon than the rationality of economic man. It encompasses consideration of appropriate ends, relationships between means and ends, non-selfish behavior, and considerations that cannot be reduced to a single value.

Because we are concerned with rational organizational decision making in the sense of what firms ought to do to choose the best alternative given their ends, it makes sense to start with the rational economic man notion of rationality. However, as we will see, there's only a limited amount of progress that can be made before we must abandon this concept of rationality for a more suitable one.

The set of alternatives

Models of rational decision-making behavior have generally started from the notion of a decision space, e.g. a two-dimensional point space in which each point represents one of the set of all possible alternatives (Simon 1955: 102). Let us say that none of the alternatives in this space have features going beyond the existing state of technological and organizational knowledge; all can be discovered without truly creative or innovative activity. Of course, it is conceivable that decision makers in considering alternatives will make creative new connections between old elements and see previously unseen relationships (whether or not explicit research and development activity is involved). This activity may make possible previously unimagined alternatives that are beyond the current state of the art. Thus, the decision space must include a third dimension in order to enclose all the possibilities that decision makers are capable of conceiving.

Subjective expected utility theory

Subjective expected utility (SEU) theory is the dominant theory about how rational economic man makes decisions. In accordance with SEU theory, decision makers in a static world will select the very best alternative from the two-dimensional space. As Simon (1955: 102–3) and others have pointed out, this involves selecting the alternative with the maximum expected payoff taking into account knowledge of the outcomes of the alternatives, the probabilities of these outcomes and the utility or value placed on these outcomes. In a dynamic context, optimizing is in principle no different; it simply means selecting the alternative with maximum subjective expected utility from a three-dimensional space, which is larger and less clearly defined than the two-dimensional one.

The problem with subjective expected utility theory

Is SEU theory a satisfactory positive or normative decision making theory? According to Simon:

> There is some indication that when the situation is very simple and transparent, so that the subject can easily see and remember when he is being consistent, he behaves like a utility maximizer. But as the choices become a little more complicated—choices, for example, among phonograph records instead of sums of money—he becomes much less consistent.
>
> (1959: 258)

However:

> in typical real-world situations, decision makers, no matter how badly they want to do so, simply cannot apply the SEU model. If doubt still remains on this point, it can be dissipated by examining the results of laboratory experiments in which human subjects have been asked to make decisions involving risk and uncertainty in game-like situations orders of magnitude simpler than the game of real life. The evidence, much of which has been assembled in several articles by Amos Tversky and his colleagues, leaves no doubt whatever that the human behavior in these choice situations—for whatever reasons—departs widely from the prescriptions of SEU theory....The principal reason...for this departure...is that human beings have neither the facts nor the consistent structure of values nor the reasoning power at their disposal that would be required, even in these relatively simple [laboratory] situations, to apply SEU principles.
>
> (Simon 1983: 16–17)

For a good explanation regarding the nature of and limitations of human information processing abilities (especially the storage and retrieval of information from short-term and long-term memory), see Simon (1981: ch. 3–4). It is important to note in this connection that the performance of a given decision-maker will be highly dependent upon the amount of relevant information stored in long-term memory, how the decision situation is represented in the mind, and what calculating skills and tools have been acquired.

There are several other reasons why SEU theory is not satisfactory as a theory of organizational decision making for complex, ill-structured situations. First, it is rarely possible for people to generate all the relevant alternatives (Nutt 1976: 88). Second, as Frey and Foppa (1986: 156) point out, "individuals —except perhaps people trained as economists and statisticians—do not work with, nor do they understand well, the concept of probability." Of course, people do have some notion of the kind of events that occur and do not occur, but this is quite different from knowing and manipulating probabilities. Third, the cognitive psychologists who formulated prospect theory have found much evidence that the heuristic devices that people use to deal with complexity introduce major systematic biases into their decision making (for a brief overview, see Etzioni 1988: 117–22; for a review of this and related issues, see Machina 1987). Fourth, organizations face severe limitations with respect to the time, energy and resources that they can afford to devote to decision-making activities (more on this later). Thus, it is obvious that if cognitively limited decision makers do not have the time to explore all possible alternatives, they will be unable to select the optimum one as predicted by SEU theory. This, however, does not mean that decision makers are not rational. It means that decision makers are not rational economic men and that a concept of rationality better suited to our purposes is needed.

Rational decision making

In relation to organizations, a more general concept of rationality such as Herbert Simon uses is helpful. According to Simon (1957: 5), organizational decision-making behavior "is rational in so far as it selects alternatives which are conducive to the achievement of the...[organization's] goals." Because substantive rationality, the type of rationality synonymous with selecting the optimum alternative, is impossible as indicated above, we are concerned here with procedural rationality (Simon 1976; Simon 1978: 8–9). Procedural rationality is a matter of degree. An organization with a higher degree of procedural rationality than another is one in which the probability of making higher quality decisions (decisions whose characteristics are closer to optimal as determined by an objective observer) is higher than in the other.[2] The probability of a certain quality of decision making depends on the quality of the organizational processes related to decision making, particularly the degree to which those processes promote openness to evidence and openness to reason as well as conscious deliberations in order to draw proper conclusions (Etzioni 1988: 136, 144–6).

It is because of bounded rationality that procedural rationality is important. Behavior that is boundedly rational is very much rational in the sense that it is intentional or purposive, i.e. guided by general goals and objectives. However, it is limitedly rational (Simon 1957: xxiv) because it falls short of omniscience on account of "failures of knowing all the alternatives, uncertainty about relevant exogenous events, and inability to calculate consequences" (Simon 1979: 502). Also, normative commitments and affective involvements introduce systematic decision-making bias because they "shape to a significant extent the information that is gathered, the ways it is processed, the inferences that are drawn, the options that are being considered, and the options that are finally chosen" (Etzioni 1988: 94). The important concepts involved are illustrated in Figure 4.1 by arraying them along a horizontal line.

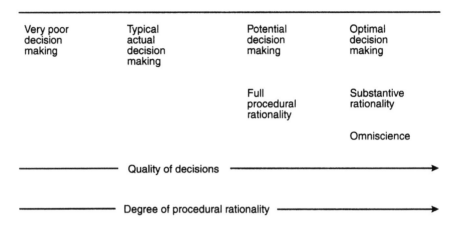

Figure 4.1 Actual versus potential quality of decisions

Moving to the right along the line means improvement in the quality of decisions as the degree of procedural rationality increases. Improvement of organizational processes makes possible better quality decisions through more procedurally rational functioning, but optimal decision making or substantive rationality is not within reach. The best that humans can do given their cognitive limitations and the nature of organizations is indicated as potential decision making or full procedural rationality.

A socio-economic model of decision making

The socio-economic model of organizational decision making developed here explains about the organizational processes and efforts necessary to achieve full procedural rationality, and indicates that this level of organizational functioning typically does not occur. The model applies to large, complex, ill-structured (not amenable to mathematical solution) decisions, i.e. it applies to the real world where the concept of substantive rationality is inapplicable. The model is designed to indicate the processes, structure and culture that an organization must have in order to make the highest quality decisions possible given the inherent limitations of humans and their organizations. The theory has three main elements:

1) the activities involved in information processing;
2) the organizational influences that regularize decision-making behavior;
3) the quality of the mental activities performed by members of the organization.

Information processing activities

Steps in decision making

To achieve best possible decision making, decision makers in the organization would have to follow the eight steps below to the best of their abilities.

1) recognize the need for a decision: opportunities, problems and crises;
2) decide about the decision process;
3) diagnosis: what are the nature of the issues and problems?
4) survey the organizational goals and the values implicated by the choice, and determine decision criteria;
5) search for existing alternatives and/or design new alternatives;
6) evaluate the positive and negative consequences of the alternatives;
7) selection: deliberate on and make a commitment to an alternative;
8) authorization.

It is not necessary that the steps be taken in precisely the sequence indicated, that every step be taken in all decision situations, or that the steps be taken only once.

Mintzberg, Raisinghani and Theoret (1976) have found in their empirical research on organizational decision making that the first step, recognizing the need for a decision, is evoked by situations that are opportunities, problems or crises. On one end of this continuum are opportunities, usually an idea for a significant new activity, and on the other end are crises that present themselves suddenly and require immediate attention. In the middle are problems involving milder pressures than crises.

Once the need for a decision is recognized, Step 2 involves deciding about the decision process. This means deciding (1) what decision strategy will be used and (2) who should decide. First, the organization must decide how much time, resources and effort will be devoted to this decision, and how analytical and systematic their approach will be. They may determine a rough schedule of activities and develop an image of the ideal solution (Mintzberg, Raisinghani and Theoret 1976; Beach and Mitchell 1978). Second, the organization must decide about whether the decision will be made by an individual or a group, and if the latter what the composition and inputs of the members will be.

Step 3, diagnosis, involves efforts to determine the nature of the problem, to clarify or define the issues, and to figure out what needs to be known. In Step 4, the decision makers need first to remind themselves of their organization's goals and values, and second to determine decision criteria that will enable them to relate these goals and values to characteristics of decision alternatives.

The next step (5) is to locate alternatives that would resolve the problem or crisis or would take advantage of the opportunity. In some cases, this merely calls for searching for ready-made solutions. In other cases, it requires the design or development of custom-made solutions or the modification of ready-made ones. Designing custom-made solutions is generally a complex, expensive and time-consuming process (Mintzberg, Raisinghani and Theoret 1976).

In Step 6, the positive and negative consequences of the alternatives are evaluated. In some cases, this may involve the bringing to bear of a great amount of systematic analysis of collected information, and in other cases it is a more intuitive and judgmental process. Regardless, it is helpful if the decision maker has a systematic method for arraying and comparing the consequences of different alternatives such as the decisional balance sheet suggested by Janis and Mann (1977: ch. 6). This procedure is not very different from the tally sheet of pros and cons that Benjamin Franklin proposed over two hundred years ago; he called it "moral or prudential algebra" (Janis and Mann 1977: 149).

Once the alternatives have been compared, the decision maker needs time in Step 7 to deliberate, i.e. time to gradually come to comprehend the complex issues, and then to commit to the best alternative. If this selection process is not done by decision makers who have the authority to commit the organization and its resources to the selected course of action, then authorization (Step 8), acceptance or rejection of the whole solution, will be done by someone higher up in the chain of command.

Selecting a decision strategy

It does not take long for decision makers dealing with large, complex and ill-structured situations to come to the realization that the information processing activities required for optimization, or even an approximation to it, would be prohibitively expensive. For this reason, decision makers have sought ways to make their information processing tasks feasible and manageable. They have, for example, sought decision strategies "based on rules of thumb or 'heuristics' [that] tend to guide the search into promising regions, so that solutions will generally be found after search of only a tiny part of total space" (Simon 1979: 507).

A decision strategy consists of a procedure that utilizes rules of search, rules of choice and rules of learning (Beach and Mitchell 1978: 439–40; Grandori 1984: 193–4). Satisficing is a decision strategy where alternatives are examined as they become available and the first one that satisfies all of the decision maker's requirements is chosen for implementation. Consider the rules involved in a satisficing strategy compared to the rules for an optimizing strategy (Grandori 1984: 195–6). The satisficing choice rule is to compare the consequences of each alternative to the decision maker's aspiration level, rather than comparing alternatives directly. The satisficing search rule is based on the principle of only partially exploring the decision space, instead of generating all possible alternatives. The satisficing learning rule is to adjust aspiration levels or the set of considered alternatives depending on whether there are too many or no acceptable alternatives. The essential difference between optimizing and satisficing is the "difference between searching a haystack to find the sharpest needle in it and searching the haystack to find a needle sharp enough to sew with" (March and Simon 1958: 141).

Satisficing and other "simplistic" decision strategies are essentially short cuts that lower drastically decision-making costs relative to the optimizing strategy, but also lower the expected decision quality because of less adequate information processing. The savings involved in the short cut strategies may make sense to the extent that the organization can still achieve acceptable decision quality. Moreover, an organization might learn over time to improve its degree of procedural rationality by adopting successively better short cuts, ones whose net benefits (considering the benefits of quality decisions and the costs of the information processing activities) are higher than previously selected ones.

The trade-off with respect to decision quality and cost is very clear in the theory developed by Beach and Mitchell (1978). In their analysis, decision makers experience utility loss as they move to more analytic strategies requiring greater personal resource expenditure.[3] Correspondingly, this move increases the probability of a correct decision in which case the decision makers gain utility. Given time and money constraints that may make infeasible certain strategies, decision makers will choose from among the remaining strategies in their repertoires the strategy perceived as yielding the maximum net utility gain. This strategy selection process takes into account the difficulty inherent in the decision situation, the importance attached to making a correct decision, and the characteristics of the decision maker(s). Thus, in the view of Beach and Mitchell, there is no single decision strategy that is correct for all situations or all organizations. The most appropriate or rational strategy is contingent on the decision situation.[4] It should be noted that the calculation of net gain is not and could not be a precise one. Thus, this strategy selection process is not a case that demonstrates the optimality of selecting non-optimal decision methods.[5]

Prominent among the short cut decision strategies are: satisficing, elimination by aspects, incrementalism and muddling through, and mixed scanning (Janis and Mann 1977: 31–41) as well as heuristic, cybernetic and random strategies (Grandori 1984).[6] In the case of driving on an unfamiliar highway and noticing that one's car is nearly out of gas, satisficing would no doubt be an appropriate strategy to decide where to stop and fill up with gas. This is because the cost of searching for more alternatives is high relative to the expected payoff from finding a better alternative (gas station). In other kinds of situations, different short-cut strategies would be appropriate. When decision making requires the design of a custom-made solution, the time and expense involved may mean that it is, again, appropriate for the organization to consider only one alternative (for empirical analysis related to this point, see Mintzberg, Raisinghani and Theoret 1976: 256).

The above should not be construed as meaning that the use of short cuts in decision making is always justified and rational. The use of a short cut would presumably be irrational in the sense of not being conducive to achieving the organization's goals if it were the outcome of an impulsive, emotional response without the benefit of adequate thought (Simon 1976: 131).[7]

Even allowing for the necessity of using short cuts, it is clear that achieving close to full procedural rationality in the information processing part of decision making is not easy to do. Given that organization members typically exert less than their full efforts to decision making, it is expected that relatively few organizations will realize close to their full procedural rationality in this aspect of decision making.

Influences that regularize organizational decision-making behavior

Regardless of the steps taken or strategies used in information processing, decision making will not be rational (oriented to organizational goals) unless decision makers take the organization's goals—not their own or others' goals—and other relevant information into account. In *Administrative Behavior*, Simon (1957) has developed what has come to be called the "rational man" (not the same as rational economic man) view of the influences brought to bear by the organization and its management to insure the rationality of its members' decision making.

In Simon's view, the influence of the organization is extremely important:

> Organization refers to the complex pattern of communications and other relations in a group of human beings. This pattern provides to each member of the group much of the information, assumptions, goals, and attitudes that enter into his decisions, and provides him also with a set of stable and comprehensible expectations as to what the other members of the group are doing and how they will react to what he says and does.
>
> (1957: xvi)

If these patterns are to influence the decisions of organization members in a desirable way, it is necessary that the organization carry out substantive and procedural planning.

Substantive planning is the activity that involves deciding about the values and goals of the organization and the general methods used to attain these values. Decisions related to these matters are arranged in a hierarchy; the most general ones at the top provide the environment for the more particular ones at succeeding steps down (Simon 1957: 96–7). It is these substantive decisions that supply the values and premises that enable organization members to make decisions by drawing conclusions from them (1957: xii).

Procedural planning is the activity that involves designing and establishing mechanisms "that will direct...[members'] attention, channel information and knowledge, etc., in such a way as to cause the specific day-to-day decisions to conform with the substantive plan" (Simon 1957: 96). It is through the following mechanisms of organizational influence that an individual comes to act as a member of an organization in the sense that "he applies the same general scale of values to his choices as do other members of the group, and...his expectations of the behavior of other members influence his own decisions" (151). First, the organization divides work and assigns tasks, thereby directing and limiting the attention of the member to that task. Second, the organization establishes standard practices, which means that it is not necessary to decide each time how certain recurrent tasks will be done. Third, the organization transmits decisions downward through its ranks by establishing systems of authority and influence. This takes the form of a hierarchy of formal authority as well as an advising function. Fourth, the organization provides formal and informal channels of communication running in all directions through which information for decision-making flows. Finally, the organization trains and indoctrinates its members. This might be called the "internalization" of influence, because it injects into the very nervous systems of the organization members the criteria of decision that the organization wishes to employ. The organization member acquires knowledge, skill and identifications or loyalties that enable them to make decisions, by themselves, as the organization would like them to decide (Simon 1957: 102–3).

In sum, organizations' control over and integration of decision making is achieved through "regularizations of the behavior of individuals through subjection of their behavior to stimulus-patterns socially imposed on them" (Simon 1957: 109). In the case of authoritative influence, it is important to note that for behavior to be governed by authority, members must relax their own critical faculties and permit the communicated decisions of others to guide their decisions (1957: 151). Individuals are willing to accept authority and other aspects of organizational membership "when their activity in the organization contributes, directly or indirectly, to their own personal goals" (1957: 110).

Even when successful, organization members are likely to feel that more could have been done to bring appropriate influences to bear on their decision-making personnel. Other businesses may also fall far short of success in this area. Because of this, it is expected that relatively few organizations will realize close to their full procedural rationality in this aspect of their decision making.

The quality of mental activity

Suppose that in its decision making, an organization always follows all the suggested information processing steps, uses appropriate decision strategies, and brings to bear influences that lead organizational decision makers to take organizational goals and subgoals into account in a consistent way. The quality of decision making in such an organization could still be substantially below potential if the quality of individual and/or group mental activity involved in certain of the decision-making steps is below potential. This leads us to inquire concerning the nature of this mental activity and the factors determining its quality. To begin, let us consider findings from the growing amount of research on brain activity related to decision making.

Intuition, the right brain and creativity

Up to this point, our conception of mental activity has largely been confined to storage and retrieval of information from short-term and long-term memory as well as to calculation and logical analysis. Recent research indicates that these functions reside in the left hemisphere of the brain, but also that equally important, often neglected functions reside in the right hemisphere.[8] Right brain activity makes possible a different form of knowing, called intuition.

The nature of intuition

According to Frances Vaughan, intuition is a psychological function—like sensation, feeling and thinking—and thus is a way of knowing: "When we know something intuitively, it invariably has the ring of truth: yet often we do not know how we know what we know" (1982: 16). The intuitive function includes such phenomena as precognition, telepathy, psychokinesis, clairvoyance and remote viewing. People with extremely highly developed intuitive abilities are known as psychics. The average person is believed to have considerable, albeit undeveloped, intuitive ability.

According to Agor:

> Intuition, fully developed, then, is a highly efficient way of knowing. It is fast and accurate. Our system will process a wide array of information on many levels, and give us an instantaneous cue how to act. We have the answer even though we do not understand all the steps, or know fully all the information our system processed to give us this cue. The more open we are to our feelings, the more secure we become through practice in their ability to give us correct cues, and the less we project our own personal desires and wishes for a particular situation or person to be other than they really are, the more efficient our intuitive clues will become.
>
> (1984: 6)

Intuitive cues come to people on four different levels: physical, emotional, mental, and spiritual (Agor 1986: 6).

One aspect of intuition is that sudden, illuminating, "I've found it" flash such as experienced by scientists (such as Archimedes and Einstein) at the moment of a breakthrough (Rowan 1987: 4). According to Rowan (1987: 6–13), the brain puts things together, compressing years of learning and experience, retrieving fragments of knowledge buried in the subconscious and fusing this with new information, and in a flash it is available without conscious effort. While Herbert Simon (1983: 25–8) does not doubt the validity of the "aha!" experience and that the resulting problem solutions are frequently correct, his view is that these experiences are akin to pattern recognition and only come to people who possess the appropriate knowledge stemming from a long period of preparation (for example, chess masters).

Using intuition in decision making

According to Agor (1986: 5), intuition is a "highly rational decision making skill—… a subspecies of logical thinking—one in which the steps of the process are hidden in the subconscious portion of the brain." One piece of evidence in support of this comes from the research of Douglas Dean and John Mihalasky (1973: 70–2). They found that among presidents who were both chief executives and chief corporate decision makers for at least five years, every man who improved his company's profits by 100 percent or more scored above average in the precognition test they administered, a remarkable correlation between high profit making and precognition, the ability to predict future events (1973: 71).

Similarly, Agor (1986: 18) finds that "when executives in top management positions who also score in the top 10 percent in intuitive ability are tested, the results overwhelmingly indicate that these executives do use their brain skill to guide their most important decisions."

> Also … when these top managers intuitively "know" they have reached the correct decision, they share a "consensus set" of feelings that tell them so: a sense of excitement—almost euphoria; a total sense of commitment; a feeling of total harmony; warmth and confidence; a burst of enthusiasm and energy like a bolt of lightning or sudden flash that "this is the solution." Alternatively, when they sense an impending decision may be an incorrect one or that they need to take more time to adequately process the cues they are receiving, these managers speak of feelings of anxiety, mixed signals, discomfort, or an upset stomach.
> (Agor 1986: 18)

Top executives find intuition is most helpful in making key management decisions in the following situations:

1) there is a high level of uncertainty;
2) there is little previous precedent;
3) variables are often not scientifically predictable;
4) "facts" are limited;
5) facts do not clearly point the way to go;
6) time is limited and there is pressure to be right;
7) there are several plausible alternative solutions to choose from, with good arguments for each;
8) new trends are emerging (Agor 1986: 18, 29).

A very common way for executives to use their intuition is in attempting to generate unusual possibilities and new options (1986: 35) or to identify problems to be solved (Leavitt 1975b: 14). Alternatively, many executives use their intuition as a synthesizer and integrator in the "process of digesting and sifting through the information they have consumed before reaching their final decision" (Agor 1986: 35). In the same vein, Mintzberg (1976: 57) points out how the right side of the brain is very useful to managers in using soft (feelings, impressions, hearsay, gossip, etc.) and speculative inputs into decision making; he also points to its usefulness in the diagnosis stage of decision making. For an analysis of the relative usefulness of left brain, right brain and integrated brain skills at different steps of the decision making process, see Agor (1984: 78–81). Agor views true creativity as stemming from an integration of both the left and right side of the brain (1984: 81).

Some of the most successful businesspeople have had extraordinary extrasensory perception. Vaughan (1982: 18) refers to "many successful entrepreneurs who have an uncanny ability to know what will happen next in their businesses."

> "Both Leon Hess of Hess-Getty Oil and Conrad Hilton of the Hilton hotel chain admit their hunches have often given them a clear-cut indication of what the other sealed bids will be, and enabled them to make the winning, profitable bid"
>
> (Dean *et al.* 1973: 137).

For other business and finance examples of ESP, see Dean *et al.* (1973: 137–40). Obviously, business people with the ability to use their intuition to see into the future, to learn what competitors in other places are doing, to become aware of new possibilities, to detect and diagnose problems, etc. will have the capability of making superior decisions without having spent an inordinate amount of time processing information in conventional ways.[9]

Organizational blocks to intuition

There is considerable consensus among researchers on the organizational factors believed to block or inhibit an organization's intuitive decision-making ability. First, organizations may emphasize left-brained, analytical abilities and performance at the expense of intuitive abilities. According to Leavitt:

> If analytic education drives out imagination, and we want "imaginative" problem finding, problem solving, and problem implementing, then we had better be careful about over crowding our organization with analysts and about maintaining an organizational climate dominated by the analytic tradition.
>
> (1975b: 18)

James March (1976) suggests that in this type of climate the exaggerated insistence upon consistency and other rules of rationality may often be dysfunctional. Such organizations may experience "analysis paralysis," delaying decisions and avoiding use of intuitive approaches until its too late in the belief that more information and analysis are needed (Rowan 1987: 91–4).

Several other factors associated with organizational climate have been identified as intuition inhibitors. First, in Agor's (1986: 79, 99) view, organizations that are inflexible, highly hierarchical, and not encouraging of new ideas or experimenting tend to drive out or suppress intuitive talent. Second, evidence from experiments performed by Douglas Dean and John Mihalasky (1974: ch. 6) strongly suggest that the intuitive abilities of women in male-dominated groups were significantly below the level of their abilities in situations where domination was not a factor. Perhaps this and other forms of dominance in organizations thwarts the intuitive abilities of certain groups of people. Third, Dean and Mihalasky find that "any sort of psychological or physiological stress appears to turn off intuition" (1974: 171).

Another intuition blocker is "the hurly-burly of tender offers, leveraged buyouts, white knights, and greenmail [which] is not conducive to the thoughtful contemplation that produces great insights" (Rowan 1987: 19). Also cited by Rowan as a blocking factor is managerial gamesmanship in organizational meetings (1987: 19).

Fostering intuition in organizations

The first approach to fostering an organization's intuitive decision-making ability is what Leavitt (1975b: 20) has called the "fertilizer approach." This involves "managing the conditions under which man thinks about the problem." One aspect of this is creating appropriate organizational relationships and climate. First:

> if we have a good, open, trusting set of human relationships in this organization, the Organizational Development argument goes, people

will not only feel more committed and work harder, they will also become freer to think more creatively and solve problems better.

(Leavitt 1975b: 16)

Second, creating a relaxed or nonstressful, informal, fun-type climate is helpful (Agor 1984: 68). March (1976) emphasizes the value of playfulness, "the deliberate, temporary relaxation of rules...[where] we challenge the necessity of consistency." This in Robey's (1986: 558) view will succeed if it temporarily shuts down the "safeguarding logic of the left" and permits some relief from control and coordination. Such an environment will encourage new ideas and experimentation. Intuition will also be fostered when organizations eliminate rules that inhibit individual judgment (Rowan 1987: 178).

Third, intuition is greatly encouraged by the right type of leadership, goals, vision and ideals. The most effective leaders in this sense develop and communicate visions of the future in such a way that it "captures people's hearts" and focuses their efforts (Agor 1984: 98–9). Masatoshi Yoshimura, a Japanese business leader, believes that "when everyone in an organization aspires to higher goals and ideals, and untiringly strives to reach them by overcoming numerous difficulties, each can undoubtedly succeed in finding himself exalted in the superrational domain," i.e. they are able to achieve a high degree of intuitive perception, which is spiritual in nature (Dean *et al.* 1974: 188). Relatedly, it takes a charismatic leader, one who can inspire his followers to high achievement, to bring out their highest intuitive abilities (Rowan 1987: 169–71). The truly excellent companies are the ones whose leadership and organizations reflect many of these right-brained considerations (Peters and Waterman 1982: 60–2, 81–6).

A second approach to fostering intuition is to use test instruments to measure employees' intuitive abilities and their use of these abilities and then through seminars, special training and so on to help employees to develop these abilities (Agor 1984). If an organization has reached the point where it knows its employees relative intuitive and analytical strengths, it can use a third approach involving the formation of appropriately staffed decision-making teams (Agor 1986: 88–90, 113–14). According to Agor:

> the quality and quantity of output will be dramatically increased in organizations if groups are formed first guided by brain skill assessments, and then sequenced so that each brain skill type [e.g. intuitive or thinking/analytical] is put on the problem at the stage in the process where their skill is most appropriate.

(1986: 114)

Not surprisingly, intuitives are best at generating new venture ideas, and thinking types are best at evaluating them.

A fourth approach to fostering the use of intuition in decision making is to structure the group's decision-making activity so as to get the most from the intuitive talent that exists. One important example of this is brainstorming, where people addressing a problem are asked to mention anything that comes to mind and to defer from criticizing others' ideas (Rowan 1987: 31; Leavitt 1975b: 19). This technique and other newer ones such as the Crawford slip technique (Agor 1986: 87–8) have been found to generate many more ideas per hour than groups not using such techniques. For completeness, it should be noted that such activities as sabbaticals, job rotation, guided imagery and visualization, meditation and so on have been found to have value in fostering the organization's intuitive ability.

Emotion, motivation and decision making

Another reason why decision-making mental activity, whether deriving from the left or right side of the brain, may be deficient is related to the quality of organizational relationships and interactions. It is the influence of these relationships on the emotions of organization members that affects the quality of their mental functioning. This viewpoint derives from the human relations approach to organizational behavior and the related practice of organization development.

The human relations perspective.

According to Chris Argyris (1960: 10), man is capable of great growth; he is capable of becoming a mature, self-actualized adult "who can give 'of' himself without giving 'up' himself."[10] However, in modern scientifically managed enterprises, the formal organization inevitably makes demands upon workers that frustrate their capacity to grow toward maturity. To some degree, these demands are the same as what was referred to earlier as the influences that regularize decision-making behavior. Because of the lack of congruency of these demands with the higher needs of humans, organizational participants, according to Argyris (1960: 15–23), will experience short time perspective, an orientation toward part of the organization rather than the whole, low psychological energy and disinterest, perceptual bias, a narrowing of the individual's range of tolerance for new ideas, distorted logic and stifled creativity. In other words, in organizations that frustrate individual self-actualization, decision-making efficiency will be far below the capability of these organizations due to low-quality mental activity.

Organization development

What the practitioners of organization development (OD) have learned is that it is possible by developing the organization's culture to counter the deadening influence of the formal organization. Because Blake and Mouton's version known as Grid OD is widely known and much written about, the discussion here will focus on it. According to Blake and Mouton:

> The problem of management is not solely to ask men to think logically, though that is a prized outcome of good management. The problem of managing men is to manage their emotions so that they can think logically and to reduce or eliminate distortions of logic that are provoked by intense emotions.
>
> (1969: 65–6)

In order to manage emotions in such a way that organization members are logical, motivated and creative in decision making (and other tasks), Blake and Mouton (1985, 1969) advocate an organizational culture characterized by high concern for production (getting results) and high concern for people, i.e. the 9,9 leadership style. The 9,9 style emphasizes free and open communication, trust, high worker participation (especially in decision making), facing and jointly resolving conflicts, enthusiastic experimentation and learning, a climate of approval, and commitment and identification with the organization's goals.[11]

Emotions, pressure and decision making

Harvey Leibenstein's (1987: 20–2) emotion spillover theory provides another perspective on the role of emotions in individual decision making. Emotions, which are unrelated or only partly related to decision situations, may interfere with optimal decision making by "distracting one's attention or distorting one's assessment of the options" (1987: 21). Thus, optimal decision making requires two types of control to eliminate these undesirable effects. The first is emotional organization. This refers to the effort required to call forth feelings that contribute to inner balance and clear focus. The second is repression of contaminating emotions. This consists of the effort required to constrain those more enduring emotions that give a false view of the world. At too low levels of pressure or stress, these individual efforts are not sufficient; but at too high levels of pressure, the pressure itself brings forth emotion that contaminates and disorganizes the decision-making activity. Only at an intermediate level of pressure is optimal decision making fostered.

Leibenstein's analysis is similar to that of Janis and Mann (1977). Janis and Mann's analysis focuses on explaining the circumstances under which people will not be "vigilant" in carrying out important decisional information processing. They find that both "extremely low stress and extremely high stress are likely to give rise to defective [nonvigilant] information processing" (1977: 52). For example, unless (1) a moderate degree of stress is present owing to the importance of the decision, (2) decision makers believe it is possible to find a better solution to the problem, and (3) sufficient time is available to search for and evaluate a better solution, decision makers either will not be aroused sufficiently or will succumb to panic, and thus will fail to process information satisfactorily; that is, their information processing will be too little, too defective or both (Janis and Mann 1977: ch. 3).

Realizing the potential quality of mental activity

Most of us know that we have rarely realized the quality of mental activity that we are capable of. This may be because our emotions usually interfere, or because our mental abilities are not developed sufficiently, or because of organizational blocks or organizational processes that do not draw the best from our mental resources. Whatever the reason, it is expected that few organizations will realize close to their full procedural rationality in this aspect of their decision making.

The model in perspective

Developing the organization as suggested in the sections above should raise the expected quality of the organization's decision making, and thus, increase the organization's internal efficiency or X-efficiency. In effect, through changes in its processes, structure and culture, the organization is able to increase its aggregate decision-making effort (for more on the nature of this effort, see Etzioni 1988: 152–7). Changes in these intangibles, mostly "soft" organizational factors, are crucial to raising the quality of decision making. Because developing these long-lasting intangibles requires time, energy and resources, their development should be considered to be an investment in organizational capital (a type of human capital and social capital) (Tomer 1987). Moreover, it tends to be true that some organizational investments that businesses could have made will not be made. Furthermore, given the investments they do make, firms' decision-making efforts will often be lower than they could be. For these reasons, the quality of business decisions will typically be below full procedural rationality. This means that at least some internal inefficiency (or X-inefficiency) in decision making will be the usual state of affairs.

An important implication of the model follows from the fact that high-quality decision making requires types of discipline not easily acquired or appreciated. Because full procedural rationality requires a high level of organizational investment and effort, and because firms are expected to vary with regard to these, a significant variation in decision-making quality among firms is expected. The variation will be lessened to the degree that competitive forces cause firms with the worst quality of decision making to fail.

It should be noted that the socio-economic model developed here uses the concept of rationality (procedural rationality) in a more holistic, more inclusive way than has generally been the case. Rationality as used here considers both the limitations of man as a calculator/analyser and man's capabilities deriving from his right brain, unconscious, and even superconscious. The model indicates that the best in leadership, management and organization enables people to draw on their unconscious, the right side of their brains and their highest capabilities in decision making. When decision making is as rational as it is possible to be, it is not simply because every possible alternative has been analyzed using every possible calculation. It is because decision making has been done not only carefully, but enthusiastically and inspiredly, drawing on unconscious and intuitive knowledge.[12] The ultimate in decision making thus occurs when experienced, trained and committed members of the organization make the greatest possible use of all the resources at their disposal, especially their various mental resources. This decision making ultimate is another facet of what has been called Theory Z management or simply Z-management in a Z-firm (see Tomer 1987: ch. 8).

It should also be noted that this decision-making model is not an alternative to substantive theories of decision making in the firm, either orthodox or behavioral. These theories offer explanations of how firms will make decisions in specific, short-run situations. For example, orthodox theory explains how firms will set prices or quantity produced in order to maximize profit, and behavioral theory may similarly explain about how the firm decides (using certain decision rules, algorithms and so on) about certain considerations given the goals to which it aspires (see, for example, Cyert and March 1963). These theories dealing with short-run adjustment-type decisions in a static context are inevitably very different from theory concerning large, complex decisions in a dynamic context. Economic theory has largely dealt with the former and neglected the latter. This is unfortunate because the latter decisions are crucial to the competitive success of businesses and a key to understanding important aspects of resource allocation. Perhaps the reason for economists' neglect of these large, complex decisions is that understanding them requires an interdisciplinary effort involving considerable complexity, not to mention a huge literature search. Moreover, the theory concerning firms' strategic decision making does not fit with the orthodox theory of the firm; it requires a socio-economic theory of the firm.

Decision making may be viewed as one stage of a problem solving process that is preceded by clarification of goals and values and followed by implementation. An organization's decision-making activity could benefit or detract from these other stages. For example, highly participative decision-making processes are known to build member commitment to the decisions made, thereby enabling a faster, less difficult (and lower cost) implementation stage. Similarly, insights stemming from decision-making deliberations may contribute to clarification of the organization's goals and values, thereby benefiting this earlier stage. Although not considered above, a complete theory should consider the possibility of these "spillovers."

Conclusion

As Robert Townsend (Janis and Mann 1977: 40) has noted, large decisions, for example, the decision to build a new product or relocate a factory should be made slowly and carefully, drawing on the participation of many people and using substantial resources if necessary: "But the common or garden-variety of decision—like when to have the cafeteria open for lunch or what brand of pencil to buy—should be made fast." According to the socio-economic model developed above, organizations that aspire to full procedural rationality in their large, complex ill-structured decision making should (1) in their information processing, follow the eight decision-making steps and utilize an appropriate decision-making strategy; (2) arrange for organizational influences to be brought to bear on individual decision makers in such a way as to insure that these decision-making efforts, collectively, will contribute to achieving the organization's goals; and (3) arrange for organizational circumstances that foster the highest quality mental activity. Because of human cognitive limitations and the nature of organizations, organizational decision making is necessarily inoptimal. This, however, does not mean that poor-quality decision making is either inevitable or the usual state of affairs. Much can be done (as the model above suggests), and is being done by some organizations, to create the conditions for highly rational decision making. Understanding the nature of the investments in organizational capital required to increase decision-making quality is crucial to business and government efforts to enhance economic competitiveness.

5 Strategy and structure in the human firm

Beyond hierarchy, toward flexibility and integration

Introduction

The need for a model of the flexible, integrated firm

In response to global competition and a rapidly changing business environment, corporate strategies and structures are becoming more flexible and integrated. Unfortunately, neither "pure" neoclassical economic theory nor its extensions provide a basis for understanding these developments. What is needed is a model of the firm that incorporates strategy and structure in a more satisfactory way. Thus, the purpose of this chapter is to develop a model of the flexible, integrated firm. The flexible-integrated (FI) firm's mode of operation represents tendencies present in high performance, global companies, particularly as these companies have been understood by leading managerial thinkers. To appreciate fully the FI-Firm, it is necessary to contrast its operations with the hierarchical (H-) firm. The H-Firm incorporates strategy and structure in a very different way which reflects the dominant operating mode of the large western corporation during much of the second half of the twentieth century. Up to the present, organizational economists have largely focused their analyses on the H-Firm; now it is time to focus on the FI-Firm.

The purpose of this chapter is to analyse the FI-Firm's competitive performance superiority over the H-Firm in the current global business environment. The FI model indicates how strategy and structure ought to be incorporated in a theory of the firm that emphasizes the intangible human capacities of the firm. The FI-Firm represents an ideal, one that has through its investments in organizational capital developed strategies and structures that enable it to realize the highest possible degree of flexibility and integration.

Defining terms

By strategy, we mean *corporate strategy* or the strategy of the entire corporate entity, which may contain any number of business units and a fair number of functional areas.[1] Corporate strategy is the common thread or underlying logic that unifies the important actions and decisions of the corporation. Our concern is with the economic aspects of strategy, particularly strategy's role in defining the nature of the firm's products and its diversification.

By structure, we mean *organizational structure* or the arrangement of relationships among the different parts of the organization. To take advantage of their similarities, certain work activities are grouped into organizational units that are differentiated from and separated from other units:

> With separation of organizational units comes the need to coordinate them, usually termed "integration." Thus integrating mechanisms must be established in a firm to ensure that the required coordination takes place. Organizational structure balances the benefits of separation and integration.
>
> (Porter 1985: 59)

A firm's strategy and structure are important in determining its flexibility and integration. *Flexibility* is the opposite of being locked into a rigid pattern; it implies quickness to adapt to environmental novelty.

Integration, generally, refers to a process by which something is made whole or complete by bringing together its parts. With respect to organizations, *integration* may mean coordination, or it may refer to other managerial actions or mechanisms that serve to unify or bring under control different elements of the organization. Accordingly, *functional integration* coordinates and unifies the firm's different functional areas (marketing, purchasing, finance, strategic planning and so on). *Product-line integration* involves coordination among the different divisions responsible for different product groups, and *geographical integration* involves coordination among the different divisions responsible for different geographical areas (for example, the U.S.A., Europe and Asia). *Vertical integration*, as economists define it, uses the term integration in a partially different way. Consistent with the above, it refers to an extension of the company's coordination and control, in this case either backward to sources of supply and/or forward to end users of the final product. In contrast to the above, it refers to bringing these activities under common ownership rather than dealing with them through arms-length market relationships.

A large company can be both flexible and integrated if, in responding rapidly and appropriately to changing conditions, it can adapt all aspects of its operations (different functional areas and different business units) in a coordinated way. Whether it can do this depends to a great degree on the firm's strategy and structure.

The hierarchical model of the firm

The hierarchical model of the firm is the stereotype of the large modern corporation with high volume, standardized production. It is similar to Aoki's (1990) H-mode which emphasizes hierarchical control within the firm. The H-Firm is the firm on which most organizational economists have focused their attention.

Organizational structure

Administrative hierarchy

In the H-Firm, the organizational structure takes three main forms: the functional or U-Form organization, the holding company or H-Form (not same as H-Firm), and the multidivisional organization or M-Form (see, for example, Ouchi 1984: 15–24). The M-Form organization (see Figure 5.1) contains four types of offices: the field unit at the operational level, the departmental headquarters which coordinates field units, the central office which administers a number of departments, and the general office where general executives and staff officers provide for the overall direction of the company and allocate resources among divisions (Chandler 1962: 9–11). The three higher level offices typically act as integrating mechanisms for the units below them. The U-Form (see Figure 5.1) has only the first three office types; there is no general office because there is only one division. The H-Form has a number of divisions like the M-Form but in its pure form it has no general office.

Vertical coordinating mechanisms

The H-Firm relies on vertical mechanisms to achieve coordination. Consider, for example, the central office that coordinates among departments. In essence this coordination is accomplished through vertical communications, up from the departments to the central office and then down to the departments. The central office uses the inputs from the departments to engage in problem solving and then not only provides knowledge and information but issues directives and guidance to departments.

Separation of thinking and doing

In the H-Firm, operating tasks are clearly separated from managerial tasks involving planning, problem solving, and decision making. When problems arise or a decision is needed with respect to an operating task, workers, whose jobs are sharply demarcated, must communicate vertically to managers for guidance. Through this process, managers attempt to exercise rational control over the operations under their jurisdiction. Maximum use of specialization is made.

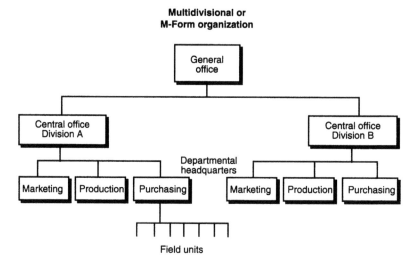

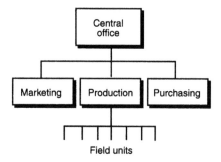

Figure 5.1 Multidivisional or M-form organization: functional or U-form
organization

Vertical integration

In the H-Firm, coordination between adjacent stages in the production
process is accomplished by vertical integration.

Structure follows strategy

H-Firms first choose their strategy and then select a compatible organizational structure. For example, companies with a strategy involving
diversification can ordinarily be expected to adopt the M-Form structure.

Corporate strategy

Deliberately designed at the top

In the H-Firm, corporate strategy is designed consciously and deliberately by the chief executive officer.

Periodic strategic reorientation

To deal with rapid, often discontinuous, change in the corporate environment, the H-Firm may engage in continuous surveillance and regularly review their strategy. The result is frequent strategic reorientation involving changes in the corporation's portfolio of businesses.

The flexible-integrated model of the firm

In the last decade or so, economists have become aware of and have begun to analyze models different from the H-Firm. One such model that has received increasing attention is the Japanese firm. The FI-Firm bears some resemblance to Aoki's (1990) model of the Japanese firm (J-mode).

Organizational structure

More complex structural forms

The FI-Firm typically utilizes more complex structural forms than the basic three (M-, U- and H-Forms). Among these complex forms are the hybrid and matrix forms that are useful when firms wish to take advantage of synergistic relationships among different product activities while not giving up some of the desired properties of the M-Form. These complex forms are defined and explained later.

Horizontal coordinating mechanisms

The FI-Firm emphasizes the use of horizontal rather than vertical coordinating mechanisms. These operate through direct communications among organizational units on the same hierarchical level, among departments, for example. Coordination is achieved through communications that enable mutual adjustments by departments or other units.

Integration of thinking and doing

In the FI-Firm, managerial tasks involving planning, problem solving and decision making are integrated with operational tasks. Workers are expected to cope with local emergencies autonomously, plan changes in their jobs, learn through job experience and share knowledge with others. Their jobs are thus enlarged, less specialized and less clearly demarcated.

Quasi-integration

Instead of vertical integration or arms-length market relationships, FI-Firms emphasize quasi-integration involving arrangements whereby independent businesses operating at adjacent stages of production agree to work closely together. The nature of the specific arrangements (minority equity investments, loans, goodwill and so on) that allow cooperation to take place are less important than that it allows for a significant degree of coordination and control. It could occur between two businesses only, or along the whole value-added chain of activities from the purchase of raw materials to the marketing of the final product as in value-adding partnerships.

Corporate strategy

More flexible strategy

In the FI-Firm, strategy derives out of a process that is partly deliberate and partly *emergent* (Mintzberg 1987), a process that allows learning to take place on different levels of the organization. Strategy on the one hand is a force for stability and control, focusing and guiding actions, and on the other hand it must allow for adaptation to external change (1987: 71). Most of the time, evolutionary change or learning occurs in the context of a given strategic orientation, within the broad guidelines set by senior management. Only rarely does a major strategic reorientation, amounting to a revolution, occur (1987: 73–4). The FI-Firm is a *learning organization* that is oriented to developing new strategic insights that enable the firm to expand its capacity and become something more than it would be if it simply adapted to the business environment (Senge 1990).

Strategic intent and core competence

The FI-Firm's *strategic intent* involves envisioning a desired leadership position; it involves ambitions that are "out of all proportion to their [companies'] resources and capabilities" (Hamel and Prahalad 1989: 64). High strategic intent involves a challenge to "employees to invent the means to accomplish ambitious ends" (1989: 76).

At the heart of the FI-Firm's strategy is development of its *core competences*. These competences are the critical and complex skills that underlie the firm's specific product activities and provide it with competitive advantage (Prahalad and Hamel 1990).

A more complex relationship between strategy and structure

In the FI-Firm, structure may follow strategy but strategy also follows structure. FI-Firms evolve a complex set of strategy, structure, systems, shared values, style and staff that mesh with each other (Pascale 1984: 63–71).

Comparing organizational structures

Which model of the firm is better adapted to an age characterized by global competition and a rapidly changing environment? Is there an economic basis for believing that the FI-Firm is superior to the H-Firm? This section provides a comparative analysis of the organizational structures of the FI-Firm and the H-Firm. The following section compares their strategies. Because of the space limitations of a chapter, our analysis is necessarily suggestive rather than exhaustive.

Four types of comparative analysis are undertaken in this section. First, the FI-Firm's more complex structural forms are compared to the H-Firm's M- and U-Forms. Second, the horizontal coordinating mechanisms of the FI-Firm are compared to the vertical ones of the H-Firm. Third, separation of thinking and doing (H-Firm) is compared to integrated thinking and doing (FI-Firm). Finally, vertical integration (H-Firm) is compared to quasi-integration (FI-Firm).

Administrative hierarchy

Before proceeding directly to the first comparison, it is necessary to review the nature of the M- and U-Forms and synergy as well as certain analyses of them.

M-form versus U-form

Given the existence of diversification and vertical integration in large modern corporations, Williamson (1971, 1981) argues that the M-Form or divisional organization will inevitably be selected over the U-Form or functional organization because of its superior efficiency. This follows from the view that when large firms shift to the M-Form from the U-Form, the resulting sum of production and transaction costs will be lower, even though for smaller firms the U-Form may be satisfactory.

Bounded rationality and opportunism are the key to the problematic behavior of the U-Form for large corporations. Because of bounded rationality, the top managers of diversified corporations face a level of complexity that they are unable to handle (Williamson 1981: 1555). This complexity arises from the simultaneous demands of long-run entrepreneurial and short-run operational administrative activities. The M-Form's structure contains features that make it possible for managers to successfully deal with or prevent these problems (1981: 1555–6). Thus, Williamson and others find that for large corporations (H-Firms, presumably) the M-Form is optimal and will inevitably be selected over the U-Form.

Synergy

Synergistic relationships among different product activities are an important reason for corporate diversification. Synergy is present when the combined earnings of two jointly operated activities exceeds the sum of their earnings for separate operations (Ansoff 1988: 58; Oster 1990: 163). In order for this to occur, there must be some crucial relationship between the activities that enables the superior joint outcome (see for example Porter 1987: 54–7; Ansoff 1988: 58; Kay 1982: 41). Synergy can be dynamic rather than static if it involves interrelationships between product activities in the context of ongoing technological or organizational change.

Comparing the more complex forms with the M- and U-forms

Given the existence of diversified firms with varying degrees of synergy between product activities, what organizational forms (M-Form, U-Form or other) should they adopt? As indicated earlier, the choice for large firms, following Williamson, is between the M-Form and the U-Form, and, almost inevitably, the M-Form will be found to be optimal and selected. It should be noted, however, that Williamson (1971: 357) does recognize that where operating divisions are not fully independent, M-Form organization will involve costs associated with ignoring their interdependence.

Contrary to the main thrust of Williamson's theorizing, Kay (1982: 61–71) believes the choice of the M-Form is not inevitable; in his view, firms will choose either the M-Form, the U-Form or a hybrid of the two, depending on the situation. First, where synergistic interrelationships among product units are strong, realizing that potential requires developing "horizontal" links between the related functions. In this situation, firms will choose the U-Form organization in which the functional (sales, R&D, manufacturing) personnel of different product activities can interact relatively frequently and easily at the expense of interactions among functions for a given product activity. While the U-Form is preferred in this case, this choice does forgo the "superior strategy formulating and internal control properties of the M-Form" (Kay 1982: 66). Second, in the opposite situation where synergistic interrelationships are relatively weak or nonexistent, the M-Form will be preferred. Third, if a firm has only one functional area, for example R&D, in which the interrelationship is strong, a *hybrid* form (see Figure 5.2) may make sense. Suggested here is a structure which has (1) independent divisions which do not contain any of the interrelated functional activity (such as R&D) and (2) a centralized functional activity (R&D)

supervised directly by the general office (Kay 1982: 67–8). This hybrid takes advantage of the desirable properties of the M-Form but allows for the frequent, easy interaction of functional (R&D) personnel associated with the different product units. Use of the hybrid form is one of the ways FI-firms take advantage of synergistic possibilities.

The *matrix* organization (see Figure 5.2), a relatively recent development, is an extension of the hybrid form and utilizes both coordination within divisions and intrafunctional coordination across divisions (Oster 1990: 135–7). It is an alternative to the U-Form that makes sense where there are strong synergistic relationships among product units but it is desired to obtain the advantages of the divisional form. It should be noted that the complexity of the matrix form has made it difficult to manage, and thus, some corporations that have used it have found that its disadvantages outweigh its advantages.

Other problems with the M-form of the H-firm

Another issue relating to integration within the firm involves the fact that the use of the M-Form has become problematic for large hierarchical firms, especially American ones. According to Jacquemin:

> In order to supervise and direct the various operational divisions...financial control, which is based on the common denominator of monetary return, has taken a dominant position in the organization, whereas the importance of managers specialized in marketing, technology, and human resources has declined. This evolution has resulted in an excessive weight being given to financial criteria...
>
> (1987: 150)

Moreover, management of the product activity portfolio has come to resemble management of the financial portfolio in which the emphasis is on minimizing risk taking and favoring rapid returns (see also Hayes and Abernathy 1980). Relatedly, the influence of strategic planning on professional managers has led them to be "less concerned with the efficiency of a particular production line than with how profitably the firm's pool of resources could be allocated among production lines" (Reich 1983: 86).

Another problem with the H-firm's use of the M-form and the procedures that typically accompany it is that it "has forced managers of related divisions...to compete with each other rather than cross-fertilize each other" (Franko 1983: 128 as quoted in Auerbach 1988: 134). This, along with the increasingly fine compartmentalizations of responsibility for divisional units, has led the product visions of western managers to become progressively narrower (Auerbach 1988: 135). Thus, in a number of ways, the

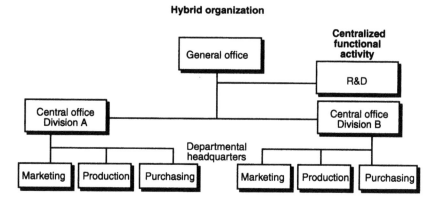

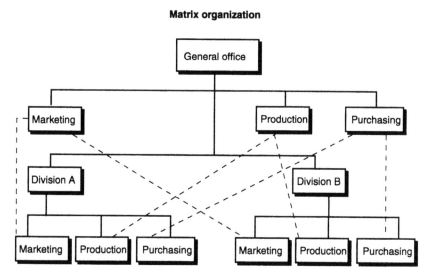

Figure 5.2 Hybrid organization, matrix organization

operating mode typically associated with the M-form in western H-firms has lead to dysfunctional integration.

Horizontal versus vertical coordinating mechanisms

Generally speaking, the horizontal integrating mechanisms of FI-firms are more flexible than the vertical ones of H-firms. With horizontal mechanisms, actions can be taken more quickly by knowledgeable people lower in the hierarchy without time-consuming and information-distorting vertical communications. With fewer vertical communications, firms find that their hierarchies flatten as they need fewer managers and fewer levels of hierarchy. It should be noted, however, that FI-firms need to develop the kind of organizational features that facilitate the desired horizontal integration. Ideally, organizational units that require coordination will develop in their members an understanding and awareness regarding how their unit's and other units' activities jointly contribute to producing the final output.

A number of leading managerial writers, while differing somewhat in their visions of the future workplace, nevertheless believe the future will contain much more horizontal integration. Peters (1987: 554) advocates a " 'horizontal style' of management, which minimizes up and down (vertical) communications and replaces it with fast, front-line cooperation across functional boundaries." Peters also advises that "the self-managing team should become the basic organizational building block" (1987: 357). In Walton's commitment strategy for the workplace, lateral coordination and control are based to a great degree on shared goals, values, and traditions (Walton 1985a: 79–81). In Kanter's view, "the new managerial work" involves flexible work assignments and "communication and collaboration across functions, across divisions, and across companies whose activities and resources overlap" (1988: 92). Finally, Drucker (1988a) envisions the information-based organization, an organization populated with knowledge specialists, that functions like a large symphony orchestra with little or no middle management and is held together by a common vision.

Separation versus integration of thinking and doing

When in the H-firm operational tasks are separated from managerial tasks, rational technocratic control may be elusive for a number of reasons:

> If the quality of information is poor, the manager may be slow and imprecise in recognizing the problems to be handled. Also, subordinates, by not being included in decision making, may lack the motivation to report problems and to implement the hierarchical order in a precise and swift way. Thus using the hierarchical system involves the cost of monitoring due to the bounded rationality of the supervisors, and the cost of implementation due to the lack of incentives of the subordinates.
>
> (Aoki 1986: 973)

In contrast, the FI-firm's horizontal coordination gains efficiency from the use of "on-the-spot knowledge and rapid problem solving through learning by doing" (Aoki 1986: 973). Subordinates in the FI-firm are more motivated and have internalized the organization's goals. It should be noted, however, that the ability of subordinates to coordinate production activity is "limited by their partial understanding of the whole mechanism operating within the firm," and their problem solving ability is "limited by the lack of centralization of information concerning emergent events" (1986: 973).

In conclusion, the relative efficiency of the H-firm and FI-firm in this regard will depend on such factors as the learning and communicating ability of FI-firm workers, the ability of FI-firm workers to grasp their company's big picture, and the ability of H-firm management to identify accurately and quickly emergent problems and to enforce implementation of desired solutions. Thus, there is reason to believe that because of its integration of thinking and doing, the FI-firm has efficiency and flexibility advantages over the H-firm.

Vertical integration versus quasi-integration

The inflexibility of vertical integration

In contrast to the other types of integration, vertical integration, especially that in hierarchically controlled firms (for example, the U.S. steel industry) has been associated with inflexibility. According to Johnston and Lawrence, one reason is that

> In the process of exploiting their distinctive competences, many large, [vertically] integrated companies emphasize one competitive dimension. In an integrated company, such focus can actually be a liability, because the strong culture that supports that focus makes it hard to perform tasks that require distinctly different orientations and values. A business that emphasizes low cost, for instance, may run its factories well, but its R&D, design, or marketing functions may have trouble innovating.
>
> (1988: 98–9)

Because vertically integrated firms' (H-firms) innovativeness is likely to be suppressed in those areas that do not fit with the common focus, these firms cannot be expected to respond flexibly to environmental challenge.

Value-adding partnerships: an important example of quasi-integration

Recall that for FI-firms quasi-integration is the alternative to H-firms' vertical integration. A value-adding partnership (VAP), an important and growing form of quasi-integration, is "a set of independent companies that work closely together to manage the flow of goods and services along the entire value-added chain," thereby effectively behaving "as one competitive unit" (Johnston and Lawrence 1988: 94–5). McKesson Corporation, once a wholesale distributor of drugs and health care products, is an important U.S. example of a VAP. To compete with the large drugstore chains, McKesson has forged close and productive links with its customers, the independent drugstores, and has gone on to develop partnerships with the consumer goods manufacturers that supply it, the insurance companies that process medical claims, and the final consumer (1988: 95). McKesson, as the key player in this VAP, has looked beyond its corporate boundaries to improve the competitiveness of the entire VAP.

Japanese trading companies are another important example of a VAP. They buy and sell goods at every stage of production from raw material extraction to end user, but the essence of their role is that of a coordinator. They:

> integrate the activities of separate firms into a production system, helping them realize the benefits of administrative coordination on a large scale while enabling them to retain their formal independence and some consequent flexibility associated with market-form coordination.
>
> (Yoshino and Lifson 1986: 42)

Quasi-integration and flexibility

In contrast to vertical integration, quasi-integration (in FI-firms) relies more on horizontal coordinating mechanisms than vertical ones, and therefore, would be expected to be the more flexible form of integration (recall our earlier discussion). Consider, for example, VAPs. According to Johnston and Lawrence, VAPs offer:

> the coordination and scale associated with large companies and the flexibility, creativity, and low overhead usually found in small companies. VAPs share knowledge and insight but are not burdened with guidelines from a distant headquarters....They can act promptly, without having to consult a thick manual of standard operating procedures.
>
> (1988: 99)

In sum, FI-firms using a variety of forms of quasi-integration are superior to H-firms because FI-firms are able to realize a higher degree of integration and flexibility along with efficiency than can be achieved with vertical integration.

Quasi-integration and transaction cost economics

According to Coase's (1937) and subsequently Williamson's (for example, 1981) analysis, transaction costs determine whether a firm will organize a separable stage of economic activity within the firm (vertical integration) or utilize market exchange. If transaction costs associated with the market alternative are high, firms will choose vertical integration. This analysis does not consider any other organizational alternatives. Jacquemin (1987: 146), however, points out that, "there is a whole range of possible organizational modes that in no way can be reduced to a choice between the market and the firm."[2] The most prominent alternative to these two is, of course, quasi-integration. Quasi-integration makes sense when high transaction costs preclude a market relationship, and high internal organizing costs preclude vertical integration (1987: 147–8). In this situation, firms that desire to coordinate adjacent activities, exploiting their interdependence, can do so using arrangements involving more flexibility and less heavy cooperation than does vertical integration (1987: 148).

Aoki's analysis of subcontracting groups

Aoki's (1986, 1988, 1990) analysis focuses on a particular form of quasi-integration, the "subcontracting group," which reflects the kind of interfirm relationships typical of a major Japanese manufacturing company and its many subcontractors. These relationships are systematic, formalized, long-term (or quasi-permanent) and stratified. Although subcontractors' policies may be influenced in important ways by the parent corporation, they nevertheless maintain substantial autonomy with respect to their control of production, and their operations are integrated with the parent largely through the use of horizontal mechanisms rather than hierarchical ones (Aoki 1986: 974).

Aoki compares the efficiency of coordination in these subcontracting groups to that in hierarchically coordinated, vertically integrated firms (H-firms). The comparison is in many respects the same as the comparison of the horizontal coordination mechanisms of the FI-firm and the vertical mechanisms of the H-firm. For example, in such subcontracting groups, actions can be taken more quickly by knowledgeable people lower in the hierarchy without time-consuming and information-distorting vertical communications. According to Aoki, a key element arguing for the superior efficiency of subcontracting groups is that:

> The savings on information and transaction costs resulting from the horizontal coordination of operations in the subcontracting group and autonomous problem solving by its member firms dramatically manifests itself in the functional hierarchy of the prime manufacturer in Japan, which is much simpler and smaller in comparison with that of the large American integrated firm. This is made possible because fewer personnel are needed for planning and monitoring (such as accounting and supervising).
>
> (1988: 215)

This analysis should apply fairly straightforwardly to other forms of quasi-integration (used by FI-firms) where coordination of semiautonomous firms is accomplished largely through horizontal mechanisms rather than hierarchical ones. It should also be noted that, unlike the predictions of Williamson's transaction cost economics, quasi-integration (Japanese style at least) appears to mitigate opportunistic behavior (Aoki 1986: 975; 1988: 217).

Comparing corporate strategies

This section compares the corporate strategies of FI-firms and H-firms by marshaling evidence and arguments that indicate their relative advantages.

Shortcomings of deliberately designed strategy

According to Mintzberg (1990: 184–7), the "deliberately designed by the CEO" style of strategy (H-firms) is inflexible in that it is intolerant of deviations from the strategy once formulated and fails to allow for organizational learning other than by the chief executive and his staff. While Ansoff's version of H-firm strategy, which emphasizes periodic strategic reorientation, is flexible in the sense that it is oriented to accommodating regularly to a changing environment, there is nevertheless a difficulty with this approach. What is needed, it turns out, is less flexibility of this kind and more flexibility in the sense of allowing modifications after the initial formulation: "The trick is to manage within a given strategic orientation most of the time yet be able to pick out the occasional discontinuity that really matters" (1990: 74). Thus, Mintzberg argues with the view that the organization should be frequently reorienting its strategy; he believes this perpetual instability is dysfunctional and creates insensitivity to the real change that requires a major adaptation (1990: 71, 73).

Strategy in a learning organization

It is important to underline the idea that FI-firms are learning organizations. A number of authors have embraced the idea that "the rate at which organizations learn may become the only sustainable source of competitive advantage" (Stata 1989: 64; Senge 1990: 7; De Geus 1988: 71). In this view, the role of leaders in FI-firms is to foster the conditions under which strategic learning takes place.

According to De Geus, then head of planning at Royal Dutch/Shell Group, "the real purpose of effective planning is not to make plans but to change…the mental models that these decision makers carry in their heads" (1988: 71). Thus, De Geus advocates a number of specific techniques that will help planners be facilitators, catalysts and accelerators of organizational learning. Organizational learning, in contrast to individual learning, occurs when shared insights, knowledge and mental models are built into organizational memory, that is, incorporated into institutional mechanisms such as policies, strategies and explicit models (Stata 1989: 64). Stata has found that the values and culture of the organization have a significant impact on the effectiveness of the learning process (1989: 70).

Adaptive learning which is about accommodating, coping, and fitting the environment is not sufficient (Senge 1990: 8). What is needed is generative learning which is oriented to originating, expanding capability, coming up with systematic fundamental insights and developing new visions.

Evidence on strategy in excellent organizations

Several research findings strongly suggest that the corporate strategies of FI-firms are superior to those of H-firms. Richard Rumelt's comprehensive study of diversification in large American businesses found that the best overall financial performance was attained by companies

> neither totally dependent upon a single business nor true multi-industry firms. These companies have strategies of entering only those businesses that build on, draw strength from, and enlarge some central strength or competence. While such firms frequently develop new products and enter new businesses, they are loath to invest in areas that are unfamiliar to management.
>
> (1986: 150)

Echoing these findings, Peters and Waterman (1982: 293) advocate that companies should "stick very close to their knitting." "The most successful of all [corporations] are those diversified around a single skill—the coating and bonding technology at 3M, for example."

Michael Porter (1987: 43–6) finds that companies whose strategic planning involves frequent strategic reorientation along with numerous acquisitions and divestitures have a dismal track record. He

> studied the diversification records of 33 large, prestigious U.S. companies over the 1950–1986 period and found that most of them had divested many more acquisitions than they had kept. The corporate strategies of most companies have dissipated instead of created shareholder value.
>
> (1987: 43)

Finally, Prahalad and Hamel (1990: 81) find that companies who conceive of themselves as a portfolio of competences generally outperform those who conceive of themselves as a portfolio of businesses. Examples of the former include NEC's investment in skills at the convergence of computing and communications, Sony's capacity to miniaturize and Philips's optical-media expertise. According to Peters (1987: 616), "Any useful strategic plan or planning process, must focus upon the development and honing of these skills [or core competences], which translate into readiness to seek and exploit opportunities," i.e. flexibility.

The strategy and structure sequence

Alfred Chandler's (1962) thesis that structure follows strategy is well known and widely accepted. The evidence gathered by him and others suggests that it applies best to H-firms in decades prior to the 1960s. In Chandler's view, businesses first changed their strategies to accommodate to or take advantage of new patterns of demand, and subsequently, operating inadequacies dictated the development of new structures. The evidence accumulated by Chandler comes from his in-depth historical studies of Du Pont, Sears Roebuck, General Motors and Standard Oil of New Jersey as well as less intensive study of close to one hundred other large industrial enterprises. He found that "where business diversified into wholly new lines for quite different customers with quite different wants, then more reorganization was needed" (1962: 393). In particular, unless these large organizations adopted the M-form structure, "it became increasingly difficult to coordinate through the existing structure the different functional activities to the needs of several quite different markets" (1962: 393). In short, M-form structure follows diversification strategy. The notion that new corporate strategies require for success innovations in organizational structure continues to be a central and important element in the thinking of many leading authorities on strategy (see, for example, Ansoff 1988: 8; Porter 1985: 23–5).

Later empirical analyses have largely supported Chandler's findings. Caves (1980) survey of many of these studies finds that they:

> nearly all agree on two propositions: 1) correctly matching strategy to opportunities and structure to strategy increases a firm's profits and presumably increases the efficiency with which society's resources are used; 2) certain strategies [diversification] and structures [M-Form] have diffused as innovations, with large firms progressively moving toward choices that make the best of their opportunities.
>
> (1980: 79)

Rumelt's (1986: 149) empirical investigations support Chandler's findings strongly for the 1950s, but he finds that later many firms turned to the M-form because it was the "fashion" to do so. In the 1960s, even corporations that were not highly diversified were splitting their operations into semi-autonomous divisions.

As strategies and structures become more flexible and integrated, the old dictum about their relationship is being questioned. Structure may follow strategy as Chandler concluded, but strategy also follows structure. This is because strategy must be based on the organization's capabilities many of which inhere in its organizational structure. Mintzberg believes the emphasis on structure following strategy has been misleading because it suggests the ability of the firm to freely alter its structure. "Structure may be malleable, but it cannot be altered at will just because a leader has conceived a new strategy.

Many organizations have come to grief over just such a belief" (1990: 183). Similarly, Pascale (1984: 63–71) emphasizes that successful firms (FI-firms) evolve a complex set of strategy, structure, systems, shared values, style and staff (socialization of members, etc.) that mesh with each other. He believes that "change efforts that shift only one or two of the factors and leave the remainder alone almost always fail" (1984: 71). To be successful, major change requires movement along all six fronts, and this occurs infrequently.

Conclusions from the comparisons

While definitive conclusions are not possible, the above provides a strong case for the FI-firm's superiority over the H-firm. If, as seems to be the case, it has become imperative for firms to be flexible and to adapt quickly to local and global shocks in order to be competitive, and if it is less important to achieve scale economies along with a high degree of specialization, then the FI-firm's mode of operation is superior to that of the H-firm. Organizational economics needs to focus on the type of organizational arrangements found in FI-firms. Increasingly, these arrangements:

1) are horizontal in nature, not hierarchical;
2) discourage opportunism and rely on trust and long-term understandings;[3]
3) involve integration of thinking and doing;
4) incorporate learning and problem solving at the lowest levels;
5) provide synergistic linkages among product activities, and;
6) involve coordination of adjacent production activities through various forms of quasi-integration.

Given the rapidly changing, global nature of today's competition, these organizational arrangements provide the kind of flexible, integrated responses required for economic survival.

Investing in flexible, integrated arrangements: organizational capital

Compared to H-firms, FI-firms' features are radically different and represent the best possible adaptation to a very different competitive environment. These features are embodied in firms' people relationships, that is, they are embodied in its corporate strategy, organizational structure, culture, organizational procedures, etc. Investing in these relationships is usefully viewed as an investment in organizational capital (Tomer 1987), a kind of capital vested not so much in individuals but in the intangible linkages between people. It may be considered as both a type of human capital and social capital. Thus, for example, when firms use up resources to develop (1) synergistic relationships between product activities,

(2) horizontal coordinating mechanisms, (3) long-term understandings miti-
gating opportunism, (4) strategies emphasizing the development of core
competence, or (5) the firm's organizational learning capacities, they are
making the kinds of investments in organizational capital critical to
building the economy's capacity.

In my view, the concept of organizational capital is the most useful one to
convey the intangible organizational nature of these changes in firm
capacity. However, it is important to note that other authors have used
similar conceptions. MacDuffie (1988: 13), for example, uses the term
"humanware" to characterize workplace practices that "integrate technology
and human resources in a production system." With respect to organizational practices, the humanware concept is similar to organizational capital,
but it is a narrower concept with a less explicit link to human capital.

From evolutionary theory comes the concept of *routines*, the deeply
ingrained, not readily changed repertoires of firms (Winter 1987: 163).
Although these may be the outcome of learning, routines are more akin to
habit and impulse insofar as they determine behavior in not so conscious
ways. Drawing on metaphors from biology and control theory, Winter sees
routines as subject either to a kind of natural selection process or the effects
of control variables that change their state. Routines relate to a broad range
of phenomena; they encompass individual skill, knowledge, technology and
organizational considerations. The routines concept, being more closely
associated with a firm's behavior than with its capacity, is thus not as useful
for thinking about designed changes in organizational capacity. For these
reasons, the organizational capital concept seems to capture better the firm's
organizational relationships that embody its strategy and structure.

Flexibility and integration in the emerging economy

In the view of a number of leading economic thinkers, economies, not just
firms, will become much more flexible and integrated than they have been.
Let us now consider the main elements of a number of these visions.

In *The Next American Frontier*, Robert Reich (1983) sees many difficulties standing in the way of a needed U.S. transition from high-volume,
standardized production to flexible-system production. In contrast to the
stability and rigidity of the former, *flexible-system production* is highly
adaptable to the kind of ever-changing circumstances characterizing global
markets today. Flexible-system production features highly skilled employees,
flexible technologies, flat organization structures, employment security, a
high degree of teamwork and cooperation, integration of traditionally separate business functions, a less rigidly delineated relationship between
management and labor, integration of thinking and doing in the workplace,
more on-the-job training, more custom-tailored, high-valued products, and
developmentally oriented government policies toward business (1983:
129–30, 134–5, 257–9, 278).[4] Reich analyzes the obstacles that lie in the path

of this needed transformation, and recommends many policy measures to remove them.

In *The Second Industrial Divide*, Piore and Sabel (1984) envision the possibility that "flexible specialization" may come to be the dominant production system rather than mass production and its accompanying organization. The key to *flexible specialization* (not the same as flexible-system production) is workers who possess craftsman-like skills and whose capacity is augmented by their use of technologically advanced, flexible equipment. Workers and workplaces are specialized in that they are committed to a particular product or industry, but they are flexible in that they embody a capacity for continuous innovation (1984: 268–9). Flexible specialization is fostered by "an industrial community that restricts the forms of competition to those favoring innovation" (1984: 17). Piore and Sabel believe that the current period offers a second chance ("the second industrial divide") to choose between mass production and flexible specialization, the superior alternative.

Like Reich, Piore and Sabel, Michael Best (1990) also sees the emergence of an alternative production paradigm that is in dramatic contrast to the rigid forms associated with mass production and hierarchy. His vision, *The New Competition*, distinguishes four dimensions along which the new system diverges from the old: (1) organization of the firm, (2) types of coordination across phases in the production chain, (3) organization of the sector, and (4) patterns of industrial policy (1990: 11). The first dimension of *The New Competition* includes entrepreneurial firms oriented away from hierarchy and toward innovation and learning by its members at all levels (1990: 11–14). A key feature of the second dimension is consultation and cooperation amongst mutually interdependent firms, an alternative to market and hierarchical forms of coordination (1990: 14–15). The third dimension includes sector institutions or extra-firm infrastructure that encourages an appropriate balance between cooperation and competition among firms (1990: 17–19). Finally, the essence of the fourth dimension is an industrial policy that develops economic capacity by promoting "(1) entrepreneurial firms, (2) consultative buyer–vendor relations, and (3) inter-firm associations and extra-firm agencies which facilitate continuous improvement in production" (1990: 20).

What these visions have in common is that firms with flexible, integrated strategies and structures ought to become the key components of flexible, integrated production systems. In this view, firms will be at a competitive disadvantage in the international arena unless they are accompanied by consultative coordination across stages of production, appropriate extra-firm infrastructure, and supportive local and federal industrial policy. In essence, this means that firms are likely to experience *organizational failure*[5] with respect to their adoption of flexible, integrated strategies and structures unless sufficiently supportive extra-firm elements are present to counteract the inhibiting influences of older regulatory institutions.

Conclusion

In the present state of the business world, there are many reasons for believing that the flexible-integrated model of the firm is not only more efficient but more flexible than the hierarchical model of the firm. The FI-firm, while an idealized conception, represents important new tendencies among companies that are successfully adapting to the rapidly changing, global environment. It is a firm that increasingly learns how to gain competitive advantage from its intangible and inexplicit characteristics, characteristics that are embedded in its organizational structure, culture, decision-making procedures, and communication and leadership patterns. It is a firm that is increasingly making the organizational investments necessary for success. The FI-firm is a model of an important dimension of the Z-firm, which is the full-fledged human firm ideal.

To sharpen our image of the firm, more research is needed to integrate recent managerial thinking on strategy and structure with economic theory. In particular, the idea that competitive advantage may be gained from a superior rate of organizational learning and the idea that firms can be creative and generative with respect to their environments rather than simply seeking to fit them need to be incorporated more completely into our economic conceptions of the firm. More generally, economists need to do more to integrate new managerial thinking with the theory of the firm in order to decrease the typically large gap between economic thinking about the firm and organizational realities. With closure of this gap, we can expect significant improvement in economists' policy recommendations regarding the firm.

6 Beyond the machine model of the firm

Toward a holistic human model

This chapter is concerned with the human firm's overall competitive performance and the kinds of ingredients and relationships necessary for achieving peak performance. As we will see, investments in organizational capital are an important part of the explanation, but there is much more to the story. In particular, we need to go beyond the machine model of the firm and move toward a holistic model.

If businesses are essentially machines, vehicles for transforming inputs into outputs, as economic theory suggests, it is hard to understand why a few companies achieve greatness, others fail miserably, and still others are mediocre. There are, however, lots of hints in non-economic business literatures regarding what is missing from the economist's conception of the firm. Among the missing ingredients are leadership, vision, passion, ethical principle, character, empowerment, self-realization, commitment, community and inspiration. This listing helps us understand the difficulty with the machine model. The problem is that the "hard" nature of economic theory seems incompatible with the listed "soft" factors. Is it possible to develop a model of the firm, an alternative to the production function, that incorporates both hard and soft ingredients? It is, and the task of this chapter is to indicate how.

The model developed here is a holistic model that understands the firm as an essentially human entity in which the whole is more than the sum of the parts. This model explains why peak performance can only be achieved in the presence of a critical combination of soft (leadership, spirit, etc.) and hard (management, organizational structure, financial structure, etc.) factors. Embodied in this model is the hypothesis that certain soft factors not included in mainstream economic models are essential to explaining the behavior and performance of the firm.

The plan of the chapter is as follows. Section 1 reviews the "machine" model of the firm starting with the familiar mainstream core theory of the firm and proceeding to extensions of this theory. Section 2 develops the holistic model of the human firm using the core machine model as a starting point. The model's most important new elements are two intangible soft ingredients, namely leadership and spirit. A key feature of the model is that the firm's peak or ultimate socio-economic performance is only possible when the right balance has been struck between the soft and hard factors. Section 3 provides important anecdotal evidence supporting the holistic model. Section 4 considers the model's implications for the U.S. economic decline during the 1970s and 1980s. The implications of the model for entire economic systems are considered in Section 5. Conclusions are in Section 6.

The machine model of the firm

Mainstream core theory of the firm

The mainstream core theory of the firm has two principal aspects. The first relates to production and efficiency. The second relates to ownership, goals and decision making.

First, the firm is a production function; that is, it is a machine that transforms quantities of specified inputs into output(s) per unit of time. Given inputs determine the maximum output (Q^*) that can be attained for a given production technology assuming the production process is efficient. Typical inputs include tangible assets (tangible capital, land, raw materials), labor and certain intangible assets including the human capital endowment of its laborers. Another intangible input, not always mentioned explicitly, is the activity of managers who are supposed to make sure that efficiency is achieved through their coordination, control, planning, staffing, problem solving and supervising efforts.

Second, the owners of the production machine or firm are the residual claimants in the sense that their claims (equity) on the firm are those that remain after all other contractual obligations have been fulfilled. As a result, the owners exercise residual control in that they have significant discretion regarding the use of the assets of the firm. In effect, the firm is their property, and they can use it as an instrument to achieve their objectives. It is assumed that these self-interested owners will seek to maximize their satisfactions from the firm; this is normally taken to imply maximization of profits. Owners concerned with long-term profitability will want to maximize the value of their equity, a value reflecting expectations about the firm's future profits. The owners, or managers who are their agents, are assumed to have perfect knowledge and perfect calculating ability in order to make decisions that achieve maximum profits. Doing the latter means that owner/managers act as though they were able to adjust the amount of output and quantity of inputs using marginal analysis.

To appreciate this machine model in comparison to the holistic one developed later, it is necessary to define what is meant by hard and soft aspects of reality. Hard attributes are relatively tangible, physical, measurable, capable of being expressed in mathematical relationships, visible and explicit. Soft attributes are opposite to the above and involve less definite, holistic aspects of the world. The right hemisphere of the brain is said to be better at appreciating the softer aspects, and the left hemisphere is better equipped for dealing with the hard aspects. Financial relationships, ownership and organizational structure (hierarchy) are relatively hard, whereas enthusiasm, fairness, kindness, harmony and compassion are relatively soft.

Not surprisingly, the core machine model of the firm includes only the hard aspects of reality; all soft aspects are excluded. Even the intangible factors included in this model, for example managerial activity and human capital, are hard ones.

It is interesting to view the core machine model from the perspective of the shift in scientific paradigms:

> Scientists in many different disciplines are questioning whether we can adequately explain how the world works by using the machine imagery created in the seventeenth century, most notably by Sir Isaac Newton. In the machine model, one must understand parts. Things can be taken apart, dissected literally or representationally..., and then put back together without any significant loss. The assumption is that by comprehending the workings of each piece, the whole can be understood. The Newtonian model of the world is characterized by materialism and reductionism—a focus on things rather than relationships and a search, in physics, for the basic building blocks of matter. In new science, the underlying currents are a movement toward holism, toward understanding the system as a system and giving primary value to the relationships that exist among seemingly discrete parts....When we view systems from this perspective, we enter an entirely new landscape of connections, of phenomena that cannot be reduced to simple cause and effect, and of the constant flux of dynamic processes.
>
> (Wheatley 1994: 8–9)

As Wheatley (1994) suggests, progress in many disciplines, not just in the natural sciences, increasingly requires models that transcend the machine model. Thus, there is presumably much to be gained, by building a holistic economic model of the firm. Nevertheless, it is important to note that the machine model of the firm has been very successful for some purposes, especially the purpose for which it was constructed, namely explaining market price determination. The problem is that the machine model is severely limited for other purposes.

Extensions of the core theory of the firm

Because of the limitations of the machine model, economists working in different traditions have developed a variety of theories that extend the core model, enabling it to explain phenomena outside the scope for which the mainstream model was constructed. An important thrust of this theorizing is the attempt to add realism by introducing organizational features (the "flesh") not considered in the "barebones" model and by explaining how these features are related to profitability, efficiency or competitiveness. Despite the increased realism and scope of the extended model, it basically remains a machine model wherein there is a precise quantitative mechanism translating inputs into certain quantities of output under certain conditions and little, if any, consideration of soft attributes.

One important extension (outside the mainstream tradition) is Harvey Leibenstein's (see, for example, 1976) notion of X-efficiency (internal efficiency), which is not the same as allocative efficiency. As Leibenstein points out, X-inefficiency (the opposite of X-efficiency) is the usual state of affairs. This means that there typically is a significant gap between a firm's actual output (Q) and the maximum, Q*. While there are many reasons for such inefficiency, Leibenstein has focused on why employees who are agents of the firm's principals might choose to exert an amount of effort not fully in accord with the interests of the principals. The resulting degree of inefficiency, which frequently has its origins in the firm's organizational relationships, explains how far Q falls short of Q* (the Q gap). A firm may choose to rectify this inefficiency, thereby raising its Q, by investing in organizational capital, the lasting productive capacity embodied in the relationships and patterns of activity among the firm's participants, an input not included in the core machine model. The organizational capital concept is especially valuable as a unifying concept that enables a variety of both hard and soft organizational features to be linked to firm performance.

A variety of important extensions to the core model of the firm come from mainstream organizational economics. One branch of this theorizing views the firm as a nexus of contracts, wherein the firm is a contracting entity that makes explicit and implicit contracts in order to supply itself with needed goods and services in an efficient manner. Important here are analyses of transaction costs, the principal–agent relationship, and incentives deriving from the assignment of property rights. A second branch of theorizing derives from the subject of finance; it views the firm as a portfolio of investments which must be financed. A third branch of theorizing relates to the large multiproduct firm. This literature deals with corporate strategy, especially diversification, and how the organization should be structured (multidivisional, vertical integration, the shape of the hierarchy and so on). For an extensive treatment of these and other significant areas of mainstream organizational economics, see Milgrom and Roberts (1992).

Radical economists' theorizing concerning the firm has emphasized the firm as an arena in which class conflicts—for example, between workers and owners—occur and are important in affecting the firm's operations. Other economic theorizing that is harder to classify has dealt with subjects such as bounded rationality, the game theory of the firm, worker participation, producer cooperatives, the Japanese firm, the high performance firm and so on.

The holistic model of the human firm

The need for a holistic model

The machine model is obsolete. There is a need for a holistic model in which the firm is an organic integrated whole, a model reflecting the new scientific paradigm. The needed holistic model is one that includes as an input intangible soft ingredients which are rooted in the firm's important human relationships. Many economists will be uncomfortable with the holistic model because it includes "higher" aspects of human behavior that cannot be quantified precisely or reduced to a monetary dimension. While it is difficult to integrate these aspects with economic theory, I believe that doing so is both necessary and extremely worthwhile.

Basics are the same as the machine model

The starting point for the holistic model is the same as that for the core machine model. That is, the holistic model includes as inputs tangible assets, labor and technology, as well as an expanded list of intangible hard ingredients which are suggested by a number of the extensions of the core model. The latter include the financial structure of the firm, its ownership structure (type of business organization and the identity and rights of owners), the organizational structure (hierarchy, rewards and incentives, channels of information flow and so on), and the state of training and other competence development (all types of human capital including organizational capital).

The holistic model is similar to the core machine model or production function in the sense that in both models if everything goes ideally the process of production results in the greatest possible outcome. As indicated earlier, in the production function, efficient use of the inputs and technology leads to the maximum output. Similarly, in the holistic model, efficient use of inputs and technology as well as ideal organizational functioning results in the realization of the firm's true potential outcome. The following subsections explain about the ingredients and processes necessary for the firm to realize that potential. This does not at all imply the view that firms typically or in fact ever realize their full potential. Nevertheless, much insight can be gained from understanding what is possible.

The new elements: the intangible soft ingredients

The qualities missing from the machine model are passion, inspiration, esprit de corps, enthusiasm, vigor, zest, vision, strongly held values, deep commitment, spirituality and highly ethical orientation. In the holistic model developed here, two essential soft ingredients are the key to bringing about such desirable qualities. These are spirit and leadership.

Spirit

Jack Hawley's (1993: 12–15) model of management includes an important new and hard to define element, spirit.[1] Spirit, according to Hawley, relates to our deep inner self. It

> is the *us* beyond all the things [physical body, five senses, mind, feelings, innate tendencies, etc.] we usually think are the real us….Spirit…refers to our (and our organizations') aliveness,…is the vitality that dwells in our body,…[is] the very source of that energy….Spirit refers to our other reality, our real reality, our higher reality—the one which at some inner level we know exists but at times forget that we know.
>
> (1993: 16–17)

A person or organization cannot be without spirit in the above sense, but a person or organization can lack awareness of and be out of unity with one's spirit in which case there is a lack of aliveness and vitality. This brings us to the role of leadership.

Leadership

According to Peter Vaill:

> all true leadership is indeed spiritual leadership….The reason is…leadership is concerned with bringing out the best in people. As such, one's best is tied intimately to one's deepest sense of oneself, to one's spirit. My leadership efforts must touch that in myself and in others.
>
> (1990: 224)

Because spirit is the source of energy, "releasing Spirit can bring an avalanche of energy and zest" (Hawley 1993: 32–3). Good leadership by definition involves "arousing and channeling a human system's energy" (1993: 37).

The most important function of leaders in tapping this energy is to establish a collective vision for the organization. A vision is a dream or a mental image of what the organization could be if it were realizing its highest purposes; it is not as specific as a goal. According to Charles Kiefer (1992: 177), "the *leader is the custodian or steward of the organizational vision*. The leader sees to it that the organization has a collective vision and that the members share that vision and are committed to it." The leader's custodial role is, first, to make sure that a process occurs from which "a genuine organizational vision emerges and, second, to make sure it [the vision] remains alive and well" (1992: 180). Thus, the leader is a "catalyst of the collective vision" and a "channel for the expression of that vision." This kind of leadership requires a disciplined imagination, an openness to spirit, and a cultivation of the humility to receive it so that the members can discover a vision that rings true for the organization and each of them personally (Hawley 1993: 38, 169–70). When organization members are fully enrolled in the highest purposes of the organization, they will work with powerful motivation, inspiration and focus (Channon 1992: 58).

Another way of looking at this leadership role involves the recognition that we all have two selves—our bodily or worldly self and our higher self, or spirit—and we have a need to experience a unity between these two selves (Hawley 1993: 21–2). Without this sense of unity, we feel unwhole, that something is lacking although we do not necessarily know what it is. The ideal expressed most clearly in the American Indian spiritual tradition and similarly in a number of other traditions is to live in a state of constant spiritual awareness, i.e. in wholeness and unity (1993: 23–4). When leaders are successful in committing organization members to the collective vision, when all members fully know about and share the organization's high purposes, then leadership has created "a collective state of constant spiritual awareness, a continual fusing of high things with the worldly" (1993: 173). While many will find this hard to grasp and seemingly unrelated to what goes on in actual firms, there is evidence that something like this occurs in high-performing organizations.

According to Vaill:

> all the case studies and other research results that have come out about excellence and peak performance confirm that both members and observers of excellent organizations consistently feel the spirit of the organization and the activity, and that this feeling of spirit is an essential part of the meaning and value that members and observers place on the activity.
>
> (1990: 216)

Moreover, in high performing systems:

> No one is shy in those organizations to talk about the spiritual or mystical aspects of the team, the craft, the product or service, the persona of the leader, the history and the lore of the activity, the meaning of being able to be part of such a system.
>
> (1990: 216)

Finally, Hawley refers to (and then responds to) a comment made by a well-known observer of organizations:

> that the quality improvement programs that really work are "almost mystical." It's an excellent point, but not quite strong enough. The programs that really work, the ones that give birth to major change, *are*

mystical....You can almost taste the inner meaning and importance of these programs.

(1993: 26)

Further perspective on the role of leaders with respect to vision can be gained by considering the important concept of fields which is increasingly finding applications among new paradigm scientists. Fields are nonmaterial, "invisible forces that structure space or behavior" (Wheatley 1992: 12–13). The different types of fields include gravitational, electromagnetic, quantum, morphogenic (biological) and, perhaps, organizational. Wheatley understands "organizational vision as a field—a force of unseen connections that influences employees' behavior" (1992: 13):

All employees, in any part of the company, who bumped up against that field would be infuenced by it. Their behavior could be shaped as a result of "field meetings," where their energy would link with the field's form to create behavior congruent with the organization's goals.

(1992: 54)

This insight is in sharp contrast with older versions of organizational motivation theory that have emphasized the enticements of external rewards, an emphasis more consistent with Newtonian science.

Wheatley's jazz metaphor aptly captures the basic idea of how a leader's role in developing vision as field can be effective:

Improvisation is the saving skill. As leaders, we play a crucial role in selecting the melody, setting the tempo, establishing the key, and inviting the players. But that is all we can do. The music comes from something we cannot direct, from a unified whole created among the players—a relational holism that transcends separateness. In the end, when it works, we sit back, amazed and grateful.

(1993: 44)

Besides establishing the firm's vision, the other important role of leaders is to design and maintain the soft structures that channel creative energies toward desired results. The soft structures are the organizational features that facilitate and guide member behavior, as contrasted with the hard structures, put in place by managers, that tend to control member performance. First on the list of soft structures is organizational culture, which involves shared values, sensitivities and attitudes; other soft structures include habits, belief structures, an understanding of the firm's core competences, and the firm's mission. Core competences are the key complex collective skills that underly and support groups of specific products that a firm markets (Hamel and Prahalad 1994). When leaders identify the firm's existing core competences and how these need to evolve, and link these to the organization's culture and mission, organization members' energies become powerfully focused. Thus, in a variety of ways, the soft structures created by leaders represent very important intangible productive capacity; they are a type of organizational capital.

The intermediate outcomes

In the holistic model, there is an important intermediate step that is crucial to determining how the inputs are transformed into the firm's socio-economic performance, Y. First, if the firm's leaders do a great job creating the vision and appropriate soft structures, the intermediate soft outcome will be a combination of (1) high energy and vitality (E/V) and (2) members who are fully aligned with the organization's mission and purpose (AMP). This intermediate outcome is akin to a high amount of charged electrical energy. Second, if the firm's managers also do a great job, they create intermediate hard outcomes, essentially intangible hard structures providing coordination and control. This intermediate outcome is akin to good electrical wiring. When these two intermediate outcomes (the energy and wiring) are in exactly the right balance (B*) with each other, the firm is able to realize its highest potential; it has become a high performance or Z-firm. In this situation, members' high energies are directed along paths expected to lead to the achievement of the firm's ultimate socio-economic performance, Y*. Because of the desired balance, B*, the expected outcome is greater than the sum of the inputs, a synergistic result.[2]

When B* is attained, the firm has realized its full potential organizational capability. It should be noted that B* consists of a number of interrelated component types of balance. The most important balance is the one between leadership and management, between the creators of the intermediate soft outcomes and the creators of the intermediate hard outcomes. According to Craig Hickman in *Mind of a Manager, Soul of a Leader* (1990), it is extremely important for firms to strive for an ideal balance between leadership and management:

> The words "manager" and "leader" are metaphors representing two opposite ends of a continuum. "Manager" tends to signify the more analytical, structured, controlled, deliberate, and orderly end of the continuum, while "leader" tends to occupy the more experimental, visionary, flexible, uncontrolled, and creative end.
>
> (1990: 7)

> Managers should not be required to become more like leaders, nor should leaders be required to become more like managers.
>
> (1990: 13)

Rather, what is desired is a balance wherein strong management is integrated with strong leadership.

B* is reminiscent of the Chinese yin/yang symbol depicting the unity of apparent opposites such as the male and female, the visible and invisible, and so forth. In this sense, B* depicts the desired unity not only between leadership and management, and hard and soft organizational features, but between right and left brain functioning (reason and intuition), creativity and control, short-term and long-term interests of the organization, and the interests of its stakeholders versus its own interests. This idea of balance or unity is not a new idea. Great thinkers and writers through the ages have developed similar themes. For example, in *The Prophet*, Kahlil Gibran wrote about reason versus passion:

> Your reason and your passion are the rudder and the sails of your seafaring soul. If either your sails or your rudder be broken, you can but toss and drift, or else be held at a stand still in mid-seas. For reason, ruling alone, is a force confining; and passion, unattended, is a flame that burns to its own destruction.
>
> (p. 50)

The firm's ultimate socio-economic performance

As indicated above, if everything works to perfection with desired unity and balance, the expected result is the ultimate socio-economic performance (Y^*), an outcome more complex than the maximum output, Q^*, of the machine model. Y^* includes the following elements: (1) aggregate contribution to society's material well-being (quantity and quality of output), (2) intangible contributions or net satisfactions to stakeholders (customers, owners, managers, employees, community and so forth), and (3) impact on community, society and world in the long run in the ecological, physical and mental health, and spiritual dimensions.

Figure 6.1 shows graphically the main steps involved when the high-performance (Z-) firm's activities produce Y^*. However, if things do not go well, there will be a gap between Y, actual performance, and Y^*. In the machine model, the gap between Q and Q^* was attributed to X-inefficiency, but in a context where there is a spiritual element to the process of transforming ingredients into an ultimate outcome, the term "inefficiency" seems curiously out of place. It seems more appropriate to use the phrase "unrealized potential" to refer to the Y gap. Ordinary internal inefficiency, of course, might be a part of why the firm's potential is unrealized, but there could be much more to it. Perhaps, it is because, lacking leadership, organization members have not been energized and aligned by a compelling vision.

Evidence of leadership and spirit in high performance firms

If the holistic model of the human firm is an improvement on the machine model, it should be possible to find evidence of this. Certainly, careful statis-

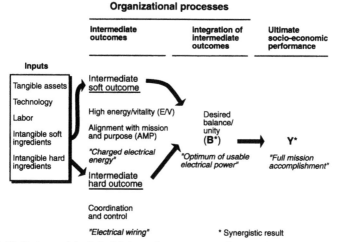

Organizational processes

Figure 6.1 Holistic model of the high-performance (Z-) firm realizing its full potential

tical analyses of the hypotheses embedded in the model ought to be possible. These, however, are beyond the scope of this chapter. What follows is anecdotal evidence supportive of the holistic model. These stories obviously do not constitute rigorous empirical investigation. Nonetheless, the reader may find that in epitomizing the leadership, spirit and balance aspects of the model, they represent persuasive support for the basic hypotheses of the model.

In the *The Soul of a Business* (1993), Tom Chappell, President and CEO of Tom's of Maine, has written a superb account about his firm's struggle to find the right balance between the practical and spiritual sides of business. Tom's produces a variety of products such as soaps, shampoos, creams and, most notably, toothpaste, all made from healthful, natural ingredients. In 1981, after about a decade of growing sales to health food stores, the company decided to enter the mass market, selling to major supermarkets and drugstore chains. This required hiring professional managerial talent with the skills to make the company more focused and analytical in its business strategy. The resulting expansion in sales growth between 1981 and 1986 was tremendously successful. However, another result was a conflict between the original company vision and that of the new managers, whose decision-making style involved rational calculation rather than gut instinct. It was during this period that Tom began to find that his "everyday business life had gone stale. Work had become an unfulfilling exercise" (1993: xi).

In his attempt to deal with and understand his unhappiness, Tom decided to attend Harvard divinity school:

> I needed to recapture what had inspired me to start the business in the first place. I needed to get back in touch with my original sense of purpose and to renew myself and my commitment to creating good products.
>
> (1993: xi)

He learned about the importance of finding a middle way involving a balance between head and heart, between spirit and the world of business. He found that "if you nurture the soul of your business, not only can you compete with the biggest players in the game, you will add meaning to your work and make a real contribution to society" (1993: xv). In other words, "you can be a hard-assed competitor and still run a business with soul" (1993: xiv). To bring back the needed balance, Tom began a process that involved developing statements of his company's beliefs and mission and incorporating these into its operations. An important part of Tom's mission is "to be a profitable and successful company, while acting in a socially and environmentally responsible manner" (1993: 33). The record to date indicates that Tom's is accomplishing its mission.

Japan's Matsushita Electric Corporation, the giant consumer electronics company whose products are sold under the brand names National, Panasonic, Quasar and Technics, exemplifies the idea of balance between spiritual ideals and the practical aspects of managing a major corporation. Konosuke Matsushita, the founder and head of Matushita for many years, writes that the mission of his company suddenly crystallized for him on May 5, 1932 after he visited a religious community (Matsushita 1984: 135–7). When he returned to his company, Matsushita's eager communications of his new vision found enthusiastic support from staff members. Today, his company is known for its strong belief system as well as its tough-minded management. Matsushita members are trained in its values, and every morning they sing its song and recite its code of values.

> The director of a major Matsushita subsidiary comments: "Matsushita's...philosophy is very important to us. It enables us to match Western efficiency without being one bit less Japanese. Perhaps the ultimate triumph of Matsushita is the *balancing* of the rationalism of the West with the spiritualism of the East."
>
> (Pascale and Athos 1981: 52; italics are mine.)

Anita and Gordon Roddick's company, The Body Shop, which sells hair and skin products such as shampoos, lotions and perfumes, is another exemplar (even if the subject of recent controversy) when it comes to leadership and spirit. Founded in 1976, The Body Shop has by any measure been a fantastic success; it had by 1991 become a global business with more than nine hundred shops in forty-two countries around the world (Roddick 1991: 23). Its success owes much to two passionately held beliefs. First, the Roddicks believe that their mission is to sell products and remedies that are made with natural ingredients and that are proven to be good for people and the environment. Second, they believe that they can do this without exploiting women or behaving immorally as the conventional beauty business has:

How do you ennoble the spirit when you are selling something as incon-
sequential as a cosmetic cream? You do it by creating a sense of holism,
of spiritual development, of feeling connected to the workplace, the
environment and relationships with one another....The spirit soars when
you are satisfying your own basic material needs in such a way that you
are also serving the needs of others honorably and humanely.

(1991: 23)

They have learned that the high motivation and inspiration of Body Shop
people derive from leadership with a large and moral vision (1991:
223–8).

Finally, leadership and spirit are a critically important ingredient in one
of professional sports' biggest success stories, the Chicago Bulls basketball
team. This is not meant in any way to demean the physical contributions
made by Michael Jordon, "the most creative player in basketball," or Scottie
Pippin, or any of the other talented players. But as coach Phil Jackson says:

the real reason the Bulls won three straight NBA championships from
1991 to '93 was that we plugged in to the power of *oneness* instead of
the power of one man, and transcended the divisive forces of the ego
that have crippled far more gifted teams.

(Jackson 1995: 6)

The essence of Jackson's leadership was his dream not just to win championships but to do it in a way that tapped the spirit of the team by creating
an environment based on the principles of selflessness and compassion I'd
learned as a Christian in my parents' home; sitting on a cushion practicing
Zen; and studying the teachings of the Lakota Sioux" (1995: 6). Another
key element in the Bulls' success was the pursuit of a kind of balance
Jackson calls the middle path (1995: 151–2). This involves neither overly
tight control of players nor giving them total freedom but trying "to
create a supportive environment that structures the way they relate to
each other and gives them the freedom to realize their potential" (1995:
152).

Implications for U.S. economic decline

Although much controversy surrounds its interpretation, the U.S. economic
decline of the 1970s and 1980s was very real and very large. During this
period, the U.S. suffered from dramatic losses in market share in many
important industries, vastly lower productivity growth, and greatly lowered
growth in real income, especially hourly wages. While economic analyses
have pointed to a number of hypotheses for the decline, much of it has not
been satisfactorily explained, and economists remain puzzled or in disagreement regarding its causes. The holistic model developed here strongly

suggests a hypothesis for the decline not seriously considered by economists, namely, a failure of U.S. business leadership. According to this view, a deterioration of the appropriate balance between leadership and management in U.S. business is responsible for the reduced industrial dynamism. Because this hypothesis emphasizes a failing with regard to one of the intangible soft factors, it is not surprising that economists have overlooked it.

While economists have neglected the leadership factor, an increasing number of business thinkers have not. For example, Hickman (1990) recognizes the importance of leadership and that it must be in proper balance with management. This means balancing managers who are more practical, reasonable and decisive with leaders who are more visionary, empathetic and flexible. According to Hickman:

> enduring results and the ultimate competitive advantage come from tapping the natural tension between managers and leaders....This requires blending strong management and strong leadership into one integrated whole where the strengths of leaders combine with, rather than clash with, the strengths of managers.
>
> (1990: 2)

When this occurs, the result is a balanced, integrated organization that is capable of producing superior synergistic (or "one plus one equals three") outcomes year after year (1990: 2, 13).

In Abraham Zaleznik's (1989, 1992) view, American industry in recent decades has lost a considerable amount of "balance" by virtue of overemphasizing professional management and underemphasizing leadership, thereby losing its competitive edge:

> The great paternal leaders of the past gave way to modern managers. Equipped with their bag of tools and their attachment to the managerial mystique, modern managers could indeed coordinate and control, but in due course lost sight of the substance of work in business. Where their predecessors in business leadership had limited views of reality, the modern manager distorted reality by displacing substance with process....The business schools...have followed rather than led business in blind acceptance of the managerial mystique. They have served as socialization plants to fit managers for the life of process found in modern organizations.
>
> (1989: 277–8)

These and related reasons are behind Vaill's (1990: 222) observation that "we have seen the spirit go out of whole institutions in our society, including *Fortune* 100 firms, government agencies, major universities, and whole professions." In sum, American organizations had become "underled and overmanaged" (Bennis 1993: 76).

Zaleznik (1992: 130) believes that if left to professional management, U.S. corporate stagnation will continue. Thus, what is needed is a strong dose of visionary leadership that anticipates the corporation's future, sets ambitious goals, inspires employees, provides a sense of purpose and direction, and energizes the organization (Thompson 1992: 213–14). This is the kind of leadership necessary for the revival and renewal of spirit that Vaill (1990: 222) has observed in some organizations. Ideally, if the right balance between leadership and management can be realized, the enterprise will have become a "learning organization" capable of responding rapidly to the turbulent global environment and "continually enhancing its capacity to create" (Senge 1993). While the ideal may be unattainable, the hypothesis outlined here suggests that the U.S. economy has much to gain from reversing the deterioration of the leadership/management balance that has occurred in recent decades. Judging by the increasing interest in and writing about leadership in the 1990s, this process has already begun.[3]

Implications for economic systems

There is reason to believe that the soft ingredients, especially spirit and leadership, are crucial factors not just for firms but for the performance of entire economic systems. Although it is beyond the scope of this chapter to develop it, what is needed is a holistic model of the economic system in which the balance between soft and hard inputs is a central element. Assuming that the basic features of such a holistic model would be very similar to the one for the firm, let us consider some of the interesting implications.

In comparing different types of economic systems (capitalism, socialism and a variety of hybrids), most have argued that the virtues and defects of a particular system derive almost entirely from its specific hard structures such as the types and features of markets, property rights, patterns of ownership, business management processes, governmental laws and regulation, and so forth. However, if economic systems function holistically, similar to firms, two societies' economic systems with the same hard structures might produce very different socio-economic outcomes. This would be so if in one the systemic structures were compatible with the true spirit of the people, and in the other they were not. Presumably, unless there is the right balance between soft and hard, the economic system would not be successful in eliciting the kind of enthusiasm and energy that would enable the realization of potential performance. Thus, a society which overemphasizes structural economic factors at the expense of such things as leadership, vision and moral ideals could wind up with a stifling economic system rather than a high-performance one.

These ideas seem very relevant to the attempt by the nations of Eastern Europe to transform their economic systems, moving from socialism to capitalism. Their headlong efforts to introduce the structures of capitalism have no doubt faltered for many reasons. One important reason may be that they have given first priority to introducing new hard structures, whether or not these reforms derived from or were consistent with the true spirit of their people. At least a few Eastern European leaders have expressed this concern. For example, in the late 1980s at the time of his visit to the Pope, Mikhail Gorbachev said that "unless the types of personal values taught by the spiritual traditions were revived in the Soviet people, they would not succeed in rebuilding the economy!" (Miller 1992: 74). In a similar vein, Vaclav Havel of Czechoslovakia said in his presidential inaugural address that "unless the people of Czechoslovakia learned to be truthful, open, and respectful with each other, they would never succeed in rebuilding the economy and country" (Miller 1992: 75). Earlier Havel had written:

> "This is not something that can be designed and introduced like a new car....A better system will not automatically ensure a better life. In fact, the opposite is now true: only by creating a better life can a better system be developed.
>
> (Miller 1992: 75).

Conclusion

The philosopher Mortimer Adler (1985: 161–3) asks whether there is a specific human nature common to all members of the species. His answer is that what is common to all humans are their potentialities. It follows that the essential nature of business enterprise is human potentiality in an organizational context. The novelty and importance of the holistic model developed here is that it offers a glimpse of this potentiality. While organizations help humans to realize their potentialities, they also frequently limit this realization. Thus the holistic model is useful not only in helping us to understand the realizable organizational potentiality, but in providing insight regarding why that potentiality is generally not fully realized.

The alternative, the machine model, does well enough as part of theories explaining price determination in specific markets and related phenomenon. Increasingly, however, economists need a model of the firm that can be used to understand more complex, intangible issues such as competitiveness. For these purposes, a holistic model of the firm that integrates soft ingredients (leadership, spirit, vision) with the conventional mix of hard ingredients is essential. Without a holistic model, it is impossible to understand why "a growing number of companies are setting off on spiritual journeys" (*Business Week* 1995: 82). The reason for this according to Lawrence Perlman, CEO of Minneapolis-based Ceridian Corporation, is that "Ultimately, the combination of head and heart will be a competitive advantage" (*Business Week* 1995: 82).

Part III

Responsibility in relationships with stakeholders

Community, employees, customers and government

Part III is concerned with understanding what determines how well the human firm exercises its responsibilities in relation to its stakeholders such as its community, employees, customers and government. The models developed in these four chapters have important implications for how to improve the responsible behavior of the human firm. Generally, improving a firm's responsibility requires investments in organizational capital. The last chapter in this part, Chapter 10, which deals with government, is concerned less with the responsibility issue and more with the question of industrial policy to improve firms' competitiveness.

7 Social responsibility in the human firm

Toward a new theory of the firm's external relationships

Under what circumstances can we expect socially responsible behavior from a firm? The theory developed in this chapter focuses on this question.

In orthodox economics, two kinds of theory depict the firm's external relationships, its relationships with stockholders, customers, employees, suppliers, creditors and the community. First, there is the theory about how markets function; second, there is the theory about how markets fail to perform optimally. The latter, market failure theory, emphasizes positive and negative externalities. These economic literatures are almost entirely unrelated to another body of thinking concerning the external relationships of firms, namely, the large and growing non-economic literature on the ethical obligations and social responsibilities of businesses. Because the latter is very different from the economic literature, economists well-trained in orthodox economics, by virtue of that training, seem unable to appreciate the arguments concerning the social responsibilities of firms. Thus, the purpose of this chapter is to develop a model of the firm's external relationships that integrates economic theory, especially theory concerning negative externalities, with non-economic insights concerning the social responsibilities of businesses. The challenge is to develop a model that, while appreciative of the broader noneconomic concerns, will allow economists to overcome the blinders imposed by their training.

Section 1 of this chapter outlines the orthodox economic viewpoint on the firm's motivation, the nature of externalities, and the firm's social responsibilities. Section 2 summarizes the noneconomic literature on the concept of social responsibility and the doctrine of corporate social responsibility. Section 3 develops a socio-economic theory of the firm's behavior that integrates theory regarding externalities and the concept of social responsibility. Using water pollution as an example, this section indicates how the firm's behavior is expected to vary widely depending on factors internal and external to the firm. Section 4 develops a number of issues related to the firm's socially responsible behavior. Section 5 outlines the normative implications of the theory, and the final section provides a brief conclusion.

The orthodox viewpoint

The firm's motivation

Although there are some well-known dissenting views, the modern orthodox microeconomic view is that the firm's motivation is to maximize short-run profit. For particular purposes such as investment decision making, orthodox microeconomists following finance theory may assume the firm's motivation to be maximizing the value of stockholder's wealth, which is generally taken to be the discounted sum of the stream of future profit. However, for most purposes, including externality theory, orthodox microeconomists continue to assume short-run profit maximization.

One reason for this is that the modern approach to economics prefers to characterize human behavior "as being based on simple and easily characterizable motives" (Sen 1987: 2–7). Thus, orthodox economics in discussing motivation ignores complex ethical considerations that earlier traditions of thinking (for example, Aristotle, Adam Smith, Karl Marx, John Stuart Mill) took more seriously. According to Sen (1987: 7) "it is hard not to notice [in economic publications today]...the neglect of the influence of ethical considerations in the characterization of actual human behavior." It is not that unethical behavior is assumed; the self-interested behavior assumed is simply devoid of ethical content. As Sen admits, for some purposes this approach has been productive, but in other instances this excessively narrow characterization of human motivation has not served well.

Externalities

Positive (and negative) externalities, also known as external economies (and diseconomies), are "events which confer an appreciable benefit (inflict an appreciable damage) on some person(s) who were not fully consenting parties in reaching the decision which led directly or indirectly to the event in question" (Meade 1973: 15). The emphasis in this chapter is on negative externalities such as when firm A harms B (the victim) as a result of its water pollution, which is a byproduct of its production activity.

In this typically abstract, orthodox analysis of the negative externality, A and B have no previous relationship with each other, nor are they part of any larger collectivity or web of relationships through which they might incur social or ethical obligations. Despite the fact that harm occurs and the result is socially inoptimal, the action of firm A is not considered immoral or unethical; A experiences no obligation of any kind to stop the pollution. Firm A, an amoral entity, is simply doing what follows from profit maximization.

Normative views

The classical creed

Milton Friedman has been the most prominent defender of the classical creed regarding the role of business in society. According to Friedman (1962), the corporation has no responsibility beyond serving the interests of its stockholders. Its only responsibility is "to use its resources and engage in activities designed to increase its profits so long as it stays within the rules of the game, which is to say, engages in open and free competition, without deception or fraud" (1962: 133). Moreover, Friedman (1970) argues that corporations that take on other responsibilities are pursuing public purposes, and their executives in effect become public employees, without having been selected through a political process (see also Baumol 1974).

Another argument for the proposition that firms should simply maximize their profits is the following empirical one. This view, cited by Howard Bowen, states that: "businessmen...are so fully imbued with a spirit of profit-making and with pecuniary standards of value that they are unable to see the social implications of their tasks—much less to follow policies directed toward the social interest" (1953: 115). Perhaps this is why most economists believe that negative externalities such as pollution cannot be corrected by businesses or market forces alone and that it is futile to expect more ethical or responsible behavior from businesses (see, for example, Blinder 1987: 139–40).

Adam Smith

Milton Friedman believes his position is consistent with Adam Smith, who sees businesspeople to be:

> led by an invisible hand to promote an end which was no part of his intention. Nor is it always the worse for the society that it was no part of it. By pursuing his own interest, he frequently promotes that of the society more effectually than when he really intends to promote it. I have never known much good done by those who affected to trade for the public good.
>
> (1937: 423)

But Sen (1987: 22–3), contrary to the conventional wisdom, points out that Adam Smith's normative view of human motivation is much broader than self-interest. Sen quotes Smith:

> Man...ought to regard himself...as a citizen of the world,...and to the interest of this great community, he ought at all times to be willing that his own little interest should be sacrificed.
>
> (1987: 22–3)

The managerial creed

In contrast to the classical creed of economic self-interest seeking is the managerial creed espoused by many corporate executives:

> In this view the actions of individual enterprises are and should be dominated by considerations of the public interest; profit-seeking takes a lesser place. If enterprises act directly in the public interest, there is much less need to rely on the competitive mechanism to demonstrate that individual actions which appear to be self-seeking are socially beneficial in the System as a whole.
>
> (Sutton 1956: 57)

The managerial creed recognizes the responsibility of the firm not only to stockholders but to employees, customers and the general public and advocates that executives' decision making should balance the often competing claims of these groups (Silk and Vogel 1976: 134–6). While the managerial creed calls for corporations to accept broader responsibilities than advocated by the classical creed, it does not expect as much from businesses as those who are calling for businesses to be socially responsible.

The socially responsible firm

The doctrine of corporate social responsibility

Although individual writers differ on specific points, there is wide agreement around the central features of what is most commonly called the doctrine (or creed) of corporate social responsibility. This doctrine, as the word "corporate" suggests, was developed particularly with big businesses in mind. Corporate social responsibility (CSR) may be thought of as a form of control of businesses, an alternative to the control by markets or government. CSR is by nature voluntary, that is, it is self-regulation or self-control in the social interest. This means that enterprises choose it without the compulsion of laws, contracts, governmental intervention or active community pressure (Bowen 1978: 116–17).

According to the CSR doctrine, corporations are social institutions, creatures of society that in effect have been chartered by society to perform certain purposes. These corporations must adopt policies and actions that are in conformity to the norms and goals of society. If not, the society that granted the charter can revoke it. In this view, businesses have a moral obligation to use their resources for the common good as well as obligations to particular groups such as stockholders, consumers, employees and creditors.

To behave in a socially responsible way, firms' decision-making processes must reflect broad societal concerns. For example, "corporations need to analyse the social consequences of their decisions before they make them and take steps to minimize the social costs of these decisions when appropriate" (Jones 1980: 65). CSR thus requires an extra degree of discipline on the part of businesses, the discipline of figuring out what it takes to align the firm's efforts with the common good in the long term.

CSR also implies accountability, the willingness of companies to be held accountable for their actions that have negative effects on others or are not aligned with the common good. Further, it implies a willingness to adjust or correct the behavior that has been found to be wanting. In sum, corporations that behave in accord with the CSR doctrine are harmonizing their behavior with the rest of society.

Changing the social contract

The doctrine of corporate social responsibility implies the existence of a "social contract" between the corporation and society. This contract:

> acknowledges the public's right to impose its preferences upon business, it also acknowledges the corporation's participation in shaping those preferences in accordance with management's judgment of its own...best interests.
>
> (Silk and Vogel 1976: 158)

As society's preferences change, this means a redefining and thus a renegotiating of the social contract, in which corporations have a right to participate as long as they do so honestly and openly (1976: 158).

The dramatic changes in social values beginning in the 1960s led to significant new public demands on businesses to be socially responsible, and accordingly to much effort to redefine the social contract. These continuing efforts and changing values are part of what defines the "new age" we live in.

The *legitimacy* of the corporation rests on the public's perception of an identity between the goals of the corporation and the goals of society (Sethi 1975: 60; Silk and Vogel 1976: ch. 5). If corporations resist public pressures on them to alter their behavior such as occurred in the U.S.A. during the 1970s, this produces the kind of crisis in which the very legitimacy of the corporation is questioned. One result of this kind of crisis is corporate efforts to legitimize their activities. Corporations in the 1990s are still experiencing significant challenges, and thus continue to be very concerned about their legitimacy.

Sethi (1975: 62–4) and others have argued that corporations in addition to becoming socially responsible should develop the capacity of social responsiveness. This means developing corporate capacity to anticipate social issues and problems before they reach crisis proportions, and to adapt their policies and programs in such a way as to minimize the disruptive conflicts that the firm might otherwise experience.

CSR as business philosophy

Although there is no uniformity of opinion among business leaders, an increasing number of them espouse a philosophy that is the same as the CSR doctrine. For example, James E. Burke, former chief executive officer of Johnson and Johnson, states:

> Aggressive social concern and higher profitability need not be at logger-heads. With creativity and commitment, they can be made entirely complementary. Indeed, businesses have far more opportunities to do good—for themselves and their communities—than is commonly appreciated.
>
> (Bollier 1996: 6)

Economists and CSR

Corporate social responsibility and ethics are generally not appreciated by economists because these concepts do not have a place in the orthodox economic theory of the firm. Socially responsible motivation does not jibe with profit-maximizing motivation, and the economic theory of externalities has a much more limited view of the firm's external relationships than the doctrine of CSR. Thus, it is not surprising that a leading economist, Alan Blinder (1987, ch. 5) for example, would argue that the environmentalists who believe pollution is a moral issue are simply wrong. Environmentalists, in contrast to most economists, are, according to Kelman (1981), concerned with societal attitudes toward pollution and the motivations of businesses with respect to pollution. He explains that "the thinking of economists allows little place for these concerns, and the case for [governmental] economic incentives ignores them" (1981: 113). This strongly suggests the need for an economic theory of the firm's external relationships that is integrated with corporate social responsibility considerations.

A socio-economic model of firm behavior: externalities and social responsibility

The purpose of this section is to develop a model of firm behavior that integrates economic externality theory with the view that firms have social responsibilities that go far beyond making a profit. The focus of the model is a firm's decision making with respect to a negative externality, namely, water pollution. The firm in question has decided to produce a new product, and it has discovered that a byproduct will be a harmful liquid requiring disposal. Will it dump the liquid in the adjacent river?

Essence of the model

The dependent variable of the model is the extent to which the firm behaves in a socially responsible way with respect to a particular sphere of activity, for example, water pollution. The firm's socially responsible behavior (SRB) is defined along a horizontal spectrum in which ideal SRB is on the far right and sabotage is on the far left. In sabotage, the firm's intention is to harm persons outside the firm to gain at their expense. Ideal SRB is defined in a later section. The purpose of the model is to explain where on the SRB spectrum a firm will locate. The degree of a firm's SRB indicates much that is important about the firm's external relationships.

There are two classes of independent variables. The first relates to behavioral characteristics of the firm; the second relates to the external situation confronting the firm. The firm's SRB is its response to the external situation, a response reflecting its internal character. Decision making about the firm's SRB is assumed to be made by a coalition of people involved with the firm, most notably top management, but the nature of this coalition is not important for this analysis. What is important are three of the firm's internal characteristics: (1) ethical orientation, (2) patience and (3) organizational capability. The first two are emphasized in the following analysis.

Internal characteristics

First, ethical orientation is defined along a spectrum with three prominent points. On the far left is a point representing opportunism; the middlepoint represents non-opportunistic self-interest; and the far right point represents high ethical principle. Opportunism, following Oliver Williamson's usage, is present when in the effort to realize individual gains in transactions individuals are willing to be sly, crafty and dishonest. Non-opportunistic self-interest is present when individuals' ethical principles do not allow them to be dishonest or otherwise opportunistic, but there is no concern for others beyond what self-interest dictates. High ethical principle is present when individuals have a sense of high purpose involving the desire to find win–win solutions in their relations with others and experiencing others not simply as means but as ends.

Second, patience is also defined along a spectrum. On the far left is the short-term orientation, and on the far right is the long-term orientation involving a high degree of patience. Patience thus refers to the ability and willingness of an individual to make short-term sacrifices for the possibility of long-term gain. It corresponds roughly to the rate of discount, a variable often used by economists to denote the rate of return used in finding the present value of future returns. On the far left of the spectrum, the rate of discount is very high, and thus individuals greatly discount the possibility of future returns. The far right is opposite to this.

The third internal characteristic, organizational capability, refers to the firm's capability for making rational decisions, innovating and learning. It is assumed in what follows that the firm's decision makers are at least average in these respects.

The three internal characteristics of the firm's decision makers are assumed to be subject to influence. For example, they can be influenced by organizational features such as the ethical climate, and they can to a degree be improved through the organization's training and development programs.

External situation

The firm is assumed to have a social as well as an economic nature, and therefore it must respond not only to signals or demands emanating from the market but from other segments of society. It follows that the external situation variables must include factors reflecting both market incentives and broad societal influences. Also included here are variables reflecting special factors related to the specific sphere of activity involved (water pollution in this case).

First, market incentives derive from the product and resource markets in which the firm participates. In the sphere of water pollution, the cost, if any, to the firm of using up collectively owned water resources through its pollution is of special importance.

Second are the broad societal and community influences reflecting societal goals and values. These non-market societal influences may be experienced in specific spheres of activity such as when a community exerts pressure for a particular kind of socially acceptable behavior.

Third are the special factors. For example, the following factors apply with respect to water pollution. It is assumed that (1) the amount of harm resulting from the pollution is known and non-negligible; (2) the damage results from this firm's pollution alone, not from combining with other pollution; (3) this type of pollution is not illegal, but it would not be considered acceptable by the people in the surrounding community (they also would not consider it the worst thing in the world); (4) immediate community activity to pressure the firm on account of the pollution is unlikely; and (5) there is no known equal or lower cost alternative way to dispose of this polluting liquid.

Nature of the model

This model is designed to apply to situations in which there is no current government involvement. In this water pollution example, the government is not involved because the possible water pollutant is a previously unknown substance. Thus, there are no laws, regulations or enforcement activities relating to it. Otherwise, government-related variables would have to be added to the model. The reason for excluding government-related variables is that governmental activity is likely to be a consequence of the firm's

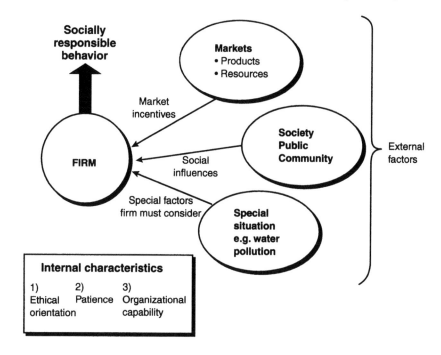

Figure 7.1 A socio-economic model of the firm's socially responsible behavior

earlier socially responsible (or irresponsible) behavior, and therefore is not fully an independent variable.

The essence of the model is depicted in Figure 7.1. In functional form, the model is

$$SRB = f(EO, P, CAP, MK, SOC, SPEC)$$

where the first three independent variables are the firm's internal characteristics, its ethical orientation (EO), patience (P) and organizational capability (CAP). The second three independent variables represent the firm's external situation, its market incentives (MK), societal influences (SOC), and special factors (SPEC). The model's theory is positive or descriptive in that it is designed to explain the degree of a firm's socially responsible behavior (SRB) in a specific sphere of activity. A particularly important and novel feature of the theory is that the firm's behavior is not simply a self-interested response to the external situation. As later analysis will reveal, the firm's ethical orientation and patience are particularly powerful determinants of its behavior. These key variables have, with rare exceptions, been excluded from economic analysis. Although the model's theory is not normative in nature, the model has important normative implications (for example for improving the firm's SRB) that will be developed later.

This model represents at least a start in developing a theory of the firm's external relationships in the sense that it involves a theory about how harmonious the relationship of the firm is with particular individuals and groups external to the firm. Among these external entities are victims, would-be victims, community organizations and leaders, and government. The key to the firm's relationship with those external to it is the degree to which its behavior is socially responsible.

To understand the model and the important role of the ethical orientation and patience variables, let us apply it to the water pollution case utilizing in sequence a number of different assumptions about the EO and P variables. Three scenarios are considered below. The first scenario is a special case that strongly resembles orthodox theory.

The classic negative externality scenario

In the first scenario, the firm's decision makers are assumed to be opportunistic and impatient (short-term orientation), values on the far left of the EO and P spectrums, respectively. Because there are no equal or lower cost alternatives to the pollution, and because of their short-term orientation, implying unwillingness to look for advantageous long-term solutions, the firm will dispose of the liquid in the river. Because the decision makers know that the pollution is unacceptable to the community, and because of their opportunism, they will not be straightforward or honest with the community or the pollution victims. The firm will make every effort to deny the existence of the pollution, will not provide information about it, will not offer assistance or compensation to the victims, and will not cooperate with concerned community leaders. In other words, it will attempt to avoid incurring cost by avoiding responsibility for the damage and attempt to maintain legitimacy through secrecy or deception.

This analysis of the classic negative externality scenario is at least superficially similar to the orthodox economic exposition, in which the firm is simply maximizing profit in a situation where there is a resource, the unpolluted river water, that is provided free to the firm rather than at a price reflecting its social opportunity cost. In both the orthodox analysis and this scenario, pollution is the expected result. However, it should be emphasized that in the present analysis, the pollution outcome is not simply due to profit maximization, it is due as well to opportunism and impatience. The firm here is not behaving in a socially responsible manner, unless, of course, one holds the view that its social responsibility is only to its stockholders. A key to the irresponsible nature of the firm's action is that the firm is out of harmony with the society in which it is a part. In the orthodox economic analysis, this aspect is completely ignored. Let us then consider another scenario.

Long-term oriented, non-opportunistic self-interest (the second scenario)

The decision

Assume that the firm's decision makers are (1) self-interested (but not opportunistic) and (2) patient. With a long-term orientation (low discount rate), these decision makers are now willing to consider sacrificing some profit in order to achieve the enhanced legitimacy that would follow from reduction of its pollution. The expectation is that the increased social acceptability of the firm's activity will over the long-term lower certain costs associated with a lack of legitimacy. The latter are called *legitimacy costs*; the nature of these costs is considered below. Because these decision makers are, in addition to not being opportunistic, not burdened with high ethical principle, the decision to pollute is for them not a question of responsibility or ethical obligation; it is purely a matter of self-interest and efficiency. Similar to an investment decision, these decision makers will presumably choose to accept the higher current expense associated with lower pollution only if this cost is expected to be less than the present value of the future stream of lowered legitimacy costs. In this view, there is a simple trade-off between efficiency and legitimacy considerations. (For an alternative approach using the prisoner's dilemma analysis, see Appendix B.)

Legitimacy costs

A company's legitimacy costs are related to the public issues life cycle (see, for example, Buchholz 1988: 6–8). This cycle begins when a gap arises between a corporation's social performance and what the public expects of it. At this stage, businesses have many options concerning how to respond to the issue. If, however, the issue grows and businesses do not respond satisfactorily, the issue is likely to become a politicized media event, putting businesses on the defensive. In the next phase, legislation is passed and regulations are promulgated. The final phase involves government action to implement the rules, enforce these and, if necessary, litigation to force compliance. "As an issue moves through this sequence, the options for business are narrowed to where they become almost non-existent" (Buchholz 1982: 415).

> The firm that takes a "public-be-damned" attitude toward non-shareholders is a likely target for harsh and perhaps even punitive legislation. The firm that ignores the interests of society in a pell-mell pursuit of profit neglects the long-run consequences that could prove to be costly or even suicidal.
>
> (Walters 1977: 42)

Thus, a firm's legitimacy costs are the price it pays for not choosing socially acceptable behavior; these costs are incurred in the long-term not only in the form of financial penalties but as reduced autonomy with increased public control.

The public issues life cycle is suggestive of the nature of many of these legitimacy costs, but a few less obvious ones should be mentioned explicitly. One cost is the discomfort or harassment, as well as reduced prestige and prominence, that executives may experience as a result of pressure from activist community groups or others external to the firm (Manne and Wallich 1972: 27). Along with this, corporations may experience reduced cooperation from a variety of external organizations, a deterioration of the business climate generally, and a more adversarial relationship with government (see Tomer 1987: 115–19). The firm may also experience lower cooperation from and motivation of its employees who find the social performance of their corporation uninspiring.

It should also be noted that firms pursuing socially irresponsible behavior will experience increased uncertainty. This is true even if no one is presently objecting to this behavior. Should societal values change, as they often do, bringing the issue to the fore, there is a high probability of starting down the public issue life cycle with its rising legitimacy costs. Thus, there is reason to believe that a firm will inevitably pay for its social irresponsibility, but the magnitude and timing of its cost will be highly uncertain.

The legitimacy costs considered above are the private costs, costs incurred by the firm as a consequence of their socially unacceptable behavior; there are also the social costs incurred by others. An obvious example is the cost incurred by the victims of the offending behavior. In addition, there may be costs of cleaning up the problem, judicial costs, enforcement costs and other costs associated with attempting to control the problem. Because these costs are not incurred and presumably not considered by the self-interested, long-term oriented firm, the firm's response to the negative externality situation, although better than the opportunistic, short-term oriented firm, is still likely to be sub-optimal from society's standpoint.

Strategic socially responsible behavior

Firms that find it in their interest to be socially responsible (the second scenario) can be expected to develop a variety of strategies for attaining legitimacy. Firms' strategies will differ according to such factors as the degree of their ethical orientation and patience. Let us consider three strategies: (1) statesmanship, (2) accommodation and (3) public relations.

In the *statesmanship strategy*, the firm's leaders not only choose to incorporate social responsibility in their actions in a way that makes sense given their expected legitimacy costs but attempt to lead and educate the public and other businesses on the virtues of their chosen strategy. This strategy is likely to require a higher degree of organizational capability than the

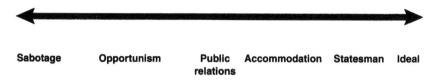

| Sabotage | Opportunism | Public relations | Accommodation | Statesman | Ideal |

Figure 7.2 Spectrum of socially responsible behavior

following two. In the *accommodation strategy*, the company's leaders are simply adapting in a self-interested way to signals from the society regarding what is acceptable and are not trying to play a leadership role. In the *public relations strategy*, the enterprise's leaders are in part accommodating and in part resisting society's demands, but they recognize that the firm requires legitimacy. To enhance the firm's legitimacy, the leaders take actions calculated to improve the public image of the firm while doing little to improve the social responsibility of the firm's behavior.

Recall the *spectrum of socially responsible behavior*, in which sabotage is located on the far left and ideal socially responsible behavior is on the far right (see Figure 7.2). The first scenario representing opportunism is on the left. The second scenario is represented by the next three positions to the right of opportunism. Starting at the middle of the spectrum and moving right, one first encounters the public relations, then the accommodation, and finally the statesmanship strategy.

Principled behavior (the third scenario)

The ideal

Ideal socially responsible behavior is not based on a self-interested calculation, not even a long-term oriented one. Ideal strategies are based on a commitment to principle transcending narrow self-interest. The difference between a strategy based on principle and one rooted in self-interest and the problem with the latter are explained by John M. Clark:

> Self-interest is not really enlightened unless it is also enlarged until it identifies itself, to some extent at least, with the interests of others. And once this enlargement has taken place, it can never treat others as mere means....And if "enlightenment" goes this far, it has become ethical. It has gone beyond the idea that "what's good for me is good for the community" and has accepted at least some part of the idea that "what's good for the community is good for me"; or that my economic relationships cannot be healthy unless they are part of a healthy community. If a businessman has gone this far, but still wants to insist that this regard for common interests is merely "good business," I have no quarrel with

him. He has broadened his conception of "good business" until it has become a moral one; that is sufficient. But if he has not gone this far, and if his enlightened self-interest is mere farsighted shrewdness, one can be sure that at some point or other the shrewdness will not be farsighted enough and trouble will result.

(1957: 207)

The ideal principled strategy is one that commits the firm to a harmonious relationship with its external social environment. Such a strategy may be a reflection of its leaders' higher self including their highest values, conscience and aesthetic sense of the business (on the higher self, see Lutz and Lux 1988: ch. 6). Finally, such a strategy may reflect the leaders' vision for the firm and their sense of sacred duty.

The solution to negative externalities

This ideal socially responsible behavior does not mean behavior that has only positive impacts on others. It means self-regulated behavior that has no socially unacceptable negative impacts. For example, the ideally behaving firm would not engage in any water pollution that the relevant affected parties find unacceptable. The firm would have to learn from society (community, government, media, etc.) what behavior (pollution) is acceptable. The firm, of course, has a legitimate right to participate in the process of determining what is acceptable, and ideally it would seek standards (for example, pollution standards) that recognize both its own interests and the interests of those affected by its activities. That is, the ideally behaving firm would seek win–win solutions. In the process, the negative externality problem would be eliminated because no appreciable damage would be inflicted on person(s) who were not fully consenting parties in reaching the decision regarding the firm's actions (recall Meade's externality definition).

Given competition in its product markets and significant costs of complying with societal standards, this ideal socially responsible firm could very well become uncompetitive if it were the only firm in its industry to behave in this way. Should this happen, it would be incumbent on the firm to take actions either (1) to gain voluntary adherence to these standards by its competitors, or (2) to pressure government to impose regulations applying to all firms in the industry. Ideal socially responsible firm behavior implies self-control, but it does not necessarily mean no governmental regulation. In situations where governmental regulation is necessary, this regulation may be expected to work much better in the presence of voluntary business cooperation than if businesses were to become adversaries to government and were to resist compliance with governmental standards.

The trade-off revisited

Do highly ethical decision makers trade off legitimacy for efficiency in the same way as self-interested decision makers? Strictly speaking, the answer is no. If the firm's principled decision makers are acting out of a sense of high obligation to the common good, it does not make sense for them to be willing to trade a little less socially responsible behavior for a little more profit. From an ethical standpoint, it is acceptable to pursue profits but only after fulfilling one's fundamental obligations to society. Of course, things may get a little murky if we inquire into the nature of these fundamental obligations. Are some obligations beyond trade off, while others can be traded? Consider water pollution. Some types of pollution are totally unacceptable and other types are partially acceptable. The notion of a trade-off might apply to some extent to the latter but not the former. Nevertheless, it is generally true that ethical obligations and efficiency considerations are incommensurable, and thus, ethical decision makers have no basis for a quantitative trade-off of one for the other. Of course, business decision makers may have to grapple from time to time with tough ethical dilemmas involving choices between incommensurables.

The model: a recapitulation

The model was applied to three scenarios which involved three different assumptions about ethical orientation and patience. Many other scenarios are possible, but these three are suggestive of the model's ability to explain differences in businesses' socially responsible behavior as well as indicating the range of its applicability. The essence is that for a given external situation, the firm's internal behavioral characteristics, especially its ethical orientation and patience, are the key to understanding its social responsibility. In the absence of these two variables, a firm behaving with a high level of corporate social responsibility simply does not make sense; at least, not from the standpoint of economic theory. There are many facets of a firm's external relationships that involve some element of social responsibility. If we assume that the firm is solely motivated by self-interest, we cannot conceive of these relationships.

Issues related to the firm's socially responsible behavior

A payoff to principle?

Although it would seem on the face of it that consciously principled behavior is anything but profitable, there is nevertheless some evidence and a considerable amount of belief among businessmen that ethical behavior pays off. According to an opinion survey of key business leaders, "almost two-thirds (63 percent) of executives are convinced that high ethical standards strengthen a firm's competitive position" (Cavanagh 1990: 172). In a study of forty-two large corporations, Clarkson found that:

> Corporations...which balanced their proactive economic orientation with a proactive social orientation were profitable at average or above-average levels in their industries.... [Whereas] unbalanced concentration on the maximization of profits was counter-productive and resulted in lower ratios of profitability than their competitors...
>
> (1990: 10)

If what these findings imply is true, then they represent a paradox. Perhaps companies that make efforts to acquire the discipline necessary to fulfill their ethical or social obligations have acquired an intangible asset that also serves them well in the traditional aspects of their business. For a similar analysis of eighty-four companies, see Makower (1993: 65–6).

An investment in organizational capital

When business leaders commit their firm to socially responsible behavior, for members of the organization, it means acquiring a kind of discipline which involves new ways of thinking and relating to others within and without the firm. Because acquiring this discipline uses up resources in the process of changing formal and informal social relationships, it may be considered an investment in organizational capital (Tomer 1987: 24). Similarly, Hattwick (1986: 91) observes that "the adoption of a code of business ethics can be viewed as an investment." Arrow (1973: 315) has pointed out that codes of ethics require discussion, incorporation in standard operating procedures, and, in the process of transmitting them from one generation of executives to the next, education and indoctrination. In Bowen's (1978: 124) view, a reason why firms adopt socially responsible behavior is to improve their intangible human relations which partake of the nature of assets. These intangible assets are believed to be the key to business success, and many "policies and actions of the firm are directed toward bettering its position with respect to these intangibles" (1978: 125).

Complicating factors

In the case of water pollution alone, not to mention other types of negative externalities, there are many complicating factors. A few of these should be mentioned. First, there are many instances when the pollution of a body of water occurs because of the combined effect of multiple sources of pollution. This tends to obscure the role that any one firm plays in the pollution. Firms lacking high principle will see the possible advantage to be gained if they can avoid being held accountable and, thereby, avoid incurring any legitimacy cost. This obviously discourages social responsibility.

The second complicating factor is that the pollution harm may not be known or knowable. Victimization could take a long time to become apparent; perhaps the victims will be members of the next (unborn) generation. Moreover, the water pollution harm may depend on the uncertain dilutive capacity of the river in which it is disposed. Such factors give unprincipled businesses further opportunity to avoid being socially responsible.

Socially responsible investing and buying

Interest in corporate social responsibility has spawned two kinds of relatively new activity: explicitly buying from and investing in companies perceived to be socially responsible. This buying and investing is believed to reinforce the socially responsible behavior of these companies and to provide an incentive for other companies to become socially responsible. The amount of socially responsible investments is estimated to have grown from $50 billion in 1985 to over $700 billion by 1992 (Miller 1994: 54). Investors now have available to them an impressive array of mutual funds and pension funds that apply a variety of "social screens" before choosing the companies they invest in. For those who want to do their own social investing, there is an increasing number of advisers and sources of information available. Among the most common areas used in screening investments are sin (alcohol, tobacco, and gambling), military weapons and services, effects on environment (including nuclear power), company relations with community, company relations with employees, treatment of women and minorities, product quality and consumer relations, and relations with oppressive regimes. For an excellent, comprehensive guide to socially responsible investing, see *Investing for Good: Making Money While Being Socially Responsible* (Kinder *et al.* 1993).

Social responsibility and positive externalities

In the case of positive externalities, firms confer benefits on non-consenting others for which these firms do not receive compensation. For example, if companies train employees who are likely to leave the firm in a relatively short period of time, the next company that employs these workers will reap much of the benefit without paying for it. Thus, the firm's incentive to train these employees is insufficient considering the returns to society from investment in this training. If, due to this disincentive, companies do too little training of low-income workers, productivity will suffer and this will exacerbate the social problems of poverty and inequality. Because of this negative outcome, it may be argued that the socially responsible company ought to do more training. This could make sense, even for the self-interested firm, because doing this would enhance the firm's reputation, and thus its legitimacy. This is very similar to saying that a firm ought to do more pollution control (reduction of a negative externality) in order to reduce its legitimacy costs (become more legitimate). Whereas negative externalities relate to the negative impacts (pollution) of firm behavior, positive externalities relate to the absence of positive impacts (training benefits) from the firm's behavior. Thus, socially responsible firms might contribute more to the solution of social problems through positive accomplishments than would be expected from considering the usual economic incentives.

A normative view: fostering social responsibility

If through socially responsible business behavior significant progress toward solving social problems involving externalities is possible, then it is necessary to consider what needs to be done to foster this. Therefore, the following briefly summarizes the normative implications of the preceding analysis. It is beyond the scope of this chapter to indicate precisely the nature of the governmental programs that could help achieve these ends.

The character of the decision makers

The most obvious implication of the analysis is one that many economists are likely to be uncomfortable with; the need to improve the ethical orientation and patience of the firm's decision makers. Instead of the typical call for governmental incentives which appeal to self-interest, and if anything, strengthen self-interest motivation, the implication here is that we would be better off if decision makers were less self-interested and more motivated by obligations to others, or, as Paul Davidson puts it, more motivated by internal incentives. According to Davidson, in a monetary system, self-interest motivation is likely to be stronger and more durable than "civic values."

> The latter is, like a delicate, fragile flower, easily trampled and lost in any money-utilizing system of production organization—unless the society makes special efforts to nurture the belief in civic values....A civilized society will try to sustain a productive harmony between external and internal incentives through the development of...human institutions.
>
> (1989: 44)

To improve the humanity of the firm and its social responsibility requires ethical discipline on the part of organization members. First, this calls for an organizational environment that will foster ethical behavior. A key to this environment is a humanized strategy that communicates the values, hopes and vision of the company's leaders. Ethical behavior will thrive when members feel proud of the organization, are willing to be patient and persistent in applying the corporation's values and principles, and when members are encouraged to pause and reflect on where they are going and how they are going to get there (Blanchard and Peale 1988: 125–6). A second key to ethical discipline is the character and quality of the organization's members, especially the top management (Andrews 1989: 100–3). Character relates to a person's values and capacity for moral judgment. It is important that the corporation make an explicit effort to select people of high character. Other qualities such as the competence to recognize ethical issues and think through their consequences and the confidence to seek out different points of view are qualities that the organization can develop (1989: 100). Developing ethical discipline in the organization may be viewed as an investment in organizational capital.

Fostering positive social influences

The case of very highly toxic pollution is instructive when considering how to improve the external social influences on the firm. If society's goals for elimination of less toxic types of pollution were just as high and clear as those for the highly toxic types, firms would more readily set high pollution elimination goals aligned with those of society. Similarly, if the legitimacy costs associated with less toxic pollution were just as high as in the highly toxic case, this high socio-political cost would provide more disincentive to this pollution. In general, socially responsible behavior is encouraged by high, clear goals and high legitimacy costs associated with the firm's negative external effects.

Back in 1989, Edward Woolard, Chairman of the Board of Du Pont, announced at the American Chamber of Commerce in London that Du Pont's goal was to reduce their air and water pollution to zero by the year 2000. Even though we may harbor skepticism about Du Pont's motives and their ability to achieve this goal, the setting of high goals such as this requires several positive societal responses. Du Pont needs support, encouragement and praise for their high social aspirations. This development, along with specifics on Du Pont's plans and strategies, needs to be communicated to other firms in order to encourage them to set similarly high goals. In a variety of ways, institutional support needs to be given for corporate actions leading to the elimination of their negative external impacts.

Changes in social structure and process that would permit greater cooperation and coordination among economic institutions are also needed. It should be emphasized that this and other resource-using efforts to foster the social influences that encourage corporate social responsibility may be considered investments in organizational capital.

Governmental incentives

The issue of what to do about negative externalities like water pollution has often been posed as a choice between a tax on pollution (governmental incentives) or direct governmental controls involving pollution standards to be met by all firms. When posed in this way, the overwhelming majority of economists opt for incentives, either in the form of effluent fees or marketable pollution permits (see Blinder 1987: ch. 5). This makes sense given the orthodox theory of the firm that assumes self-interested, short-term profit maximizing behavior and an absence of ethical principle. If decision makers are rational in this way, the only possible way to reduce pollution is to raise the cost of pollution to the firm. Incentives are better, i.e. more efficient, than controls at doing this because firms with low pollution reduction costs will take on more of the pollution reduction task than those with high costs.

Assume now that the firms' decision makers are highly ethical or potentially so. What these decision makers need to know are society's standards, that is, what is acceptable and what is not. Leaders of these firms also need encouragement and support for their socially responsible behavior and discouragement for their unprincipled behavior. If these are provided, many firms may be expected to voluntarily comply with the pollution standards. But if instead the main government anti-pollution initiative is to place a tax on pollution, the government is implicitly communicating that pollution is acceptable behavior, albeit a more costly behavior than before. While such incentives may help by increasing the efficiency of pollution reduction, they may actually discourage corporate social responsibility. Because pollution taxes are based on the assumption of short-term, opportunistic firm behavior, they effectively sanction or legitimize this behavior. This hurts, because the war on pollution cannot be won without the willing cooperation of corporations. This is not to say that governmental incentives, especially pollution penalties, should not be used. If, however, incentives are to be used, they must be made compatible with socially responsible business behavior.

It should be noted that pollution taxes involve substantial government monitoring and enforcement costs and cannot deal with previously unknown sources of pollution. With these taxes, the government is always trying to catch up and extend its incentives to new areas, some of which are not amenable to incentives. In contrast, the socially responsible firm would voluntarily decide either to eliminate new sources of pollution before they ever came into existence, or to cooperate from day one with government on efforts to find pollution solutions.

Conclusion

Economic theory has for too long been dominated by an overly narrow conception of self-interest and has not appreciated that individuals and organizations are of society and, accordingly, must align their interests with the common interest. Because of this, economics' theory of the firm's external relationships has not been satisfactory. This chapter has attempted to remedy this deficiency by integrating the concept of social responsibility with economic theory. In the revised model of firm behavior, the ethical orientation and patience of the firm's decision makers are important variables explaining the firm's socially responsible behavior. This model enables better understanding of the business–society relationship and enables considerable perspective on what needs to be done to deal with pressing social problems such as environmental pollution. A key to this is investing in intangible relationships and patterns of activity (a variety of types of organizational capital) that are most likely to bring about socially responsible firm behavior.

Appendix A: social responsibility and U.S. competitiveness

The lack of social responsibility of U.S. corporations and the lack of governmental policies to encourage socially responsible behavior appear to be damaging U.S. international competitiveness. According to Robert Reich (1990: 57–8), American companies do not feel a "special obligation to serve national goals." For them, short-term profitability comes ahead of national interests:

> Nor does our system alert American managers to the existence of such goals, impose on American managers unique requirements to meet them, offer special incentives to achieve them, or create measures to keep American managers accountable for accomplishing them.
>
> (1990: 58)

Therefore, too many U.S. multinational companies in the interest of their own competitiveness have moved the base of their operations to foreign countries and have done too little to invest in the skills of the American workforce, actions which are damaging to U.S. competitiveness.

Appendix B: the prisoner's dilemma analysis

An alternative way to view the second scenario (involving long-term oriented, non-opportunistic self-interested decision makers) is using the prisoner's dilemma analysis. The firm in this analysis has two choices: (1) cooperate with the community (do not pollute) or (2) non-cooperation (pollute). Similarly, the community has two choices with respect to its behavior toward the firm: (1) cooperate through actions toward the firm that are non-controlling and non-penalizing, or (2) non-cooperation involving behavior that is controlling and penalizing. If the firm's decision makers are opportunistic and short-term oriented, the predicted short-term outcome is that the firm pollutes and the community cooperates. The firm is acting as a free rider and taking advantage of the community. With the passage of time, however, the community will surely shift to non-cooperation, the ultimate result being the prisoner's dilemma solution, a jointly disadvantageous situation.

If the firm's decision makers are long-term oriented and self-interested (though not opportunistic), the decision makers may anticipate that the community's initially cooperative stance may degenerate if they choose to pollute. As a result, the firm may find it in its interest to cooperate by not polluting. At least, this is likely to be true in circumstances where the firm's payoff with community noncooperation is very low compared to the mutual cooperation scenario. Thus, the prisoner's dilemma analysis comes to essentially the same conclusions as our earlier analysis which focused on legitimacy costs.

8 The human firm in the natural environment

A socio-economic analysis of its behavior

Introduction

Whereas Chapter 7 was concerned with understanding the essence of social responsibility, this chapter applies and builds on these insights in order to understand the firm's behavior with respect to the environment. The analysis is directed toward answering two key questions. Under what circumstances will the firm behave environmentally responsibly? And how can a firm's environmentally responsible behavior be fostered?

New realities are leading an increasing number of businesses to discard their old managerial perspectives and practices with regard to the natural environment. Growing public alarm about environmental degradation, hostility toward the businesses involved, stiffer environmental regulations, consumer preference for products that are not harmful to the environment, and opportunities arising from new technologies are among the realities that have challenged firms to develop new managerial approaches to the environment.

As desirable as the new approaches are, the environmental behavior of these firms cannot be explained by the neoclassical model of the firm that underlies the environmental thinking of practically all economists. To understand this behavior requires a socio-economic model of the firm which incorporates managerial, social, environmental and ethical realities not found in the neoclassical model. The socio-economic model developed here not only incorporates these added human dimensions but indicates how government policy makers can foster highly responsible, environmentally appropriate firm behavior. It is anticipated that this model will help to understand, reinforce and extend a number of policy-making initiatives already underway.

This chapter explicitly focuses on firm behavior because firms' behavior with respect to products, technologies and pollution control determines much about the environmental quality of our societies. Thus, it is imperative that we seek a better understanding of the factors that contribute to firms' decisions and learn how to have a favorable influence on them.

The focus here is on those environmental problems that come under the

heading of pollution. That is, our main concern is with the harmful byproducts, notably air, water, land and noise pollution, deriving from the
production and consumption of firms' goods and services. This chapter does
not directly address the problem of resource exhaustion because this issue is
related more to the functioning of the entire economic system than to the
behavior of individual firms.

The chapter is organized as follows. Section 1 presents the neoclassical
model in which the firm's environmental behavior is determined by market
and regulatory incentives. Section 2 explains how traditional managerial
approaches with regard to the environment are giving way under the weight
of new realities to new approaches that harmonize economic and environmental interests. In light of this, Section 3 explains why the neoclassical
model is deficient and why a new model is needed. Section 4 develops the
socio-economic model of the firm's environmental behavior that begins with
the elements found in the neoclassical model and incorporates important
additional elements. Section 5 develops the implications of this model for
governmental policy.

The neoclassical model of firm behavior

In the neoclassical model, the firm's behavior with respect to the environment follows from the model's behavioral assumptions. It is assumed that
the firm is perfectly knowledgeable of alternative courses of action and
chooses the alternative that maximizes its current period profit. The firm's
only social responsibility is to its owners, the profit recipients.

Because this firm is simply a profit-maximizing machine, its behavior is
an outcome of the economic incentives impinging upon it. These incentives
derive from (1) the product and resource markets in which it participates
and (2) the regulators that seek to modify its behavior. Of special note here
are the "pollutable" resources such as air and water (rivers, lakes and so on)
that are collectively owned, i.e. not privately owned. Because firms are able
to use up these resources, by disposing their harmful byproducts in them, in
many cases without paying for them, they have an incentive to use more of
them than is in the public's best interest. This "negative externality" problem
arises because the social costs of the degradation of these resources are
excluded from or external to firms' decision making. Thus, in the neoclassical model, the pollution problem is entirely a market failure, a failure of
the market for pollutable resources to provide the correct incentives for "efficient" firm behavior. The problem has nothing to do with the character or
quality of particular firms, nor does it have anything to do with societal
influences on the firm.

Because in the neoclassical model the problem is with market incentives,
it follows that the solution is to provide regulatory incentives that counteract
the problematic market ones. According to Baumol and Oates (1979: 2):
"what is needed is the design and enactment of a proper set of policies that

will provide direct incentives to consumers, government agencies, and business to protect, rather than abuse, the environment." Ideally, these incentives will force firms' decision makers to consider the full social costs of their pollution, thereby leading profit-maximizing firms to socially optimal behavior. Besides fostering allocational efficiency in a static context, desirable regulatory incentives should encourage firms to pursue opportunities for technological innovation in pollution control. In sum, the neoclassical firm's behavior with respect to the natural environment (pollution, pollution control activity) follows from the combined effect of market and regulatory incentives. Figure 8.1 depicts these determinants of the firm's behavior. Given this analysis, the relevant policy question is: which type of regulatory incentives are best to achieve specific policy goals for the reduction of pollution? Much economic analysis has been devoted to this question (for a good overview of this literature, see Oates 1990).[1]

Managerial approaches to the environment and changing realities

Old managerial approaches

Traditionally, our society has approached pollution by adding end-of-pipe pollution controls and by disposing with an 'out-of-sight, out-of-mind'

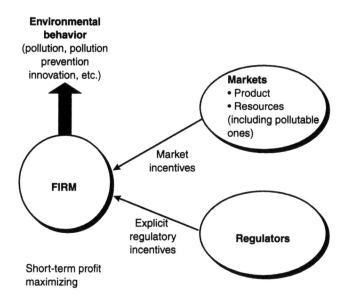

Figure 8.1 The neoclassical model of the firm's environmental behavior

perspective" (Institute for Local Self-Reliance 1986: 118). No doubt this is a stereotype, but it seems to represent an important tendency in managerial thinking about the environment. Steger (1990: 73) calls it the "defensive strategy"; it involves quick efforts merely to comply with environmental standards by adding equipment to existing production processes at the lowest possible cost. At worst, dangerous byproducts are disposed of opportunistically with as little thought as possible to the consequences. Also, businesses have tended to think of regulations as excessively burdensome demands and have not infrequently resisted them.

This traditional managerial thinking has a rough consistency with the neoclassical model of the firm. If decision makers in neoclassical firms are focused solely on maximizing short-term profit and have no other sense of social responsibility, regulation will inevitably be perceived as a profit lowering factor to be complied with at minimum cost or evaded. What neoclassical theory and traditional managerial thinking share is an opportunistic, short-term orientation to decision making.

New realities

A variety of new realities confront management today. First, the public is alarmed about the extent of environmental degradation and increasingly supports strong environmental protection efforts. Business activities that harm the environment are increasingly met with hostility. Second:

> Environmental activists of the 1990s are a different breed from their 1970s' predecessors. Those earlier pioneers lacked the scientific, technical, and legal expertise enjoyed by today's groups....They may bring to their encounters a cadre of credentialed scientists, skilled lobbyists, and legal eagles—as well as a membership numbering in the tens or hundreds of thousands.
>
> (Makower 1993: 99–100)

This has increased their ability to find technologically feasible and politically acceptable solutions to environmental problems.

Third, government has responded by requiring companies to meet increasingly stringent environmental standards. "Environmental regulations in the industrialized world have mushroomed, levying a sort of de facto tax on companies, which must devote significant resources just to fill out the paperwork" (Makower 1993: 15). Fourth, "Sometime around Earth Day 1990, a new realization seemed to strike the collective consciousness of the marketplace like a bolt from the polluted blue. There was money to be made catering to consumers' growing concern about the fate of the earth" (1993: 102).

Not only were consumers more willing to buy green products but they engaged in product and company boycotts, waste-reduction campaigns, and public education. Fifth, "new technologies have been developed that avoid or contain pollution in the manufacturing process" (Steger 1990: 72). One other not so new reality should be mentioned. This is the recognition that using our commons, our collectively owned resources, as a place to dispose of waste will of necessity have to be abandoned (Hardin 1968: 1248).

New managerial approaches

The new realities have been an important stimulus to the development of new managerial approaches. First, environmental management is beginning to be recognized as an important new functional management area which is taking its place alongside the traditional areas such as marketing, finance, R&D, and manufacturing. Now, even service and consumer goods companies are appointing senior executives to newly established environmental policy positions (Lublin 1991). Their role is to insure that environmental impacts are considered in all aspects of a company's operations. In support of this development, courses on environmental management and policy are being offered at business schools.[2]

Along with this, more companies are setting high environmental goals integrated with their overall corporate goals. 3M, Du Pont (as indicated earlier) and Xerox are among the companies that have announced ambitious environmental improvement goals. Xerox, for example, pledged a 90 percent reduction in their hazardous waste, air emissions and solid waste to landfills by the end of 1997 (*Business Ethics* 1997: 6). It should also be noted that corporations are being pressured by environmentalists and investors to conduct their environmental affairs in a highly responsible manner, for example, in accordance with the CERES Principles (Hinden 1990).[3] On January 9, 1997, BankAmerica Corporation became the first major financial company to endorse the CERES Principles. Earlier, General Motors, Bethlehem Steel, Polaroid, Timberland and Sun Oil, among others, had done so (1997: 6).

Relatedly, more and more corporations are developing environmentally oriented strategies, the purpose of which is to harmonize their environmental and economic goals and link them with the opportunities facing the company. Such companies are attuned to opportunities that enable them simultaneously to protect the environment and gain a competitive edge. That is, businesses are finding that "pollution prevention pays." Companies are making systematic efforts to produce less waste in the first place and, thus, finding that their operations are not only cleaner and safer but less costly. To prevent pollution, "five different approaches have been used: improving routine plant operations, altering production technology, recycling waste back into production, changing raw materials, and redesigning or reformulating the product itself" (Hirschhorn 1988: 55).

According to Robert Bringer of 3M, the company's Pollution Prevention Pays program has saved them more than $500 million since it began in 1975

(*ENR* 1990: 30). While American managers are largely concerned with the direct costs, "some European nations' managers see waste reduction as a comprehensive strategy to cut production costs, spur innovation, and promote international competitiveness" (Hirschhorn 1988: 55). As many firms have discovered, the payoff is typically fast. Stonyfield Farm, for example, has found that its environmental improvements, stimulated by an outside audit, led to:

> more efficient use of energy, waste reduction, packaging reduction, and pollution prevention...reduce costs in the fairly short term: "As (GreenAudit CEO) David Mager went through the audit at our mid-year review, every single audit item—and he went through some pretty wide-ranging stuff—put dollars back into our bottom line."
>
> (Reder 1995: 278)

Consider two examples. First, Carrier, a part of United Technologies Corp., decided in 1987 to adopt "clean" technologies:

> In manufacturing air conditioners, the biggest source of hazardous wastes is the "degreasing" line. There, copper and aluminum parts pass through tanks of solvents to be cleaned of oils and debris accumulated during cutting and soldering....[Carrier] first developed a nontoxic lubricant that evaporated. Next, it fine-tuned its cutting presses to cut metal coils more precisely, with less friction and less waste....The company also designed air conditioners with fewer parts, reducing the need to cut and rejoin metal. The result: Carrier eliminated the "degreasing" line, increased automation, reduced scrap and eliminated down time.
>
> (Naj 1990: A1)

They also improved the quality of their product. Herman Miller, the Michigan-based furniture maker, has also had success with its waste reduction efforts (Reder 1995: 278–82). Miller saves a quarter of a million dollars a year by selling its leather trimmings to luggage makers to make attaché cases and selling its vinyl scraps to stereo and car makers to use as sound-deadening material. It saves even more with internal recycling such as reusing solvents. It saves over $1.4 million due to packaging reduction efforts. And it saves about $350,000 through the operation of its trash-to-energy plant that burns wood scraps and sawdust, thereby supplying heat and energy to the main facility. Miller also favors "materials and processes that are energy efficient to use and emit minimal pollutants and product designs that disassemble easily so that parts can be reused or recycled" (1995: 281).

A notable factor in successes like the above is that they take an integrated, system-wide approach to waste reduction; they are not simply end-of-pipe approaches. For success, companies contemplating pollution prevention efforts should start with an environmental audit and a careful evaluation of the benefits and costs of different approaches and techniques (ILSR: 34–5), that is, they should strive to make these decisions as rationally as possible. The benefits, including reduced liability, lower disposal and cleanup costs, increased employee health and reduced material costs, are today larger and more compelling than ever.

Taken together, the different elements of the new managerial approach described above amount to a dramatic change in managerial orientation. It would not be correct to suggest that most companies are following this approach. However, there are increasing signs of company managements, prodded by the new environmental realities, starting to take such a long-term, rational, non-opportunistic, responsible approach to the way their companies' operations impact on the environment.

The problem with the neoclassical model and the need for a new model

The fact that some companies have adopted the new managerial approach and others have not indicates an important failing of the neoclassical model. Apparently, firms' environmental behavior is not simply a response to market and regulatory incentives; if it were, all similarly situated firms would behave the same way. Despite the existence of negative externalities and opportunities to evade environmental regulations, some firms have consciously chosen behavior that is nonopportunistic, long-term oriented, and responsible to interests that go far beyond those of their owners. The neoclassical model cannot account for this behavior.

What is needed is a model that explains the whole range of environmental behavior, not just the worst case. We need a model that helps us understand the beneficial aspects of the new managerial approach, a model in which the neoclassical model is a special case of a more general model. Moreover, we need a model that (1) incorporates managerial, social, environmental and ethical as well as economic considerations and (2) has clear alternative policy implications.

A socio-economic model of the human firm's environmental behavior

The socio-economic model of the firm's environmental behavior is quite different from the neoclassical model. In both models, however, firms are affected by the same market and regulatory incentives. In both, there is a market failure stemming from negative externalities, which provide the economic incentive to pollute the commons.

In addition to market and regulatory incentives, the human firm's environmental behavior is determined by:

1) the environmental opportunities confronting it;
2) its internal organizational capabilities;
3) the "macro" societal influence;
4) the "micro" social influences of extra-firm institutions and infrastructures; and
5) other regulatory influences.

In other words, the firm's organizational capabilities determine the firm's capacity to take advantage of opportunities for improving its environmental impact, and the macro and micro social influences as well as other regulatory influences encourage or discourage the firm from undertaking these environmental activities. Let us consider the five factors above one at a time.

Environmental opportunities

Environmental opportunities are known or knowable developments that firms can utilize to improve the environmental impact of their operations. Firms may or may not find these opportunities financially rewarding. First are opportunities associated with "clean technologies," particularly those that enable firms to avoid or contain pollution in the manufacturing process. Second are the opportunities related to consumer desires for environment-friendly or "green" products. These are products that have been:

> reformulated to reduce solid waste by using less packaging and recycled or recyclable packaging; to reduce hazardous waste by eliminating or reducing the use of toxic materials or chemicals; to reduce harm to the ozone layer by avoiding use of chlorofluorocarbons (CFCs), and so on.
>
> (Schorsch 1990: 6)

Third are the opportunities stemming from the development of new knowledge and approaches to environmental management.

Internal organizational capabilities

Six internal organizational capabilities are the key determinants of how a firm responds to the opportunities and incentives confronting it. They are its capabilities for:

1) integrating environmental management with other aspects of management;
2) rational organizational decision making;
3) socially responsible behavior;
4) entrepreneurial behavior;
5) organizational learning; and
6) environmental concern and awareness.

These human capabilities embodied in the firm derive to a considerable degree from the firm's investment in human and organizational capital.

Integrating environmental management relates to the firm's capability for incorporating environmental considerations into all aspects of the company's operations. Particularly important here are (1) integrating environmental goals with overall company goals and (2) developing environmentally oriented strategies that harmonize the firm's environmental and economic goals and link them with its opportunities. This is a capability that many firms are now striving to develop.

Rational decision making is the second organizational capability. In the neoclassical model, decision makers are assumed to be substantively rational in the sense that they are able to select the optimum alternative utilizing perfect knowledge of all the alternatives and perfect ability to calculate the consequences of each. Following Herbert Simon (1979), the socio-economic model assumes, somewhat more realistically, that a firm's decision makers are boundedly rational. This recognizes that although human decision makers intend to make the best possible decisions, their decisions are often far from optimal because their mental abilities and knowledge are limited. Nevertheless, the quality of decision making in organizations, and thus its procedural rationality, can be enhanced by improving the organizational processes related to decision making. Firms with a higher degree of procedural rationality will be able to make better decisions concerning environmental alternatives because their organizational processes are conducive to systematic, clear-headed deliberations (see Chapter 4). Firms can thus improve the rationality of their environmental decision making through investments in organizational capital.

Social responsibility is the third capability. The socio-economic model, in sharp contrast to the neoclassical model, assumes that decision makers in firms differ in their (1) ethical orientation and (2) patience, and that these determine the degree to which the firm is socially responsible, i.e. responsible to societal goals and values (recall Chapter 7). Ethical orientation varies among firms along a spectrum starting from opportunistic (low) through nonopportunistic self-interest (middle) to high ethical principle (high). Patience, the ability and willingness to make short-term sacrifices for the possibility of long-term gain, also varies among firms along a spectrum from a short-term orientation (impatience) to a long-term orientation (highly patient). The short-term oriented, opportunistic firm is the same as the neoclassical firm whose only social responsibility is to maximize profits for its owners. The worst socially responsible behavior is sabotage in which the firm's intention is to harm persons outside the firm to gain at their expense. On the other end of the spectrum of socially responsible behavior is the highly patient and ethical firm whose behavior is based on a commitment to principle transcending self-interest. The latter are, obviously, few in number. But even firms less ethical and patient than this may behave with a relatively high degree of social responsibility. This will be true if they perceive the need to maintain their legitimacy in the eyes of the public, and thereby, try to avoid the inevitable costs of losing legitimacy (for example, financial penalties and tighter public control). Similar to rationality, the firm's capability for socially responsible behavior can be developed.

Entrepreneurship refers to the capability for envisioning change and carrying out the change; it requires a substantial ability to deal with risk and uncertainty. The neoclassical model has little to say about entrepreneurship. On the other hand, the socio-economic model recognizes that firms differ in entrepreneurial capability, that certain aspects of this capability can be developed, and that the creation of appropriate conditions can do much to encourage innovation. Entrepreneurship thrives when there is an openness to new approaches and the time and opportunity to try them. Environmental entrepreneurship is particularly difficult because would-be innovators must cope with the uncertainties inherent in a changing regulatory context. Excessive risk and uncertainty due to regulation can thwart the prospects for innovation.

Organizational learning is the fifth capability. Unlike the neoclassical firm, the human firm's members have the capability of learning from experience and incorporating this learning into the strategy, structure and culture of the organization. The learning capability of some firms is hampered by the overly bureaucratic nature of their organizations; other firms have developed the kind of processes and culture that enables rapid learning and flexible response at all levels. Taking best advantage of environmental opportunities requires that firms invest in their learning capabilities.

Environmental concern and awareness is the sixth organizational capability. Firms may respond more readily to environmental opportunities if their members share a special concern about and awareness of the nature of environmental problems. Moreover, if these members share a vision of a "sustainable environmental order" and how their company can contribute to it, this will undoubtedly provide strong motivation for the firm's environmental efforts. Developing such an ethic is an example of an investment in a "soft" type of organizational capital.

The macro social forces

The macro social forces are the first of two external social influences on the firm's decision makers. These are the broad community and societal influences reflecting the public's awareness and concerns, societal goals and demands, and society's generalized support for environmental improvement. These tend to encourage environmental behavior in society's overall interest but tend to be diffuse in their impact.

The micro social forces

The second of the external social influences are the micro social forces emanating from certain extra-firm institutions and infrastructures. The micro social forces operate in the local environment of the firm and, unlike the macro forces, their impact tends to be direct, immediate and salient. The extra-firm institutions and infrastructure relevant to environmental behavior include educational institutions, trade associations, consultants, the firm's suppliers (including its suppliers of pollution control technology), lawyers and lobbyists, and standard industry and managerial practices. The extra-firm social influences from these sources provide encouragement or discouragement that is often the key determinant of a firm's environmental behavior. Sometimes knowledge and advocacy from these sources can lead firms to adopt new clean technology; in other cases, it can retard beneficial innovation.

Other regulatory influences

One final type of influence on firms should be noted, which derives from regulators' administrative operations. Unintended social and economic influences from these operations may have an undesirable effect on firms' environmental behavior. For example, the Technology Innovation and Economics Committee of the Environmental Protection Agency (1990: 7) stated that "uncertainties, costs, and delays associated with the permitting of tests and of early commercial uses of innovative environmental technologies, and the unpredictability and inconsistency of enforcement, are significant disincentives that discourage technology innovation for environmental purposes." These regulatory influences should be distinguished from explicit regulatory incentives and policy recommendations for additional types of regulatory influences on firms.

An overview of the socio-economic model

In the socio-economic model, the human firm's environmental behavior is responsive to market and regulatory incentives, but, unlike the neoclassical firm, its responses to opportunities are also determined by its internal organizational capabilities and the external social and other regulatory influences upon it. The main elements of the model are shown in Figure 8.2 below.[4] Thus, the firm's behavior regarding pollution depends very much on its capacity for rational, socially responsible, environmentally aware, innovative behavior. Pollution is not simply a product of market failure but of insufficiently developed firms and lack of appropriate social and regulatory support.

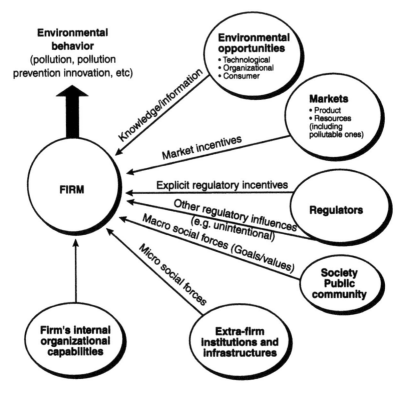

Figure 8.2 The socio-economic model of the human firm's environmental behavior

A spectrum of environmental behavior

To understand the model better, it is important to apply it to specific cases. Three main cases are considered: (1) the case of very poor environmental behavior (high pollution), (2) the case of ideal environmental behavior (zero pollution), and (3) the case where environmental behavior is relatively poor on account of a deficiency in the external social influences on the firm.

First, consider the very poor case. Suppose that the firm has not developed any of its internal capabilities; strong negative externalities exist; regulators' pollution penalties are weak; significant opportunities for improving environmental behavior exist but the firm is not aware of most of them; an intermediate degree of societal concern about environmental problems exists; extra-firm institutions and infrastructures are not capable of helping the firm deal with environmental problems; and regulators' administrative operations cause unintended disincentives to environmental innovation.

How would a firm in this situation behave? According to the model above and using some judgment, I expect the following. Such a firm would (1)

comply only with specific, strong-enough regulatory incentives, adopting end-of-pipe solutions; (2) not learn about or try any new solutions to pollution problems; (3) use public relations to seek a favorable public image of its environmental activities; (4) on occasion, evade compliance by opportunistic actions involving placing wastes out of sight and out of mind; and (5) take legal actions to block regulatory initiatives or law suits. The result is a high amount of pollution and little pollution abatement, a clear case of market failure. It is also a case of environmental irresponsibility.

The second scenario is on the high end of the spectrum. Suppose now that the firm has developed its internal organizational capabilities to the maximum; strong negative externalities exist; regulators' pollution penalties are strong in some specific instances; the firm is very knowledgeable of the significant opportunities for improving its environmental behavior; a high degree of societal concern about environmental problems exists; extra-firm institutions and infrastructures provide the latest knowledge concerning pollution prevention and advocate innovative environment-friendly solutions; and there are no unintended regulatory disincentives to environmental innovation.

The firm above should manifest ideal environmental behavior. This firm would be expected to go far beyond compliance with regulations, set high environmental goals and integrate environmental management and strategy with overall management and strategy, find ways to make innovative pollution prevention efforts pay for themselves, and seek environmental solutions in harmony with societal goals and in accord with their vision of a sustainable environmental order. The result is either zero pollution or a movement toward a zero-pollution solution. In this case, the market failure is overwhelmed by the presence of favorable factors internal to and external to the firm. The firm is behaving in an ideal environmentally responsible manner.

The third case involves a socio-economic failure of the firm (recall Chapter 2). Suppose that the firm has developed its internal organizational capabilities to an intermediate degree; strong negative externalities exist; regulators' pollution penalties are moderate to strong; the firm has some knowledge about significant opportunities for improving its environmental behavior; a moderate to high degree of societal concern about environmental problems exists; extra-firm institutions and infrastructure embody old traditional approaches and are not progressively oriented; and there are no unintended regulatory disincentives to environmental innovation.

This firm has sufficient internal capability and knowledge to take advantage of opportunities for environmental improvement, but the retarding influences from extra-firm sources are expected to be decisive in discouraging the firm from undertaking any innovative environmental actions. Thus, this firm is expected to comply with regulations in a traditional manner and do just enough to seek a favorable public image of its environmental activities. Presumably, the external retarding influence reflects a failure of extra-firm institutions to keep their services and programs up-to-date. It could also reflect prejudices deeply held or even a dramatic change in the prevailing paradigm that has left behind obsolete institutions and infrastructure. In any case, the micro social forces from extra-firm sources are the key to why these firms are expected to succumb to market failure rather than find innovative and economic ways to improve the environment. The result is a moderately high level of pollution and little pollution abatement. It also involves a low level of environmental responsibility.

There is evidence of a socio-economic failure of the firm in the example below relating to environmental consultants:

> Some observers contend that firms now peddling pollution prevention services are still wedded to traditional techniques. "The majority of advice [that] companies get from the pollution control sector is oriented toward treatment techniques rather than prevention."
>
> (*ENR*1990: 30)

Second, there is general agreement that the "conservative" attitudes of managers and engineers have been a problem and that there is a need to reprogram their thinking.

In contrast to the above, it should be noted that extra-firm institutions may encourage desirable environmental behavior. For example, *ENR* cites the "hope that new industry support groups such as the American Institute of Pollution Prevention and the Global Environmental Management Initiative will spur technology transfer and convince more CEOs to jump on the bandwagon" (1990: 31).

Implications for governmental policy

The purpose of this section is to outline the main implications of the socio-economic model for governmental policy, especially the implications that differ from those of the neoclassical model. It is beyond the scope of this chapter to provide a comprehensive set of policy recommendations.

Recommended nonregulatory government roles

Four main governmental roles follow from the socio-economic model: (1) encourage the development of firms' internal organizational capabilities; (2) provide firms with knowledge of environmental opportunities or opportunities to learn about them; (3) identify and reduce the undesirable micro social influences emanating from extra-firm institutions and infrastructures, strengthen their desirable influences; and (4) identify and reduce the undesirable, unintended influences from regulators' administrative operations. These four roles are depicted in Figure 8.3 below by the four dashed lines originating at the oval labeled "Recommended nonregulatory government roles."

Coaching is a useful metaphor for thinking about most of these governmental efforts (Hampden-Turner 1988). Just as a coach nurtures and facilitates the development of his or her players, the government needs to coach the various players (firms, extra-firm institutions, etc.) in order to develop the systemic capacity for desirable environmental behavior. If these players are performing below their capacity or relating to each other in dysfunctional ways, the coach should intervene to facilitate the proper development of the system. Ultimately, the government as coach should foster ideal environmental behavior by doing what is necessary to see to it that firms have the knowledge and capability to take advantage of environmental opportunities and are not discouraged from doing so.

Encouraging the development of internal organizational capability is the first nonregulatory government role. Inevitably, firms themselves must take the responsibility for developing their internal organizational capabilities, but government can provide some incentives, encouragement and guidance

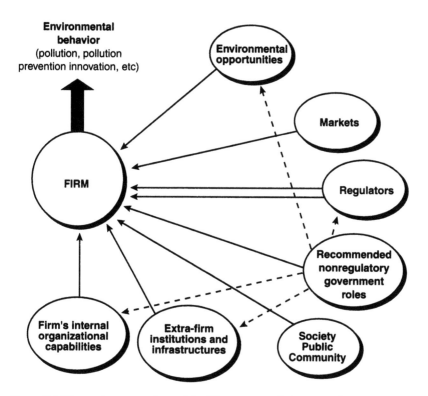

Figure 8.3 The socio-economic model with recommended nonregulatory government roles

regarding what needs to be done. Conferences, workshops, publications, audio and visual materials and consultants are among the things that could help firms appreciate how improving their capabilities would help both themselves and the environment.

In addition to the above (including efforts to develop firms' capabilities for environmental entrepreneurship), policy makers can encourage entrepreneurship by creating conditions that foster it or at least eliminating conditions that thwart it. First, entrepreneurship can be encouraged by reducing excessive risk and uncertainty due to the unintended effects of regulators' administrative operations. Second, various types of forbearance may foster innovation. Because innovation requires more time for rethinking/reorienting than existing regulations typically allow, it makes sense, for example, to offer compliance "waivers" to companies considering new approaches (Naj 1990). Third, technological entrepreneurship will be encouraged by providing aid to the development, testing and demonstration of new environmental technologies (Technology Innovation and Economics Committee 1990: 8ff). An example is the establishment of testing centers. Fourth is "strong, predictable, targeted enforcement [that] triggers a problem solving mentality and is...supportive of the development and use of both pollution control and pollution prevention technology" (1990: 12). Fifth, because firms' innovative efforts flourish in the presence of public trust and support, the public should be informed about innovative environmental efforts and encouraged to participate in these at appropriate times (1990: 13–14).

Providing knowledge of environmental opportunities is the second governmental role. Firms, obviously, must be knowledgeable about environmental opportunities if they are going to take advantage of them, and government can help by providing knowledge and advocating useful approaches. Technical assistance of various kinds has been provided for many years by both federal and state governments. There is, however, a need to go beyond technical assistance in order to awaken firms to a broader range of environmental opportunities, notably ones relating to managerial change and new and changed consumer goods.

Reducing undesirable extra-firm influences is the third governmental role. Because extra-firm institutions and infrastructures can encourage or retard firms' inclinations toward progressive environmental behavior, it is important first to assess the quality of these influences. If, for example, the environmental knowledge provided by educational institutions or consultants is out of date, efforts to strengthen these institutions would make sense. For example, encouraging colleges to adopt new environmental curricula and offering special training and seminars for consultants might be warranted.

Reducing undesirable, unintended regulatory influences is the fourth nonregulatory government role. Because the unintended effects of regulators' administrative operations have in the past discouraged firms from taking the risks associated with environmental innovation, it is important to identify and neutralize these effects. EPA's Technology Innovation and Economics Committee (1990) has made a number of valuable recommendations designed to deal with this problem.

Other governmental roles

In addition to the four main roles considered above, the government can help in a number of other ways to improve the incentives experienced by firms. Let us consider two. First, the federal government could (perhaps in cooperation with a nonprofit organizations) award seals of environmental approval to products determined to be especially environment-friendly, thereby encouraging consumers to use them (Schorsch 1990). Second, the government could make available to communities information regarding the pollution and other environmental effects of local firms. In a number of cases where this has occurred, the resulting community pressure caused these firms to undertake dramatic new pollution reduction initiatives (Smith 1991).

Conclusion

The neoclassical model that has guided economists' environmental analyses and policy recommendations is highly unsatisfactory because it leaves out the social, organizational and ethical context in which economic forces operate. The socio-economic model developed here provides an alternative explanation of the firm's environmental behavior. This model indicates that although negative externalities are an unhappy fact of economic life, firms need not succumb to them; in fact firms can, under the right conditions, discover and choose behaviors that are both profitable and environment-friendly. Although there are many obstacles in the way of such an outcome, the socio-economic model clearly identifies them, and thus allows understanding of the necessary governmental corrective measures. Ultimately, conquering environmental problems will require firms with the capacity for rational, learning, socially responsible, environmentally aware and innovative behavior, and the socio-economic model allows an appreciation of this. Hopefully, this model will lead to better understanding of, reinforce and extend a number of business and government policy initiatives that are now beginning to bear fruit.

9 Beyond transaction markets, toward relationship marketing in the human firm

A socio-economic model

Users "are incredibly bonded to this product [Lotus Notes]," says James Moore, president of GeoPartners Research Inc., a Cambridge, Mass., management consulting firm. "It's a very robust community of allies, all tied together by this product with a shared destiny and a shared fate."

(*Wall Street Journal*, June 7, 1995)

This chapter is concerned with the variety of relationships between the firm as seller of goods and services and its customers. Three key questions are addressed. What type of marketing relationship will the firm choose? Will the firm choose to behave responsibly toward its customers? And should this customer responsible behavior be fostered?

When economists think of product markets, they generally think of transaction markets, where the goal of sellers is, pure and simple, to make a sale. Although long-term buyer–seller relationships are not new, relationship marketing, where sellers aspire to develop long-term, symbiotic, learning partnerships with customers, is emerging as an important new phenomenon. There is good reason to believe that with relationship marketing, markets function not only differently but better. Thus, it is important for economists and others to understand (1) the nature of these markets, (2) under what circumstances selling firms can be expected to choose this type of relationship, and (3) whether society ought to encourage this development.

The chapter is organized as follows. Section 1 considers the variety of buyer–seller relationships and defines a spectrum of marketing relationships starting with the transaction orientation and ending with relationship marketing. This section also considers how economic theory has depicted marketing relationships. Section 2 considers the emergence of relationship marketing in the context of the business paradigm changes now occurring. Section 3 develops a socio-economic model of the human firm's marketing behavior. The focus of this model is to explain the selling firm's choice of a particular marketing orientation and why firms with the opportunity to choose relationship marketing might not do so. Section 4 considers examples of marketing practices involving elements of relationship marketing. In Section 5, a number of the economic implications of relationship marketing are explained. In the sixth section, the implications for governmental policy are developed. The final section provides conclusions.

The variety of buyer–seller relationships in product markets

Evolution of marketing relationships

One way to understand the variety of buyer–seller relationships in product markets is to consider the evolution of marketing. According to a leading marketing text (Evans and Berman 1995: 11–12), marketing has evolved through a sequence of five eras: barter, production, sales, marketing department and marketing company. In the earliest era, marketing simply involved ways to trade good for good (barter); in the second, the essential marketing task was to increase output through the process of industrialization in order to meet demand (production). In the sales era, firms sold products without first determining consumers' desires and then used advertising and their sales forces to "make the desires of consumers fit the attributes of the products offered" (1995: 12). The marketing department era developed as firms facing stiff competition for customers found that they could not prosper without marketing input. Thus, these firms created "marketing departments to conduct consumer research and advise management on how to better design, distribute, promote, and price products" in order to satisfy customer demands better than their competitors (1995: 12). Finally, in the marketing company era, marketing has taken on a central role in all aspects of firms' operations. In these present-day companies, marketing typically involves aggressive, integrated, goal-oriented, systematic pursuit of customers (see also McKenna's 1991: 66–7, view of marketing evolution).

A spectrum of contemporary markets

To better understand contemporary markets, it is useful to consider a continuum of market orientations from the transaction orientation on the left to the relationship marketing orientation on the right (see Shapiro 1993: 128–31). When a market is *transaction oriented*, "exchange is generally quite discrete, with a product or service moving from seller to buyer and money moving in the other direction after a period of negotiation and information transfer....[It is] a one-time exchange or a continuing series of exchanges" (1993: 128). In transaction-oriented markets, the aim of sellers is to close a specific sale with a customer, nothing more.

In contrast, in the *relationship marketing orientation*, the aim of the seller is to have a long-term, broad relationship with the buyer in which the occurrence of a particular transaction is only a minor event in a long history. The seller's goal is to win loyal customers to which they provide a variety of goods and services.

Relationship marketing

Basic relationship marketing

The following are additional defining characteristics of the essence of relationship marketing (RM) as used in this paper. First, RM requires an investment of time, energy, and attention to create and sustain a bond between buyer and seller. Second, in RM, there is a partnership between the provider and customer which involves a mutual commitment to doing business with each other, and thus a willingness of both to forsake alternative transactions offering opportunities for short-term financial advantage. Third, RM is an important part of the seller's business strategy, and, at least in the case of a business buyer, the customer's strategy as well. Fourth, RM involves continual communication, a dialogue, between the provider and customer. This communication enables learning, and thereby the continuous improvement of the goods and services in terms of their ability to satisfy the needs of the customer. This implies continuing product customization. It should be noted that different authors define RM in slightly different ways (see, for example, Evans and Laskin 1994, Peppers and Rogers 1993, and Pine *et al.* 1995 for authors with definitions very similar to the one used here).

A good example of RM is Individual Inc.'s service of providing published news stories specifically selected to fit the constantly changing interests of its customers (Pine *et al.* 1995: 104–5). Individual first determines the type of information the customer wants and assigns a person to manage this client's business. Then descriptions of the desired information are entered into the software system that searches for the pieces matching the client's needs, and these are delivered. Each week, Individual asks customers to rate the relevance of the received articles, and the responses are fed into the system. In this fashion, Individual gradually increases the relevance ratings of the articles sent. Individual also responds to client requests for new sources and ways of receiving information. These two way communications allow Individual to learn continually about its clients' needs and respond in a customized way. Individual enjoys a customer retention rate of 85 to 90 percent.

In some cases, companies that desire a long-term relationship with their customers have taken actions that are steps toward RM but not the full-fledged version. For example, some companies provide positive reinforcements for long-term customer loyalty in the form of cash or special privileges for high frequency among their flyers, long-distance customers, car renters and so on. Other companies have ongoing dialogue programs using newsletters or special twenty-four-hour 800 numbers. Some companies attempt to create a sense of family or membership among its customers, such as when Saturn invited its customers to a Homecoming at its manufacturing facility.

Ultimate in relationship marketing

The ultimate in RM involves features going beyond the basic defining characteristics of RM indicated above. First, it involves relationships that are not only long lasting but authentic and deep (see, for example, Mandel 1993). Second, the buyer and seller are involved in a win–win relationship; both are active coequal partners in achieving common goals. Third, the relationship is oriented to providing what customers really need; not just what they want. It follows that there is genuine communication and intimacy in the relationship. Fourth, the partners utilize the best of flexible information technologies to aid the learning and customization processes.

Limitations of relationship marketing

Although this paper focuses on the ideal aspects of RM, it is important to note a number of negative aspects. First, a strong RM bond might preclude establishment of new and possibly better relationships. Second, actual RM relationships would presumably reflect the psychological pathologies common to all human relationships.[1]

Strategic relationship marketing

When the customer is a business and the relationship has great mutual and strategic importance to both parties, a close lasting alliance, i.e. one involving strategic relationship marketing, may result (Shapiro 1993). This occurs when the relationship requires sharing intimate technological, design and operating information over a long period of time. Further, it occurs when there is a need for integration but the company is not able to develop the requisite skill and resources to supply itself. To work, strategic relationship marketing must involve extensive communication between vendor and customer staff members, a sharing of business values and culture, and financial integration such as significant shareholding in each other, a formal joint venture arrangement, development contracts, supply contracts, licensing and so on. An example of strategic RM is the mutually beneficial joint venture between Fujitsu Fanuc, the Japanese robot vendor, and General Motors: "General Motors needed Fanuc's factory-automation skills to survive and prosper in a competitive environment; Fanuc needed a large worldwide base of leading-edge, high-volume customers, advanced applications knowledge, and factory involvement to develop its dominant position in robots" (Shapiro 1993: 146).

In some instances, strategic RM involves not just one buyer–seller pair but a chain of such relationships. That is, it involves a "'value-adding partnership'—a set of independent companies that work closely together to manage the flow of goods and services along the entire value-added chain" (Johnston and Lawrence 1988: 94). One example is how McKesson

Corporation, originally just a distributor of drugs, health care products and other consumer goods, transformed itself into a manager of an entire chain of companies including the manufacturer, distributor, retailer, consumer and third-party insurance supplier (1988: 94–6). In a very real sense, this entire value-adding partnership (VAP) acts as one competitive unit. Japanese *keiretsus* frequently function as VAPs. In some cases, trading companies play the managing role; in others, it is a leading manufacturing company. Other VAPs include segments of the textile industry of central Italy and parts of the U.S. construction and book publishing industries (1988: 98).

It is important to note that the *raison d'être* of strategic alliances and VAPs is usually different from that in typical relationship marketing. Consider the Japanese trading companies' role in system organizing/coordination among all the separate companies in the steel industry from mining raw materials to delivery of a finished steel product. A key reason for the existence of this VAP is that it enables not only risk reduction but the achievement of economies of scale that the separate companies could not provide themselves (Yoshino and Lifson 1986: ch. 3). This is different from typical relationship marketing in which learning and continual improvement/customization are the key reasons for its existence.

Economic theory and marketing relationships

Mainstream economic theory

Economic theory mirrors actual marketing relationships but very imperfectly. For example, economists' model of perfect competition is reasonably useful at capturing the essence of transaction-oriented markets, but it fails badly where the relationship marketing orientation prevails.

As depicted in the model of perfect competition, sales are discrete transactions. This means that there is no long-term relationship between buyers and sellers, each of whom are distinctly separate entities. There is no opportunity here to develop warm human bonds. According to theory, in each sale the customers impersonally evaluate expected benefits and costs and make their decisions to buy or not accordingly. Sellers make similar evaluations that determine their willingness to sell. The aim of a selling firm is to complete a transaction; once it is accomplished, little or no attention is focused on customers to whom the sale has already been made.

Economic theory contains little information about communications between buyers and sellers in competitive markets. However, one can infer from theory that communications between buyer and seller are typically brief, impersonal and oriented to transmitting transaction relevant information (for example, price, quantity and quality) prior to anticipated transactions. Perhaps in some situations, there are communications involved in negotiating the terms of the deal. In perfect competition, products are assumed to have a given quality; thus, there is really not much to communicate about.

In imperfectly competitive markets as depicted in theory, there is more leeway for different relationships and communications because goods and services are differentiated. Advertising and sales communications are important here and largely oriented to increasing demand (and ultimately profits) for the output firms have already produced. These communications reflect the more personal, and frequently opportunistic and adversarial, nature of the buyer–seller relationship in imperfect competition. Thus, such communication may not be honest, straightforward representations regarding sellers' products. To the extent that economists have begun to incorporate competitive strategy into their depictions of imperfectly competitive markets, theory is beginning to capture more of the nuances of modern marketing relationships. However, mainstream economic theory still is much better at representing marketing relationships on the left or transaction end of the spectrum of contemporary markets and does not deal at all with relationship marketing.

Enduring relationships in heterodox theory

Although he did not write about relationship marketing, Arthur Okun's (1980 and 1981) analysis of seller's long-term relationships with customers is in marked contrast to the mode of operation in transaction markets, and thus it is of interest here. In Okun's view:

> firms promote patterns of recurrent purchases seeking to convert buyers into regular customers by establishing the reliability, predictability, and generally satisfactory character of pricing and services.
>
> (1980: 8)

In these "customer markets," firms seek to establish a reputation and build a clientele by, for example, eschewing price increases in order to retain customers when markets ease (1990: 7). Through these means, firms foster "understandings and conventions involving fair play and good faith," i.e. implicit contracts, with their customers, not legal contractual obligations (1990: 8). While Okun's "invisible handshake" may take place in the context of mass production, mass marketing and one-way (seller to buyer) communication, it is similar to RM in that it involves the creation of a buyer–seller bond that inhibits opportunism and promotes trust and fairness.

Paradigm changes and changing market relationships

The paradigm change in manufacturing

As many are aware, a transformation is going on in manufacturing as many firms organized according to the principles of mass production/scientific management (MP/SM) gradually and sometimes hesitantly are changing to a new ideal type, the continuous improvement firm (CIF) (see, for example, Cole and Mogab 1995). MP/SM firms are those that produce high volumes of standardized products, use narrowly specialized labor, and use technology largely developed external to the firm. The goal of MP/SM firms is profit maximization, and thus its owners will decide to acquire new organization or technology if its profitability can be established. Laborers are the agents of owners and are hired or laid off according to short-run profitability.

In contrast, the CIF's ultimate competitive goal is providing increasing customer value through a constant stream of improvements in both product quality and the production process without sacrificing low cost. These improvements involve endogenous, incremental technological and organizational change. In contrast to MP/SM firms, CIFs are flexible in that they produce a range of customized products, a development owing much to the use of advanced information technology. In the CIF, labor is the principal stakeholder, labor hires capital, and the firm relies for its success on its long-term relationship with highly motivated, trained and less specialized (or generalized) laborers who have internalized its goals. Unfortunately, all too often, especially in western countries, the logic and superior features of production organized according to the principles of the CIF paradigm have not been appreciated because the MP/SM paradigm, which had provided a vision and concepts to guide progress, now serves as a set of blinders (Cole and Mogab 1995: preface and introduction).

A similar paradigm shift in marketing

Similar to what is occurring in manufacturing, a new paradigm is emerging in marketing. The shift is from mass marketing (including sophisticated marketing company era versions) to relationship marketing. This is not to suggest that all marketing will eventually become RM; transaction markets and mass marketing are unlikely to disappear totally. Nevertheless, the key features of RM appear to define the emerging marketing paradigm, and these features are very similar to the CIF paradigm. While in manufacturing the shift is toward production flexibility, product customization, continuous improvement through learning, long-term nonopportunistic relationships, less specialized and more empowered workers, and the use of advanced information technology, much the same is happening in marketing. Of course, in marketing, the focus is on buyer–seller, not employer–employee, relationships and it is firms' communications with customers that are becoming more flexible, thereby contributing to product customization.[2,3]

A global paradigm shift?

The paradigm shifts in manufacturing and marketing mentioned above may be part of a more global paradigm shift. As all scientists operating from the new paradigm tell us, there is a whole-ness and connectedness between all living things. Everything and everyone is connected in some way to everything else. In business this means that the watchwords for this period are connection, creativity, compassion, and intuition....The old, or scientific, paradigm is best typified by Newton's mechanistic, clockwork view....In the new paradigm, the key challenge is therefore to apply inner knowledge, intu-ition, compassion, and spirit to prosper in a period of constant and discontinuous change.

(Ray 1993: 5–6)

With respect to marketing, Terry Mandel (1993) would like to see the language of the heart brought into the marketplace. "Instead of glorifying transactions at the expense of relationships, business can re-energize itself as a high-voltage conduit of human connectedness" (1993: 169–70).

A socio-economic model of the human firm's marketing behavior

Despite these ongoing paradigm shifts and some notable RM successes, firms with the opportunity to do so might not choose an RM orientation. Societal resistance to change is significant, particularly because old paradigms blind decision makers to the benefits of change. Therefore, firms' decisions presumably reflect the balance of socio-economic factors favorable and unfavorable to choosing RM. The model developed below explains how these factors affect firms' choices. It is important to note that this model includes a significant number of factors normally left out of mainstream economic models. In this respect, the model is similar to the socio-economic model developed by the author to explain the firm's environmental behavior (Chapter 8).

Marketing orientation: the dependent variable

The model's dependent variable is the selling firm's choice of a particular marketing orientation located along the spectrum starting from the transac-tion orientation on the left to the RM orientation on the right.

The explanatory variables

In the model, the human firm's choice of marketing orientation is deter-mined by:

1) the economic incentives from markets it which it participates;
2) the customer's orientation;
3) the internal organizational capabilities of the seller;

4) the "macro" societal influence;
5) the "micro" social influences of extra firm institutions and infrastructures;
6) special factors related to the nature of the product; and
7) the technological opportunities available to the seller.

No governmental factor has been included in the model; however, it is at least conceivable that a significant government regulatory presence in the industry could affect the firm's choice of marketing orientation.

Economic incentives

Buyers and sellers will experience different costs and benefits depending on the choice of marketing orientation. For instance, in transaction oriented markets, transactions costs are likely to be significant, and in RM, switching costs are likely to be substantial. The sections below consider the nature of these two costs.

Transaction costs

Those transaction costs associated with making an explicit legal contract between the buyer and seller are of particular concern when the product is complex and when sellers are believed to be opportunistic. Then customers will want to protect themselves (through the use of contractual provisions) from the consequences of the product failing to live up to the promises made by the seller. Sellers are most likely to behave opportunistically in transaction oriented markets, and thus, transaction costs would be expected to be highest there. As one moves along the continuum toward RM, transaction costs should decrease as buyers and sellers become more trusting of each other and more bonded. After all, there is little point to spending a lot for extensive legal protections against someone who is trusted. The lowering of transaction costs with the move toward RM is very much akin to lowering transaction costs via a move from a market transaction between buyer and seller to common governance of the two separable activities.

Switching costs

Switching costs refer to the costs incurred by the customer should the customer decide to change to another provider. In other words, it is the customer's net short-term loss due to the switch. To an extent, switching costs (SC) are an outcome of product and market realities. If, for example, there are many sellers of a homogeneous product such as in perfect competition, SCs are likely to be low to nil. If, however, there are few sellers of very differentiated, complex products, SCs are likely to be high because the customer typically will find the process of adapting to a new provider and products costly (see Kotler and Armstrong 1993: 459–60).

Customer switching costs will be higher still when either buyers or sellers or both have made an investment in the relationship, an investment inevitably reflected in goods or services improved in their ability to satisfy the customers' needs. The seller may also incur SCs should customers switch. This would be so if the seller's investment in adapting to a current customer were incompletely usable in the seller's relationships to future customers.

When the seller makes an investment in the relationship, the following types of activity are typically involved:

1) accumulating the initial information about the customer's needs and what it will take to satisfy them;
2) discovering or inventing ways to carry on a continuing dialogue with the customer;
3) learning from the acquired information about the changes in product mix and features necessary to bring about greater customer satisfaction; and
4) spending the time, energy and attention necessary to create an enduring bond or partnership between buyer and seller.

When the customer makes an investment in the relationship, the following types of activity are typical:

1) providing information regarding the customer's need to the seller;
2) providing resources that can help to upgrade the vendor's capability; and
3) spending the time, energy, and attention to build the mutual commitment.

Generally, the outcome of these investment activities is to move the buyer–seller relationship to the right along the continuum toward RM. As a result, switching costs increase, reaching their peak at RM. These investments are in good part investments in organizational capital, or perhaps in this context inter-organizational capital is a more appropriate term.

Consider the customer's decision to switch to a product(s) of another vendor. If the customer makes the switch, the first period loss is the amount of the SC. The switch would make economic sense if the present value of the future net gains in satisfaction from the new product(s) exceed the SC. Thus, for the customer, the decision to switch is like an investment decision. Because of this, it is understandable that present suppliers would like SCs to be high in order to prevent switching and retain their customers. Conversely, prospective suppliers can be expected to make efforts to lower SCs by making their goods very similar to those of present suppliers and, more generally, by providing an easy, low-cost path for would-be switchers.

The seller's choice of marketing orientation involves a decision concerning whether it pays to invest in the organizational capital necessary for RM. From a strict economic standpoint, it would pay if the present value of the benefits, reflecting the extra sales due to the lengthened time the customer is retained and the lower risk of losing the customer due to greater buyer loyalty, exceed the investment cost. Before choosing this option, the seller needs to compare the rate of return on the above investment with another one. The seller could alternatively spend money to acquire new customers, say in transaction-oriented markets. The latter might make more economic sense, but a number of knowledgeable marketing experts believe that the rate of return to acquiring new customers is significantly lower than it is for developing improved relationships with existing customers (see, for example, Kotler and Armstrong 1993: 459–60).

It should be noted that whenever there are significant transaction costs there will be significant SCs associated with them. This is because when a customer in a transaction market switches to another seller, there will be costs associated with breaking and renegotiating the legal contracts. In contrast to the SCs discussed earlier, these SCs, along with their corresponding TCs, will become lower for firms moving closer to RM on the spectrum. This is a move away from the protection of legal contracts toward the formation of implicit contracts involving mutual genuine commitment.

In sum, depending on the seller's choice of marketing orientation, both buyers and sellers will incur TCs and/or SCs that influence the profitability of their relationship. Although these economic incentives are significant, attention must now be given to the other important factors that determine the selling firm's choice of marketing orientation.

Customer orientation

It only makes sense for a seller to try to establish RM with a patient customer. Patience here entails two characteristics: the ability and willingness to make short-term sacrifices for the possibility of long-term gain (in effect, a low discount rate), and a long time horizon. For RM to work, customers must be prepared to reciprocate the seller's commitment/ investment by making a corresponding commitment/investment. Patient customers will reciprocate in this way because they will consider the gains from RM over a very long period and give substantial weight to them.[4] On the other hand, an RM orientation does not make sense (but a transaction orientation does) for customers who have short time horizons and require quick payoffs, i.e. customers who are likely to switch quickly to commodity sellers offering advantageous short-term financial deals.

Several other customer characteristics are important. The seller is more apt to choose RM when prospective customers have the ability to make lasting commitments, a preference for harmonious, non-opportunistic relationships, and a preference for customized products and high service suppliers.

Internal organizational capabilities

Four internal organizational capabilities are the key determinants of how the selling firm will choose in responding to market incentives and other external factors and opportunities confronting it. These behavioral attributes are the firm's (1) ethical orientation, (2) patience, (3) awareness of and orientation to paradigm shifts, and (4) learning/creativity/ entrepreneurial abilities. These human capabilities embodied in the firm derive to a considerable extent from the firm's investment in human and organizational capital.

First, ethical orientation varies among firms along a spectrum starting from opportunistic (low) through nonopportunistic self-interest (middle) to high ethical principle (high). Opportunism indicates a willingness to be dishonest in order to realize individual gain. Non-opportunistic self-interest implies that dishonesty will not be resorted to but that there is a lack of concern for others. High ethical principle is present when individuals have a high sense of purpose and a desire to find win–win solutions in their relations with others.

Second, patience, as defined earlier, also varies along a spectrum from a short-term orientation (impatience) to a long-term orientation (highly patient). The third capability is a firm's awareness of and orientation to the ongoing paradigm shifts in manufacturing and marketing as well as what some see as a global paradigm shift. A firm high on this capability will be very open to paradigmatic change possibilities and alert to new information about these.

The three capabilities described above determine the firm's capacity for exercising *customer responsibility*, that is, socially responsible behavior toward customers. When a firm exercises the ultimate in customer responsibility, it is not only being highly ethical and patient but it is behaving in a way that really is in the best interests of the customer. It is trying to know and respond to the buyer's "true" preferences, not merely the wants of the consumer. Conversely, the firm is trying to avoid influencing customers toward consumption antagonistic to their best interests. Customer responsibility also implies a responsibility for maintaining and developing the relationship or bond between seller and customer, i.e. nurturing, protecting and facilitating the growth of this relationship.

The fourth internal organizational capability is the firm's learning/creativity/entrepreneurial ability. To establish full-fledged RM with a customer, a selling firm must have the ability to learn from customer communications about the buyer's needs, must have the creative ability to envision new or modified goods and services to satisfy these needs, and must be able to carry out such changes as well as cope with the uncertainty involved in doing so.

The macro societal influence

The macro societal influence refers to the broad community and society influences reflecting the public's awareness, attitudes and concerns, goals and demands, and generalized encouragement of marketing relationships akin to RM as opposed to the transaction orientation. These influences encourage or discourage firms from choosing RM, but they tend to be diffuse in their impact.

The micro social influence

The second source of external social influences are the micro social influences of extra-firm institutions and infrastructures. The micro social forces operate in the local environment of the firm and, unlike the macro forces, their impact tends to be direct, immediate and salient. The extra-firm institutions and infrastructure relevant to marketing relationships include educational institutions, trade associations, marketing consultants, advertising firms and standard industry marketing practices. Not infrequently, the social influence from these sources, either encouraging or discouraging ones, can be the key determinant of a firm's decision regarding marketing orientation. When the influence reflects an acceptance of the emerging marketing paradigm as well as knowledge of and advocacy concerning RM, firms are more likely to adopt RM; in other cases, their influence can inhibit firms' choice of RM.

Special product related factors

Relationship marketing makes more sense for certain types of products. Simple, cheap products with unchanging characteristics lend themselves to transaction marketing. On the other hand, RM makes more sense for large, complex products for which the amount of service time to selling time is high (see Shapiro 1993: 128–9). Also, it is generally true that RM is more appropriate for those customers whose spending is high enough to justify investing time and attention on them.

The availability of technological opportunities

Another important factor affecting the firm's choice of marketing orientation is the availability of efficient technological opportunities to facilitate the dialogue between provider and customer. Without the ability to automate the dialogue, RM communication, which enables continual learning and product customization with a large number of customers, would not be possible. What is needed for RM are communication technologies that are interactive in that they have the ability to receive messages from individual customers and send customized responses. Peppers and Rogers (1993: ch. 7) have described how companies can use a variety of communication technologies in innovative ways to build "one to one" relationships. For example, firms can learn to exploit the capabilities of the telephone by using features such as voice mail, pre-recorded addressable voice messages and "bulletin boards." Similarly, they can learn how to use many heretofore relatively unutilized capabilities of facsimile machines and addressable video.

An overview of the socio-economic model

In the socio-economic model, the human firm's choice of marketing orientation for a given product category does depend on economic incentives (notably transaction costs and switching costs) as mainstream economic analysis presumably would emphasize, but its choice is also determined by external social influences (macro and micro), the customer's orientation (especially patience), the communication technologies available to it, and the seller's internal organizational capability (notably its ethical orientation, patience, awareness of the new marketing paradigm, and entrepreneurial ability). The main elements of the model are shown in Figure 9.1.[5] Thus, a selling firm with a suitable product, customer and available communication technology will choose RM if this firm is interested in developing long-term, win–win relationships, has the ability to do it, and is encouraged enough, or at least not sufficiently discouraged, by societal attitudes and social pressures from significant outsiders.

Utilizing the model: three cases

To understand the model better, it is important to apply it to a number of specific cases. Consider three situations with three very different choices of marketing orientation by the selling firm. The first case is the ideal situation where relationship marketing is chosen. In the second case, the opposite factors hold, and the firm chooses the transaction orientation. The third case is a mixed situation in which RM is not chosen because of a deficiency in the external social influences on the firm.

In the first case, suppose that the products in question are complex and highly differentiated, high switching costs exist, the customer is patient and has the ability and inclination to make lasting, non-opportunistic relationships with sellers, the selling firm is highly ethical, patient, aware of the emergence of a new marketing paradigm, and has high learning and creative ability, societal attitudes are highly supportive of RM, extra-firm institutions and infrastructures are encouraging of RM, and many efficient communication technologies are available to facilitate the buyer–seller dialogue.

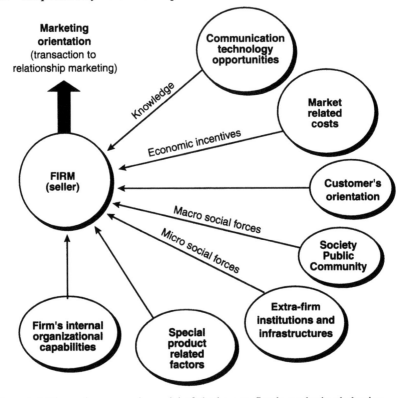

Figure 9.1 The socio-economic model of the human firm's marketing behavior

What marketing orientation would this firm choose? According to the model above and using some judgment, it is not difficult to surmise that this firm would choose RM; all the factors point in that direction. In this case, the firm should be able to develop a creative, lasting relationship with the customer in which it can continually learn about the customer's needs and continually improve the product(s).

The second situation is on the opposite end of the spectrum. Suppose now that the products in question are simple with unchanging characteristics, low switching costs exist and the customer is relatively impatient with little inclination or ability to develop a long-term relationship with sellers, the selling firm is also impatient, not particularly ethical and has low innovative ability, societal attitudes are not supportive of RM, extra-firm institutions and infrastructures tend to discourage RM, and the firm has little knowledge of how communication technologies might be utilized efficiently in their relationships with customers.

The firm in the situation above would be expected to choose a transaction orientation with its customers. Neither the firm's nor the customer's capabilities and inclinations suggest that they are likely to develop a mutual, lasting relationship. And, in the absence of any economic or social incentives encouraging relationship building, the firm presumably will settle for a focus on individual transactions.

The third scenario is a mixed case. Suppose that products in this category are reasonably complex and differentiated, switching costs are relatively high, the customer is relatively patient and has some ability and inclination to form relationships with sellers, the selling firm is relatively ethical and patient and has a reasonable amount of entrepreneurial ability, neither the society nor the local community are particularly interested in RM, certain of the extra-firm institutions which have significant dealings with this firm believe that RM is not worthwhile, and the firm has a sufficient knowledge of the communication technologies that can aid the buyer–seller dialogue.

This situation is less clear. On the one hand, factors one through four and seven indicate that RM could work. On the other hand, factors five and six indicate that crucial external social support for RM is missing. While a definite answer is not possible, there is a strong likelihood that the firm will fail to choose RM on account of the lack of societal encouragement and the discouragement from a number of the significant extra-firm institutions. The phenomenon illustrated in this case is an example of what has been called the socio-economic failure of the firm (see Chapter 2).

Outcomes of the firm's choice of marketing orientation

When RM is chosen and the selling firm works with the customer to create a mutually satisfactory long-term relationship, a *market bond* is created. Market bonds involve a strong mutual commitment, a high degree of trust and a recognition of the buyer's and seller's common destiny. While this connection between buyer and seller has a similarity to Arthur Okun's implicit contract concept, it goes beyond that idea. Whereas the essence of an implicit contract is unspoken understandings regarding mutual fairness, market bonds basically involve explicit agreements deriving out of the continual communication between buyer and seller. Thus, market bonds provide a much stronger constraint against opportunism, and even non-opportunistic self-interest seeking, and thereby strongly encourage customer responsibility on the part of the seller and similar responsible behavior by the buyer. It would be expected that both the buyer and seller joined by a market bond would willingly forsake enticements from prospective partners offering deals providing short-term financial advantage.

As an alternative to choosing RM, a selling firm might choose to develop a marketing relationship that falls short of RM (but goes far beyond the transaction orientation). Suppose that the seller is not highly ethical. One case is the seller who is patient but nonopportunistically self-interested. This seller may seek a long-term relationship with the customer as a way to gain buyer loyalty, but view this relationship basically as an instrument for achieving long-term profitability, i.e. much less than a win–win proposition. Another case is that of the opportunistic seller. Is it possible for such a seller to induce certain customers into one-sided relationships where the seller gains at the expense of the buyer in the short-term if not the long-term?

Relationship marketing in practice

To gain a better perspective on RM, it is important to consider some noteworthy examples of marketing practices which involve elements of RM. First, Waldenbooks offers a service called Preferred Readers which is designed for people with special interests who spend more than $100 a year at its stores (Pine *et al.* 1995: 110–11). Those who sign up and pay a $10 annual fee receive a discount on book purchases. Because Waldenbooks tracks these customers' purchases, it enables them to learn about customer preferences and to inform these readers when books of interest are available or when special authors will appear in the area.

According to Robert A. Peterson, one key to what makes customers committed to companies and their products is not simply customer satisfaction but "love":

> Customers with genuine affection for an institution are loyal customers—me and Federal Express are a case in point. Others may be quite "satisfied," but unless there's an emotional bond,…such satisfaction doesn't necessarily translate into future sales.
>
> (Peters 1992: 722)

Another key to customer commitment is what Tom Peters calls customerizing, allowing and encouraging the customer to be the initiator and participant, not just a passive recipient of the seller (1992: 740–1). A good example of both these points is Ikea, the Swedish furniture retailer (1990: 750–1). Customers who visit their huge out-of-town stores typically spend three hours and look on it as a day's outing. Customers are not only attracted to the style and low cost of the furniture but enjoy store amenities such as child play areas and in-store cafe. Shoppers save money because their activity allows Ikea to economize on shipping, storage and assembly. Customers use the catalog and a "customer tool kit," pull flat boxes of unassembled furniture from the shelves, place them on a cart, and push the carts to their cars. Ikea's customers get excited about their participation and love the idea of great-looking furniture at unbelievable prices. Ikea is, it seems, building a long-term relationship with its customers.

Finally, consider Peapod, a grocery-shopping and delivery service (Pine *et al.* 1995: 109). For the initial cost of a software application, a $4.95 per month service charge and a per-order charge of $5 plus 5 percent of the order amount, Peapod provides customers an abundance of information on food items available in their supermarket, allowing them to make intelligent shopping choices without ever leaving their homes. After delivery of the food, Peapod uses a customer survey to try to learn how well they did and how they could improve their service. Peapod also makes significant efforts to learn about particular customer's needs, thereby customizing their service.

Some economic implications

In markets where full-fledged RM exists, there is reason to believe that shortages and surpluses will be practically non-existent. Consider why shortages and surpluses exist in transaction markets. They exist because sellers' supply decisions and consumers' demand decisions are made largely independent of each other, certainly with little or no direct communication. The amount sellers bring to market is in part based on a forecast of demand. Because these forecasts are often wrong and because demand can shift unexpectedly, the quantity supplied can easily be substantially greater or less than the quantity demanded. If, however, buyers and sellers are continually communicating not only regarding how much is needed but about the nature of these needs as in RM, sellers' forecasts of current period demand are unlikely to contain much error, and thus, supply should always approximate demand. Furthermore, sellers can be expected to know how demand and customers' future needs are changing and will be able to adjust their capacity accordingly, thereby tending to avoid future shortages or surpluses.

The second implication is that price fluctuations should be substantially less in full-fledged RM markets than in other types of markets. The first reason follows from the above analysis. If shortages and surpluses are practically non-existent, price rises or declines will not occur on account of them. Second, when buyers and sellers are partners sharing a mutual commitment to each other, their joint decisions regarding price will reflect what is best for the long-term health of the relationship, not short-term market strains or opportunities. Thus, a high degree of price stability in RM markets is to be expected.

Implications for governmental policy

What's the problem?

Is there a problem with firms' choices of marketing orientation? First, conventional market failure does not seem to be the problem. Selling firms apparently have an adequate profit incentive for investing in long-term relationships with their customers. Due to these investments, their customers should realize significant long-term benefits, and they would be expected to reciprocate with loyalty and payments commensurate with the benefits received. If so, there are no external benefits, benefits to external parties not accruing to the seller, that would lead the seller to underinvest in these relationships. An alternative possibility is that sales in RM will be smaller than has been true in traditional marketing orientations because RM sellers will refrain from selling goods unless customers really need them. If so, this suggests that the benefits to customers are greater than those that can be realized by the seller; in other words, a positive externality exists, leading the seller to underinvest in these relationships. In my judgment, even if the latter is true, it is doubtful whether the market failure is sizable.

Nevertheless, it can be argued on grounds other than strict market failure that society would be better off if more firms adopted RM instead of traditional marketing approaches. What is the problem with the old notions of marketing? According to Regis McKenna (1991: 69), "the heart of it is image making—creating and projecting a false sense of the company and its offerings to lure the customer into the company's grasp." Traditional marketing strategies bombard people with lies, play on their fantasies and fears, are insulting and intrusive, and produce cynicism (Mandel 1993: 165). Thus, "most people think marketing with integrity is an oxymoron, like jumbo shrimp, or honest politician." If more firms chose RM, this would greatly help in lessening the negative effects of traditional marketing on business culture. With greater trust and honesty in the marketplace and with sellers striving to serve customers' real needs, this should greatly lower consumer lawsuits and lessen the need for extensive regulation of consumer goods and services. Thus, when businesses fail to develop the potential of their relationships with customers, society incurs not only cultural damage but a significant resource cost.

Obstacles to greater use of relationship marketing

Are there obstacles in the way of greater use of RM by businesses? The obstacles, it appears, are not so much economic (lack of profitability) but social and cultural. The model developed earlier is suggestive regarding this. To achieve success with RM, firms must employ enough patient, highly ethical and entrepreneurial people. There is a real question regarding whether organizations today have the ability to select, train and socialize enough members with these characteristics. Secondly and relatedly, societal attitudes which stem from the dominant culture of capitalism may not be sufficiently supportive of RM. For example, in the U.S.A., many have claimed that there is too much value placed on short-term financial self-interest seeking and not enough value placed on developing mutuality and commitment in organizational relationships. In sum, there are good reasons to believe that social and culture factors are the biggest obstacle to the growth of RM.

The government role

The role that government ought to play is suggested by our analysis of businesses' failure to invest sufficiently in their buyer–seller relationships and the obstacles to this. To realize the potential benefits in this area, what is needed is government playing the role of coach, as in industrial policy (Hampden-Turner 1988). Ideally, the coach should act to foster the development of desirable seller–customer relationships and to help businesses overcome the obstacles to this. Many will surely judge that a failure in marketing relationships is not as compelling as, for example, environmental failures involving high levels of ecological degradation and significant threats to health and safety. Nevertheless, the societal benefits to improved buyer–seller relationships, while less tangible and vivid, are very real and substantial. Thus, it is recommended that government ought to be involved in promoting relationship marketing. Government programs could help by fostering patient, ethical, committed behavior among buyers and sellers, by stimulating awareness concerning RM, providing knowledge relating to RM, and by helping firms learn about how to use appropriate communications technologies. To the extent that these programs are successful, it should be possible to lower the government resources committed to consumer regulation and the legal protection of consumers. It is beyond the scope of this chapter to provide a more complete set of policy recommendations.

Conclusion

As transaction markets and old marketing relationships recede and dynamic, bonded buyer–seller relationships grow in importance, it is interesting to consider what this means for the idea of consumer sovereignty. The emergence of relationship marketing implies an increasing number of sellers who are engaged with their customers in a dialogue from which they learn about customer needs and respond by customizing their goods and services. In these relationships, consumers are sovereign in the sense that sellers are actively seeking to satisfy their real and changing needs. However, there is a sense in which the term consumer sovereignty does not apply. In RM, the consumer is not the king, and the seller is not the subject. In RM, the seller and customer are partners sharing a common fate and a mutual commitment; they are coequal collaborators for the long term. It follows that we ought to cherish RM wherever we find it and foster its development where its growth encounters obstacles. Investing in the kind of organizational capital necessary for RM will generally be a good investment both for the firm and society.

10 A new rationale for industrial policy

Developing the capabilities of the learning firm

Introduction

Chapter 2 has argued that U.S. firms failed to adapt to important new competitive realities especially during the 1970s and 1980s. That is, that the rate of organizational learning was insufficient to maintain competitiveness during that time. The three chapters of Part II have focused on how firms' competitiveness is related to several different organizational capabilities, each of which is a product of their investments in organizational capital. Also, Chapter 6, the last chapter of Part II, has argued that a deterioration of the appropriate balance between leadership and management in U.S. business bears some of the responsibility for the competitiveness decline. The present chapter considers the implications of these earlier chapters for government policy and makes the case that government industrial policy should attempt to reverse these organizational failures through actions designed to accelerate organizational learning and stimulate needed investment in organizational capital.

Is government intervention justified in order to raise a nation's competitiveness? Contemporary economists are deeply divided on the answer to this question. The infant industry argument has provided a long-standing rationale for such interventions, but economic theory, the prospect of political difficulties, and the practical problems of policy implementation have considerably undermined this argument. Thus, the answer of orthodox economists tends to be a negative one. On the affirmative side, however, there is the undeniable success of Japanese-style industrial policy. Writers such as Robert Reich and Chalmers Johnson have argued that the U.S.A. and other western countries ought to learn from and adopt the general thrust and spirit of Japan's industrial policy, if not the specific methods used. The problem is that the arguments of the latter authors frequently do not fit comfortably with orthodox economic theory. Thus, proponents of industrial policy have not, in the eyes of many economists, provided a convincing rationale for government efforts to raise national competitiveness. What is needed is a rationale based on the kind of social science that is at once understandable, acceptable and compatible with economic theory.

At the heart of the new rationale developed here is the insight that firms are capable of both organizational learning and being economically responsible to society. Recently, there has come recognition that the firm's rate of organizational learning may be its most important source of competitive advantage and that this in turn may be the key determinant of the rate of a nation's productivity growth. Therefore, the important question becomes: can government interventions successfully influence the organizational learning of a nation's firms? And if so, under what circumstances? The purpose of this paper is to develop a rationale for industrial policy that builds on recent literature on learning organizations and takes account of Japanese and American experience with industrial policy. In regard to the latter, America's success in the case of Harley Davidson is noteworthy. To begin, it is first necessary to consider the traditional industrial policy rationale.

The traditional industrial policy rationale: the infant industry argument

Early advocates

Early advocates of industrial policy based their arguments on the notion that "infant industries" required protection and encouragement. For example, Alexander Hamilton, in his "Report on Manufactures" written in 1791, said that subsidies (or tariffs and other measures) were, "in most cases, indispensable to the introduction of a new branch" of industry and that this would be "essential to the overcoming of the obstacles which arise from the competitions of superior skill and maturity elsewhere" (1961: 18). According to Friedrich List:

> Every "suitable" nation can reap an advantage, at a certain stage in its cultural and economic development, by fostering manufacturing, until it reaches large proportions, through protective tariffs. But the tariffs should be only temporary. They should be removed after they have performed their function of "nursing," and have built up a supply of skilled workers, technicians, and entrepreneurs, and have enabled a number of industries to become established and able to stand upon their own feet.
>
> (as quoted in Haberler 1936: 279)

According to John Stuart Mill:

> The superiority of one country over another in a branch of production often arises only from having begun it sooner. There may be no inherent advantage on one part, or disadvantage on the other, but only a present superiority of acquired skill and experience. A country which has this

skill and experience yet to acquire, may in other respects be better adapted to the production than those which were earlier in the field...

([1848] 1965: 922)

Mill also stated that protection should not be continued beyond the time necessary for a "fair trial." Further, Charles Bastable (see Kemp 1960: 65) argued that protection should not be provided unless the discounted sum of the eventual cost savings are expected to exceed the discounted sum of the excess costs during the learning period. This doctrine, the classic infant industry argument, came to be recognized as the most significant of the few valid exceptions to the doctrine of free trade.

The matured firms in the new industry are expected to produce at a low enough cost to compete with foreign manufacturers once protection and support are removed. It follows that less developed countries can through this process build up a completely developed manufacturing sector. A number of nations such as Japan have followed this route.

Economic theory and the infant industry argument

Despite the fact that the infant industry argument has been accepted by such important economic thinkers as Alfred Marshall and Frank Taussig (Irwin 1991: 203), many economists have rejected it, just as the human body tends to reject transplanted organs. In part, this is because this argument has lacked the precise formulation necessary to integrate it with the main body of trade theory. Thus in recent decades, economists have sought to develop clear theoretical arguments for and against this proposition. The main arguments are briefly cited below.

First is the existence of economies of scale within the infant industry. Protection and support, it is argued, should enable firms within the industry to increase the size of their overall operations, thereby moving them down their long run average total cost curves.

Second, and at the heart of the matter, is learning which enhances the skills and knowledge of workers, owners and managers within the industry. The greater the cumulative output or passage of time, the greater is the accumulated learning or experience. This "learning by doing" shifts the long-run average total cost curve downward over time, and moves average costs lower along the "learning curve" with increasing cumulative output or time. These learning economies are strictly separate from scale economies although both may occur at the same time (see Fuller 1983).

Third, infant firms may also learn in a different way, that is, through explicit investments in the acquisition of new knowledge. Whether through R&D or other means, this learning is quite different from the type gained through production experience. Because it involves a one-time expense and is a fixed cost, increasing the output that uses this knowledge will lower average total costs as the average fixed cost portion decreases.

Fourth, are two kinds of inter-industry effects known as external economies, which can lower costs in an industry as an unintended consequence of what is happening in other industries. The first of these derives from economies of scale in industries supplying the infant industry. Second are the spillovers of knowledge to an industry from another industry. An example of the latter is Succar's (1987) analysis of how the development of dynamic industries such as capital goods can serve as a learning center in which the technical skills that are acquired are critical to the subsequent development of other industries.

Protection and support of the infant industry are thus warranted to the extent that they allow economies of scale to be achieved within the infant and supplying industries, allow time and experience for learning within the infant industry and its diffusion to other industries, and fosters explicit efforts to develop new knowledge.[1,2] This strong apparent support for the infant industry argument has, however, been qualified and/or undermined by the following.

First, if fully functioning capital markets exist, infant firms should be able to finance the profits forgone and the explicit costs of learning during infancy, and thus, should not need government assistance. In principle, this is no different than raising funds to acquire physical capital.

Second, a key question is whether the infant firms can realize the full social benefit of the economies as profit. If they can, the case for government assistance is undermined. If, on the other hand, some of the social benefit accrues to other firms or consumers due to knowledge spillovers or increased competition, the case for protection and support remains.

A third important issue is the geographical dispersion of the external economies. If the expected spillovers from the infant industry cross national borders, there is no advantage on this account to be gained from supporting domestic infant industries. This is because these benefit spillovers would also be gained from the establishment of foreign infant firms (Dosi *et al.* 1989: 8–9).

Because of the above considerations as well as the practical and political problems associated with implementing an industrial policy based on the infant industry argument, some contemporary economists have rejected this argument; others have cautiously accepted it, especially its application to less developed countries. In any case, it should be noted that the above theoretical arguments are largely based on static allocative efficiency considerations. For a better understanding of the infant industry argument and its relationship to industrial policy, it is necessary to go beyond economic orthodoxy. We must understand the firm as a learning organization.

The bases for a new rationale for industrial policy

Towards a new rationale

In making their case for U.S. industrial policy in the early 1980s, authors such as Robert Reich and Chalmers Johnson used a number of the above economic arguments but did not rely on these. At heart, their advocacy was based on the idea that structural change processes, if left to the market, are too slow and rigid, and therefore require easing, accelerating and directing activities on the part of government (see for example, Magaziner and Reich 1982: ch. 27; Johnson 1984: ch. 1). Businesses, in this view, are either too timid, insufficiently responsive to national interests, or lacking the knowledge and incentive to make the long-term investments necessary to maintain and enhance competitive advantage. A variety of rigidities internal and external to the firm were believed to be holding back the desired adjustment to worldwide structural change (Reich 1983; Johnson 1984).

Implicit in the above is the idea that the firm is potentially an efficient learning organization (defined below). Thus, developing a new industrial policy rationale involves making what has been implicit more explicit and formal. It should be noted that the relevant concept of comparative advantage in this context is a "dynamic" one which incorporates the insight that many of a nation's critical resource endowments can be developed and are a product of learning. In other words, the relevant concept is not a "static" one in which a nation's advantage derives from given geographical and natural endowments.

The firm as a learning organization

Organizational learning

The first basis for a new rationale for industrial policy is that the firm is a learning organization. According to Argyris and Schon (1978), learning is not simply information absorption. As explained in Chapter 2, learning begins when individuals discover that their mental models are in error. This is the stimulus for individuals to learn, i.e. to revise their mental models. In *organizational learning*, mismatches between expected and actual organizational outcomes reveal the error in individuals' shared mental models. Organizational learning involves a process of inquiry, reflection and evaluation in which the model is revised and becomes embedded in organizational memory as well as the regular practices of the organization. In *adaptive learning*, the organization copes with changes in the external world but does not make any central changes in its shared mental model (Senge 1990b: 8). *Generative learning*, on the other hand, is a more creative process in which capacity is expanded and significant changes in the shared mental model are made.[3]

Learning organizations

Learning organizations are ideal organizations that continuously manifest high-quality, appropriate organizational learning, and thus are continuously expanding their capacity to create and deal with the future (Senge 1990a). Learning organizations, accordingly, have mastered five key disciplines: systems thinking, personal mastery, mental models, building shared vision, and team learning. In Senge's (1990a: 5–6) view, learning organizations have been invented, but not yet innovated; there are promising experiments and prototypes, but full-fledged learning organizations still remain an unrealized aspiration. Nevertheless, the learning organization concept is useful in that it enables us to envision both what is possible and why that frequently does not occur. It enables us to understand the conditions conducive to organizational learning and the nature of organizational learning disabilities.

Obstacles to organizational learning

Some obstacles to organizational learning are internal to the organization. These learning disabilities are deficiencies in the organization's learning system; most notable are the inhibitions to high quality, generative organizational learning. Among these disabilities are: inaccessible and obscure mental models, defensive modes of behavior, lack of good team work, lack of systems thinking and lack of shared vision. Thus, it is generally "soft" organizational characteristics that either interfere with or, in other cases, foster the desired organizational learning. It follows that investments in these soft kinds of organizational capital can be very profitable.

Conditions external to the firm can also play an important role in organizational learning. For example, Porter's (1990a, 1990b) research indicates that there are a handful of broad attributes of a nation that are the critical determinants of the national environment that affects the extent to which companies learn the lessons necessary to acquire competitive advantage in the international marketplace. Among these attributes are:

1) the character of the home nation's demand (especially whether domestic buyers are sophisticated and demanding);
2) the presence of related and supporting industries that are internationally competitive;
3) the presence of strong local rivals that stimulate firms to innovate;
4) the presence of infrastructure or factors such as skilled labor that are highly specialized to an industry's needs;
5) the presence of strong favorable tendencies with respect to how companies are organized and managed (Porter 1990b: 77–82).

These attributes are suggestive of what needs to be done external to the firm to provide an environment that stimulates organizational learning, thereby leading to innovation, higher productivity and competitive advantage.

On the other hand, the social influences in the firm's external environment could inhibit the learning process. Such an organizational failure, a type of socio-economic failure of the firm, occurs when despite the sufficiency of market incentives, the social influences on firms cause firms to fail to adopt the most economically appropriate organizational features in response to new competitive situations (see Chapter 2). These social influences may, for example, derive from established groups that block efficiency enhancing changes that run counter to their interests. If management consultants, educational institutions or other groups are threatened by a prospective change from the prevailing management model, they may act in such a way as to preserve the status quo.

Organizational learning as competitive advantage

Increasingly the basis of competition is shifting to organizations' ability to learn (Porter 1990b: 73). In fact, Ray Stata (1989: 64) argues that "the rate at which individuals and organizations learn may become the only sustainable competitive advantage." Thus, the most pressing contemporary need for western companies is to improve their capacity for generative organizational learning, which should enable them to make successful adjustments to the changing realities of global competition.

Because organizational learning involves processes by which organization members' shared mental model is revised, it is a much broader conception of learning than economists have heretofore incorporated in their theories. It is, for example, broader than Malerba's (1992: 848) conception of learning which involves six major types of learning processes: (1) learning by doing, (2) learning by using, (3) learning from external advances in science and technology, (4) learning from intra-industry spillovers, (5) learning by interacting with suppliers and users, and (6) learning by searching for new knowledge. Learning of these specific, largely technological types cannot occur if the new insights are in conflict with the organization's established mental model (Senge 1990b: 14). Thus, organizational learning, which produces changes to organization members' basic perceptions of their business reality, is different from and must logically occur prior to the acquisition of specific technological and managerial knowledge.

Economic responsibility

The second basis for a new rationale for industrial policy is economically responsible business behavior. Economic responsibility is in essence socially responsible behavior in the economic realm (the sphere concerned especially with economic growth, productivity and competitiveness). Socially responsible business behavior occurs when firms voluntarily adopt policies and actions in conformity to the norms and goals of society (see Chapter 7). Correspondingly, economically responsible business behavior occurs when firms voluntarily align their economic goals and activities with society's economic goals. Conversely, firms would be economically irresponsible if they committed themselves to economic tasks incompatible with society's economic goals.

Economically responsible firms take a long-term perspective because their behavior is aligned with society's long-term interests. Such firms are willing to be role players like basketball players on a successful basketball team. It's not that they do not desire to be competitive and responsive to market signals. It is simply that they are also responsive to non-market, economic-related signals including advice and guidance from governmental economic agencies. Economically responsible firms are characterized by a willingness to participate in the process of achieving and setting national economic goals. An economically responsible firm has a particular kind of learning orientation that involves openness to societal concerns. It does not mean that these firms have adopted a submissive, follower-style mentality.

The importance of economic responsibility becomes clear when there is a significant gap between the economic performance society expects from a firm and its actual performance. This is because society ultimately will insist on closing the gap, i.e. insist on business behavior consistent with societal goals. If businesses do not voluntarily act to close the gap, society can be expected to do it using governmental regulation. Such regulation could reduce businesses' autonomy or impose penalties on them. Thus, firms might find it in their long-term interest to adopt an economically responsible mode of operation, effectively making economic responsibility a part of their business strategy. Of course, firms that are mainly oriented to short-term profitability are not very likely to choose an economically responsible pattern of behavior.

Industrial policy as fostering appropriate learning in firms

It follows from the above that industrial policy ought to foster economic restructuring through the creation of conditions that encourage firms to increase their capacity and competitiveness through appropriate organizational learning.

Learning may fail

A lack of systems thinking

The need for industrial policy arises because in many cases the profit motivation does not by itself lead to the desired learning experiences. The reason, as indicated earlier, is that internal and external obstacles keep firm members from revising their mental models despite evidence of these models' inadequacy. For example, a very important internal obstacle is a lack of systems thinking on the part of business people. In Senge's (1990b) view, business leaders typically do not have the capability for systems thinking necessary to understand the underlying system of relationships that are the cause of their problems. Instead, they frequently view the problem as either events or patterns of behavior and not as a systematic structure. Because attention is focused on symptoms including the financial distress, these firms tend to adopt symptomatic solutions rather than fundamental solutions. As a result, the problems tend to worsen and become harder and harder to solve.

The example of U.S. firms

The above kind of learning obstacle is undoubtedly a factor in the serious problems that American firms have faced especially in the 1970s and 1980s as evidenced by their declining ability to compete amidst stiffening global competition. The good news is that:

> Some American firms are responding vigorously to the new competitive challenges...[They] are developing a continuous improvement mind-set, automating, simplifying their structures, increasing employee involvement in real business issues, tying pay to performance, and improving quality.
>
> (Grayson and O'Dell 1988: 13)

These firms are learning, finding fundamental solutions, and increasing their competitiveness.

> The bad news is that as yet only a relatively small number of firms are making the kinds of changes required. The majority of American firms are not responding at all, doing very little, or engaging in a flurry of activity, much of it short-term cost-reduction, layoffs, slam-bang automation, and closings of inefficient operations. They will secure some short-term improvement but little lasting productivity growth.
>
> (Grayson and O'Dell 1988: 13)

These symptomatic solutions reflect an absence of generative organizational learning. It is unlikely that these firms will enhance their long-term competitiveness. If this slow and uneven rate of learning in American industry were to persist, the prospect would be for continued American industrial decline, a prospect presumably unacceptable to the American people. There is some evidence and considerable belief that the rate of organizational learning, and correspondingly the competitiveness, of U.S. industry have improved during the 1990s.

Industrial policy as coach

If athletic team members are not learning and responding appropriately, it is up to the coach to correct the situation. If too many firms in the economy are failing to learn and perform satisfactorily, there is obviously a need for an "economic" coach. This is the essence of industrial policy as practiced by Japan and other East Asian countries. Charles Hampden-Turner (1988) believes that in today's world the appropriate government role toward the economy is that of a coach, not a referee or abolitionist. "Only the coach sees the social market as an organism needful of independence and of nurturance, and—crucially—as a living system [of organizations] whose learning can be accelerated" (1988: 44). Thus, "governments can facilitate learning by acting as catalysts" (1988: 45). Clearly, western countries such as the U.S. are in need of an industrial policy as coach.

But this raises many more questions. When should the government/coach intervene to stimulate appropriate learning? How should the coach intervene? The answers to these questions should themselves be a product of learning, learning that in part derives from an examination of the successes and failures of past governmental interventions in different times and places. In recent U.S. history, one very successful intervention experience compels our attention.

Government intervention in the Harley Davidson case

Consider the U.S. government's intervention in the case of Harley Davidson, the U.S. manufacturer of large motorcycles. Harley Davidson:

> sought Government protection in 1982 when Japanese importers refused to cut production in the face of a declining market. The Japanese over-production led to a price war at a time when Harley could not afford it.... Special tariffs were imposed for a five-year period...in April 1983 as Harley skidded toward bankruptcy. Aimed at giving Harley time to carry out planned changes in manufacturing practices and product improvements, the tariffs followed a sliding scale that added 45 percent to the cost of the Japanese imports with engines larger than 700 cubic centimeters in 1983 with a decline to 10 percent in...1988.
>
> (Feder 1987)

By 1987, Harley Davidson had dramatically increased its profitability and market share and requested that the government withdraw the tariff protection in advance of its scheduled phase out. Harley Davidson had introduced Japanese management methods such as total quality control, just-in-time inventory methods, and statistical process control. Among the results were: (1) "raised the percentage of motorcycles leaving its production lines without defects from about 50 percent to more than 98 percent," (2) redesigned many parts to get rid of "bone-jarring vibration," (3) increased productivity by 30 percent, (4) reduced scrap and rework by 60 percent, and (5) reduced work-in-process inventory by $22 million (Feder 1987; Gunn 1987: 174). In the process, the company became a mecca for engineers from other industries. According to author and management consultant, Richard Schonberger, "'tariff protection was vital to Harley'" (Feder 1987). Another notable result is that Jim Lucas, a manager at Harley Davidson who guided many of these changes, has gone on to another company, Deutz-Allis, where as general manager he has been introducing similar changes.

In terms of our analysis, Harley Davidson in 1982 was clearly a case where desperately needed organizational learning was failing to occur. The temporary protection gave Harley Davidson sufficient breathing room to make the major managerial changes necessary for it to regain competitiveness. Thus, rapid organizational learning began at Harley Davidson with an assist from the governmental coach. Under the threat of extinction and with one more opportunity available to it, Harley Davidson had become very open to the needed learning. It should be noted that while Harley Davidson required governmental protection, it did not require a more overt governmental coaching role. To stimulate the desired change process, other firms suffering from a similar syndrome might have required more direct governmental facilitation of their learning processes.

The infant industry argument revisited

The ostensible reason for the federal government's action in the Harley Davidson case is the dumping of large motorcycles by the Japanese producers. However, the use of a high and gradually declining tariff for this good indicates that the infant industry reasoning was applied. In other words, despite the mature status of Harley's motorcycle business, this industry segment was being treated as an "infant" with the idea that some sort of rejuvenation process would occur.

In the absence of rejuvenation, such a firm can be likened to a child in a game with a grown-up competitor. Because we cannot accept the inevitable outcome of such a match, it is necessary to protect the child until he or she gains the maturity and skill of the adult (see Friedrich List's boy versus man analogy, in Haberler 1936: 278). This is true in both business and sports. It is also true for just-planted grass. We protect it by posting keep off the grass signs because it is highly vulnerable at this stage. Later on the protection may be removed because even vigorous sports activity will not bother the grass once it has acquired the hardiness of maturity. Analogously, Harley Davidson's recent performance including gains in market share relative to its Japanese competitors indicates that it has acquired the kind of hardy competitiveness that no longer requires protection.

Because of the successful revival of Harley Davidson, the natural question is whether there are other business infants that could be rejuvenated through a similar process. Also, could an accumulation of specific instances of rejuvenation lead to a more general rejuvenation of American industry?

Organizational learning and the infant industry argument

While it would be wrong to jump to too many conclusions based on it, the Harley Davidson case is nevertheless highly suggestive. It indicates that the infant industry argument when coupled with the organizational learning concept can provide at least under special circumstances a very useful rationale for industrial policy interventions.

Let us consider the kind of circumstances where this rationale makes sense. To begin, it applies where there are firms whose members' shared mental model is problematic in the sense that it is not well adapted to their current competitive environment. Second, it applies to situations where there are generally occurring, identifiable, and understandable obstacles to organizational learning. Third, it applies where the firms in question are important to the economy, and thus, it would be an unacceptable market outcome to lose these firms to foreign competition. Fourth, it applies where there is good reason to believe that coaching (protection plus stimulus) is likely to be the necessary and critical ingredient for jumpstarting these firms' organizational learning. Finally, it applies where there is no other reason why these firms cannot be competitive.

These criteria would seem to be satisfied in the case of the failure of many U.S. firms, in the face of stiff foreign competition, to implement the kind of management methods well adapted to the new global competitive realities. Many insightful management observers agree that the magnitude of the learning required of many U.S. firms to transform them into strong global competitors is great. To be sufficiently strong competitors, such firms must not only learn very new managerial approaches but substantially increase their capability for organizational learning. In effect, these firms have underinvested in appropriate organizational capital. Correspondingly, both the private and societal rates of return to governmental intervention would be expected to be very high.

To the best of my knowledge, the above rationale for industrial policy has never been used even though there are undoubtedly instances, notably the situation at Harley Davidson, where the government's rationale must have involved some similar thinking. Japanese industrial policy seems loosely based on a variety of notions of business learning, but it is not based on the concept of organizational learning associated with the thinking of Argyris, Senge and others. It should also be noted that Japanese industrial policy generally involves a coaching approach and makes extensive use of infant industry thinking. It could be argued that certain aspects of Japanese industrial policy in the late 1940s and 1950s were implicitly based on an organizational learning rationale. This was the period where the quality of Japanese goods was very poor, and their management was demonstrably inferior to that of the U.S.A. During this period, the Japanese made substantial efforts to transform their management methods in key industries and to transfer these methods to other industries. These industries were generally highly protected during this time.

It should be emphasized that the purpose of any governmental intervention involving protection and support is to strengthen the firm(s) or to encourage the creation of new firms, and thereby to raise capacity and competitiveness. The purpose is not to raise profit, certainly not the profits of owners associated with the firm's previous failure. Therefore, in devising policies that protect infant industry, the public's interests should be made paramount, not the interests of particular owners of capital. One way to achieve this would be to mandate that when a firm's profits rise as a direct result of governmental protection, this should not add to existing owners' wealth. Under such a plan, this rise in net worth (assets minus liabilities) would accrue to the government or other designated stakeholder in the firm. Later on, profit and wealth increases owing to increased efficiency would be allowed to accrue to the owners.

Toward a more general industrial policy rationale

Besides situations where the infant industry argument may apply, the concept of organizational learning as well as other types of learning could serve as a basis for a more general industrial policy rationale. A number of existing industrial policy practices may become more understandable and justifiable when they are seen as ways to enhance desired learning. For example, Japanese industrial policy makers have long sought to develop a desired balance between competition and cooperation/coordination in targeted industries. Among the lessons guiding this aspect of Japanese industrial policy are:

1) cutthroat competition is destructive in the sense that it leads to too little investment and learning;
2) a low level of competition does not provide enough pressure or prod to learning;
3) unguided competition fails to foster the type of learning that derives from cooperative or coordinative efforts among competing firms (for example, cooperation among competitors might involve joint research, and coordination might involve specialization within the industry).

Thus, these Japanese efforts to manage the balance between industrial competition and cooperation/coordination are usefully viewed as a way to foster desired learning. Presumably, it would be fruitful to link other existing or proposed industrial policy practices to their expected effect on organizational learning. However, doing this is beyond the scope of this chapter.

Conclusion

Ideally, firms under the prod of competition and the lure of profit will come close to realizing the potential of their learning efforts. Research concerning organizational learning, however, indicates that firms' learning is typically deficient; there are many obstacles to organizational learning which are not easily surmounted. If it is possible to understand these failures, it should be possible for the industrial policy maker, or government coach, to take action that will help firms overcome these obstacles, thereby accelerating their organizational learning. This will especially be true for firms that are economically responsible, that is, open to governmental guidance. As a result, firms will acquire competitive advantage, and national productivity will rise. The essence of the task is developing a country's intangible, collective human capacities in line with its economic growth goals. Industrial policy in this view is part of a larger process of accumulating the critical qualitative stocks of human capital, especially organizational capital.

Obviously, more research needs to be done in this vein. First, it would be important to know to what extent it is possible to stimulate critically needed organizational learning in declining industries without governmental coaching assistance. Second, it would be important to examine a variety of countries' experiences with industrial policy to determine whether these can shed light on the viability of the proposed rationale.

One thing is clear. If economists are to gain satisfactory understanding of the behavior of firms and how economies grow and fail to grow, it will be necessary to make learning a central part of our understanding of these subjects.

Part IV

Conclusion

11 Summing up

Firms, policies and economic systems in a new economic age

The human firm in a new economic age

Unlike the neoclassical firm, the firm analyzed in this book is a fully human one. It is fully human in that it is capable of behavior that realizes the highest human potential. But, unfortunately, it is also all too human in its typical failure to realize that potential.

More specifically, the analyses of the preceding chapters indicate the following about the human firm. The human firm is capable of fully rational organizational decision making when confronted with large, complex, ill-structured decisions, but the degree of procedural rationality attained is typically much less than that potential. The human firm is capable of ideal social responsibility, environmental responsibility and customer responsibility, but its actual behavior is usually much less responsible than this. The human firm is capable of behavior that is ideally flexible and integrated as well as manifesting a high degree of organizational learning, creativity and innovativeness. Unfortunately, actual firms rarely achieve this level of efficiency. The human firm is capable of overcoming the tendency of its members to make insufficient efforts on its behalf. Moreover, it is capable of fully aligning the interests of its individual members and the organization, but the reality generally falls far short of this. Finally, the human firm is capable of great socio-economic performance when its members are both inspired and appropriately channeled, but again greatness rarely occurs.

The human firm is a socio-economic actor, an actor partially embedded in society. Such a firm is not the independent, economically rational and entirely self-interested actor of mainstream economic theory. It is also not the purely sociological actor who behaves only in accordance with social norms, rules and obligations. The human firm is an actor that simultaneously (1) responds to economic incentives as it strives, more or less rationally, to achieve its ends and (2) responds to social influences reflecting the firm's network of social relationships. How the human firm responds to these economic incentives and social influences and to what extent the firm can attain its economic and social ends in doing so is determined in large part by the firm's accumulated stock of organizational capital.

Organizational capital, as indicated earlier, is a concept used primarily by economists to denote the productive capacity that is embodied in an organization's people relationships. Because it is embodied in people, organizational capital is properly considered a type of human capital. But it is also appropriate to consider organizational capital a type of social capital. *Social capital* is a term used, typically by economic sociologists, not simply to refer to organizationally embodied productive capacity, but also more generally to refer to the social relationships that serve as a resource enabling actors to attain their needs. According to James Coleman (see, for example, 1988), an economic sociologist notable for his role in developing the social capital concept, social capital refers to a variety of social structural resources embodied in families, businesses, other institutions, civic communities and the larger society. More so than for most types of social capital, organizational capital is likely to have been created intentionally by persons who view it as an investment from which they hope to profit.

By virtue of its organizational capital stock, the human firm has both hard and soft attributes, and correspondingly, capacities that determine its competitiveness and responsibility. First, consider some of the hard (relatively tangible, explicit and definite) organizational attributes that contribute to a firm's competitiveness. Decision making with respect to large, complex decisions is likely to be more rational when an organization's regular procedures bring to bear appropriate influences on decision makers and lead their members to use all eight decision-making steps and appropriate decision-making strategies (Chapter 4). Greater flexibility and integration are possible when a firm creates organizational structures that allow greater use of horizontal coordinating mechanisms, enable synergy among different product activities, and utilize fewer levels of organizational hierarchy (Chapter 5). Other aspects of organizational structure as well as ownership structure and financial structure also contribute to a firm's productivity (Chapter 6).

Second, let's consider some of the soft (less definite and holistic) organizational attributes that contribute to a firm's competitiveness and responsibility. One may expect greater organizational commitment and citizenship behavior from members, when during the joining-up process, a strong mutual bond between the organization and its members has been created (Chapter 3). The quality of mental activity involved in decision making is likely to be high in the presence of a non-stressful organizational climate, high ideals and leaders who communicate visions that "captures people's hearts" (Chapter 4). Social responsibility (and especially environmental responsibility and customer responsibility) is likely to be high for a firm with a highly ethical orientation and a high degree of patience (Chapters 7–9).

Further, improved flexibility and integration can be expected when a firm develops in its organizational relationships features that discourage opportunism, integrate thinking and doing, and promote horizontal relationships

(Chapter 5). Greater environmental responsibility can be expected for a firm that improves its capability for organizational learning, raises its environmental concern and awareness, and integrates environmental management with other aspects of management (Chapter 8). Greater ultimate socio-economic performance can be expected for a firm that creates (1) a genuine, collective and shared vision, and (2) the soft organizational structures (organizational culture, habits, belief structures, understanding of mission and competences and so on) that facilitate and guide member behavior. The latter applies with particular force when these soft organizational features are in balance with the hard organizational features (Chapter 6).

If the human firm has invested in all the types of organizational capital discussed in the preceding chapters to the point where its internal organizational capabilities are developed as much as possible, it will have become the ideal (or Z-) firm. The Z-firm is a socio-economic or human firm that has realized its highest potential with respect to competitiveness and responsibility. There are many reasons to believe that it should be ideally adapted to survive and prosper in the emerging new economic age.

In this new economic age, as discussed earlier, the old science, the science of machine metaphors, is giving way to a new science of holisms. With regard to organization, an orientation to short-term profitability and control is giving way to an orientation to the long term, vision and relationships. Given such paradigm changes, there is a corresponding need for a new economic conception of the firm. The prevailing mainstream economic conception of the firm as a barebones machine, a theoretical skeleton, has clearly become obsolete. That is why this book has sought to develop a socio-economic conception of the firm as a more complex human entity whose capacity is determined by the rich variety of organizational relationships which have been created in it.

According to sociologist Emile Durkheim, "organic" periods in which various social forces in a society are harmoniously adjusted to each other will be followed by a "critical" periods. The latter involve considerable turmoil and unbalanced conditions; they are periods in which the old social order is breaking down and new healthy social forces are beginning to appear (Coser 1984: xx). The critical period idea seems very much pertinent to what has been referred to here as the emergence of a new economic age. According to Durkheim, during a critical period, new types of corporations would arise. These new corporations would serve to revive the socio-economy through the creation of a new institutionalized setting involving new norms, values and moral bonds, leading to greater social cohesion. There is good reason to believe that this is what is happening today. In preceding chapters, this aspect has been an important and recurring theme in that this book has focused on (1) the firm as a socio-economic entity and (2) the firm as an investor in the social/organizational capital necessary for the revival of the economy.

Government policies in a new economic age

When economies fail to perform as expected, people may naturally turn to government for corrective measures. The kinds of government remedies recommended will depend, among other things, on the prevailing theories regarding how economic institutions work. If the accepted conception of the firm is as a human or socio-economic entity, the policy implications drawn will tend to be quite different than if the mainstream core theory of the firm is the only intellectually legitimate conception.

Economists holding mainstream conceptions of the firm almost inevitably advocate that government should perform a "regulatory" role in the sense that there should be laws, along with government agency regulations, that serve to correct problematic firm behavior. These corrections are necessary, in this view, because of positive and/or negative externalities involving market incentives that lead firms to make choices that produce inoptimal, i.e. economically inefficient, outcomes. Some who hold this view advocate corrective regulations of the "command and control" variety. But, following the advice of many contemporary economists, others advocate regulatory corrections utilizing market-like incentives (for example, taxes or subsidies) that counter the market incentives, thereby opposing the detrimental effects of the externalities.

Rather than the government as regulator, an alternative approach is the government as coach. Charles Hampden-Turner (1988: 44) has asked: "Is it possible...for capitalist free enterprise to be 'coached' to greater humanity and success?" His answer (and my answer as well) is a resounding yes. This book has argued in a number of chapters that firms' socio-economic performance can be raised through appropriate coaching. Coaching makes sense when we conceive of firms as organisms that learn, organisms that not only compete but cooperate, and organisms that are involved in complex social networks. Further, the coaching approach follows when we conceive of firms as fully human, socio-economic entities whose learning (and cooperation) can be nurtured, facilitated, prodded, and otherwise encouraged. It is through such means that the human firm's capacity for competitiveness and responsibility can be raised and, thereby, the economic failure addressed. In contrast to the regulatory approach, the emphasis in coaching is *not* to get the firm to do the opposite of what it would naturally do, but to provide the firm with plenty of opportunity and a conducive environment that will enable it to realize its highest potential in its relationship with society.

The analyses of this book have strongly suggested a number of important specific roles for the government as coach. First, consider the situation where an economy is failing because of a lack of competitiveness. There are a variety of ways the government coach could act to raise the productive capacity and, thereby, the competitiveness of the economy. Consider, for example, the analysis of Chapter 10 which has indicated that for a variety of reasons, firms organizational learning is typically deficient. In many of these situations, government might be able to provide the critical help necessary to enable firms to overcome the obstacles to the needed learning. If the process is successful, the targeted firms will have gained competitive advantage and the nation's productivity will have been raised. Such successes develop the country's intangible collective human capacities, especially its organizational capital, and should thereby enable the nation to avoid deindustrialization and reach its economic growth goals.

Alternative ways in which the coach approach can raise an economy's competitiveness are suggested by the analyses of several other chapters. For example, Chapter 5 has analyzed the characteristics of the ideal flexible, integrated firm and how, given the rapidly changing global nature of today's competition, it is economically superior to the hierarchical firm. It makes sense for firms to strive to become more flexible and integrated, but it is no mean task to orchestrate such a transformation. Thus, if the government coach could provide certain critical types of help to firms seeking to develop the specific organizational features that provide flexibility and integration, this might provide a significant boost to competitiveness.

Chapter 4 has analyzed the procedures that organizations need to follow if they aspire to improved rationality in their large, complex ill-structured decision making. Raising decision-making rationality is also not a trivial task. Quite conceivably, government coaching could supply the key assistance firms need to make more rational decisions, thereby furnishing still another boost to competitiveness. Lastly, Chapter 6 has analyzed how a critical combination of soft features (leadership, spirit, etc.) and hard features (management, organizational structure, etc.) are needed to realize the firm's potential socio-economic performance. No doubt the right kind of government coaching could help here as well, thereby raising competitiveness.

The other major role for the government qua coach is developing the firm's, and thus the economy's capacity for responsible behavior. This would address the kinds of economic failure that stem from irresponsible behavior. Chapter 7 has analyzed the factors determining the degree to which a firm's behavior is socially responsible. Two internal capabilities, the ethical orientation and patience of a firm's decision makers, were found to be the key to understanding its social responsibility. An important conclusion that emerged from this analysis was that ideal socially responsible firm behavior provides a solution to the negative externality problem. This is because the ideally behaving firm, having attained a high degree of disciplined, socially harmonious self-control, would not do anything that causes harm to others unless their consent were given. Two important implications for governmental policy follow from this. First, it might be possible to resolve the economic failure associated with externality problems without the use of regulatory incentives (market-like or not). This would be the case if more firms were to act in a fully socially responsible manner. The second implication is that the government coach could help move the economy toward this desirable state of affairs by actions designed to improve firms' internal capabilities, especially the character of firms' decision makers, and improve the external social influences on firms.

Two other chapters also focus on the responsibility of the firm's behavior and how the government coach might improve it. The socio-economic model of Chapter 8 provides an analysis of the determinants of the firm's environmental behavior. The implications of this analysis are that to improve the firm's environmental responsibility, the government coach should (1) encourage the development of the firm's internal organizational capability, (2) provide knowledge of environmental opportunities, (3) reduce undesirable extra-firm influences, and (4) reduce undesirable and unintended regulatory influences. In Chapter 9, the focus of the socio-economic model is on the firm's socially responsible behavior toward customers, i.e. customer responsibility. Ideal customer responsibility is when the firm behaves in a way that really is in the best interests of the customer. Because of the many costs to society when firms behave irresponsibly to customers, there is a strong argument that the government coach should act to foster the development of desirable seller–customer relationships and to help businesses overcome the obstacles to this.

The socio-economic model of Chapter 3 includes an analysis of the factors determining whether an organization member will behave in an organizationally responsible manner or not. When these members behave out of a strong commitment to the organization and act in accord with the organization's long-term best interests, they are behaving with ideal organizational responsibility. The analysis indicates that to improve the organizational responsible behavior of a firm's members, a firm should first select organization members with the human qualities conducive to forming satisfactory long-term organizational relationships, and second, in the process of joining-up, subject these members to the kinds of socialization experiences that will lead to a strong mutual bond between the member and the organization. Because organizationally responsible members make greater efforts on behalf of the organization (and are not as self-interested), it is in the financial interest of the firm to encourage organizational responsibility. Nevertheless, it is not a trivial task to create the organizational relationships that contribute powerfully to organizational responsibility. For this reason, there may be a need for a government coach to foster organizational responsibility within firms. If successful, improvement of organizational responsibility will increase the organizational effectiveness of firms, and thereby boost competitiveness.

Chapter 10 considers one last aspect of responsibility on the part of the firm, economic responsibility. Economically responsible firms voluntarily align their economic goals and activities with society's economic goals. In doing so, they are assuming that they and society will be better off in the long-term when their efforts are aligned. Economically responsible firms desire their own economic success, but not at the expense of society. Accordingly, they are not only responsive to signals from the market but to advice and guidance from government economic agencies. They are part of the nation's economic team, and thus are amenable to instructions from the government's economic coach. If industrial policy is to work, if the nation's competitiveness is to be boosted, economic responsibility must be present.

Up to this point, this section has considered a variety of ways in which the government as coach might make significant contributions to competitiveness and responsibility, thereby overcoming certain economic failures. These suggestions regarding the role of the government qua coach should not be considered as a detailed set of policy recommendations applicable in every case. Rather, they should be considered as a generalized philosophy or set of useful ideas. The essence is that when we conceive of the firm as a human or socio-economic entity, an entity with the highest human potential yet all too human failings, it makes sense to consider how the firm might be coached to success (both the firm's and society's). Whether any particular type of coaching is worthwhile for a nation will depend on such things as the society's priorities, the competence of its firms, and the business –government–society relationships. In other words, it will depend on whether the prospective benefits outweigh the costs of the proposed coaching activity.

With regard to government policy in the new economic age, one other thing besides the coach approach is very important. That is the balance between hard-headedness and soft-heartedness described by Alan Blinder (1987). According to Blinder, hard-headedness refers to a desirable quality of thinking that is rational, logical, sober and based on the relevant facts; it is the opposite of wishful thinking. While hard-headedness may seem like a conservative quality, it is not a quality associated with ideology. One of Blinder's examples of soft-headedness, the opposite of hard-headedness, is the Reagan administration's use of supply-side economics thinking which, judging by the discrepancy between their forecasts and actual outcomes, involved much wishful thinking and very little careful logical thinking and attention to facts. Note also that the best of hard-headed thinking involves an appreciation of both the hard and the soft aspects of reality.

Soft-heartedness, the other part of the desired balance, refers to a compassionate attitude in the sense of rooting for and wanting to help society's underdogs. Blinder associates soft-heartedness with generosity, ethical concern, fairness, a desire for equity in income distribution, and liberal Democrats. The essence is the view that we ought to soften the blows for those who play the economic game and lose, or who cannot play it at all. In contrast, the hard-hearted attitude is that our wonderful market system is so essential, and so fragile, that we must not tamper with it in order to aid the underprivileged, the shortsighted, the indolent or even the unlucky. Aiding any of these unfortunate people would be futile at best and harmful at worst. Hard-heartedness, not surprisingly, is associated with conservative Republicans. Ideally, soft-heartedness ought to transcend partisan considerations and reflect an unconditional loving orientation towards all people and an appreciation of the oneness and common humanity of all people.

Policies reflecting the right balance between hard-headedness and soft-heartedness should be focused on finding solutions to the economy's failures through the development of the hard and soft capacities of society (and especially firms). In many cases, coaching will be the key government activity involved in developing the intangible capacities essential to the achievement of the desired socio-economic performance. Further, the best policies ought to reflect a concern for the less fortunate, who too often are the victims of economic failure, and more generally, a concern for creating a just society.

Economic systems in a new economic age

The perspectives on the business firm contained in this book are suggestive with respect to economic systems. If it makes sense to conceive of firms as fully human, socio-economic entities, why not conceive of whole economic systems the same way? To make the subject more manageable, let us limit our focus to capitalist economic systems, that is, economic systems with privately owned, profit-seeking enterprises operating in the context of product, labor and capital markets. The task here is to briefly consider how "human capitalism" differs from more conventional conceptions of capitalism.

Neoclassical economists tend to conceive of capitalism as a mechanistic system that is typically either moving toward or in equilibrium. Movement toward equilibrium occurs as economic actors unfailingly make economically rational choices in their pursuit of economic gain. Capitalistic perfection, from the neoclassical perspective, occurs when the system has reached an equilibrium in which every possibility for making someone better off through changes in resource allocation, without someone else becoming worse off, has been exhausted. This abstract model of capitalism contains only hard attributes, no soft ones; there is no room for features that are not quantifiable, explicit, and definite. Further, the economic system is considered entirely separate from other aspects of society, and thus, its actors are motivated only by economic concerns.

Similar to the conception of the human firm developed throughout this book, the suggested model of human capitalism is a holistic one, containing both hard and soft attributes. It contains such specific hard features as market structure, property rights, patterns of ownership, business management processes, government laws and regulations, and so forth. But it also includes soft features such as spirit, leadership, vision, moral ideals, ethical orientation and so on. Presumably, human capitalism functions best when the hard and soft ingredients are in the right balance with each other. In contrast to the neoclassical capitalist model, human capitalism (including especially its markets) is partially embedded in society, and thus, all its economic actors respond not only to economic incentives but to social influences depending on the web of socio-economic-political relationships in which they are involved. It would seem reasonable to expect harmonious functioning of the system when its economic actors behave responsibly. The motivations of people in a human capitalist system encompass the entire range of human motivation rather than being limited to economic ones. Accordingly, human capitalism may achieve greatness reflective of the highest human potential or may be all too human in its failure.

Human capitalism as conceived here is not an ideal; it is simply more human than the neoclassical or other conventional conceptions of it. Further development of the concept of human capitalism would seem to be an extremely important task (but beyond the scope of this book). It is important because the material aspects of people's well-being, not to mention certain nonmaterial aspects, are determined by the performance of the socio-economy. Similar to firms, a socio-economy's actual performance will generally be below its potential, often far below. Recall Leibenstein's view that X-inefficiency is the usual state of affairs. The reasons for such gaps are many and complex, and are not simply economic in nature. Unless we can learn to think in a disciplined and interdisciplinary way about human capitalism, we will not be able adequately to understand these reasons, grapple with them, and resolve the complex problems involved. This is true whether we are confronting the difficulties of advanced capitalist economies, the Eastern European economies in transition, the newly industrializing nations, or less developed countries struggling to get on the growth path.

It is also of great interest to inquire about the nature of ideal human capitalism (Z-capitalism?). Robert Ozaki (1991) believes that ideal human capitalism resembles the best features of contemporary Japanese capitalism. Following Ozaki, "human capitalism" is a highly productive, people-oriented system in which human resources are the most vital capital. In this system, managers and workers in effect own firms and share information, the fruits of their work efforts, and decision making; companies both compete and cooperate with each other; and income distribution is relatively egalitarian. While interesting and useful, Ozaki's conception of ideal human capitalism is a more limited ideal than the one suggested by the analyses of this book. Although Ozaki's version of capitalism indicates how Japanese-style socio-economic relationships can produce greater prosperity and genuine well-being than conventional capitalism or socialism, it lacks an appreciation of the highest aspects of human nature. Because it leaves out of the analysis such important soft qualities as spirit and leadership, his ideal is not consonant with that of a socio-economy realizing the highest human potential.

Putting flesh on the bones of our conception of ideal human capitalism is an important subject for further research. With a clear vision of the ideal socio-economy before us, it will be possible to build the institutions and intangible capacities necessary to realizing society's human potential. Such a vision of the ideal human capitalism can provide the spark, the inspiration that is needed to energize people enabling them to achieve the highest possible socio-economic performance, which in turn can lift greatly the quality of people's lives and help realize the human potential of our new economic age.

Notes

2 The human firm in the socio-economy

1 The distinction between micro and macro social forces is not the same as Etzioni's (1988: 209–11) distinction between micro and macro social bonds, although it has some similarities.
2 Datta-Chaudhuri (1990: 33) observes that "producers and traders do not always correctly perceive the various trade or technological possibilities open to them. There is scope for imaginative intervention to alter their perceptions and thereby improve the performance of an economy."
3 The Deming statement comes from his November 6, 1981 article in *The Journal of Commerce*, as quoted in Chaiken (1982: 847).
4 Skinner's argument is similar in some ways to Michael Maccoby's (1981) thesis that societal change requires a new model of leadership that emphasizes development of people.
5 It should be noted that Skinner (1988: 279) sees "a new breed [of manufacturing manager] coming on fast," a breed who have more of the desirable competencies and who are open to change. He expects they will be coming into power in five or ten years and hopefully will be of greater assistance in bringing about desirable management changes than the current breed.
6 While lack of ideological change is no doubt an impediment to change, the positive reception of recent books on organizational innovation and Japanese management at least provides an "ideological climate favorable to serious thinking" about fundamental managerial change" (Hearn 1988: 301).
7 The Cuomo Commission (1988) has recommended a number of elements it believes this consensus should include.

3 Organizational capital and joining up

1 Among Organ's (1988: 7–13) categories of organizational citizenship behaviors are altruism, conscientiousness, sportsmanship, courtesy and civic virtue.
2 It should be noted, however, that organizational free riding is quite similar to the types investigated by Marwell and Ames (1981). If so, employees will definitely free-ride but will be constrained in how much they do so by their concept of fairness.
3 It should be noted that the basic nature of game theoretic analysis (such as Leibenstein's) is quite different from the earlier analysis of suboptimal effort, which emphasizes positive externalities.
4 In functional form, the socio-economic model is as follows:

$$ORB = f(ECON, OrgIn, MSoc, EOI, OrgK)$$

where ORB is the individual's organizationally responsible behavior, ECON represents the economic or market incentives confronted by the individual in organizational situations, OrgIn represents the organizational incentives which generally counter the negative effects of the economic incentives, MSoc represents the macro social forces, EOI represents the micro social forces of the extra-organizational institutions, and OrgK represents the stock of organizational capital (pre-organizational and linking) that joins the individual to the organization. Given the ECON and OrgIn, the greater the OrgK the more organizationally responsible (ORB) will be the behavior of the individual. ORB will also be improved when MSoc and EOI encourage it, and ORB will be worse when MSoc and EOI discourage it.

5 In Wiener's view,

> The stronger the [organizational] commitment, the stronger is the person's predisposition to be guided in his actions by such internalized standards rather than by a consideration of the consequences of these actions. Thus, committed individuals may exhibit certain behaviors not because they have figured that doing so is to their personal benefit, but because they believe that it is the "right" and moral thing to do
>
> (1982: 421)

6 It should be noted that Leibenstein's prisoner's dilemma solution can be viewed as a special case of the socio-economic model developed here.

4 Rational organizational decision making in the human firm

1 For the purposes of theoretical clarity, it is assumed that the goal determination process took place prior to the decision-making process. Although this is logical and desirable, it may not always be realistic, as accounts of actual decision making processes attest.

2 Using Janis and Mann's (1977: 40) terms, a high degree of procedural rationality implies a low likelihood of miscalculation and postdecisional regret.

3 There are obviously certain situations where the mathematical techniques of operations research, statistical decision theory and systems analysis can be employed. "But these advanced procedures remain largely the appropriate techniques of relatively small-scale problem-solving where the total number of variables to be considered is small and value problems restricted" (Lindblom 1959: 80). In any case, these are by definition not the ill-structured decisions that we are concerned with here.

4 For a somewhat different contingency theory related to selecting decision strategies, see Grandori (1984).

5 Day and Pingle (1988) explain how introducing a cost of decision making into standard theory causes Pareto efficiency to be violated. They point out that in light of these costs bounded rational choice methods may be superior to "optimizing."

6 Using rules of thumb is not the same as using decision strategies to deal with large, complex decision situations. In Baumol and Quandt's (1964) analysis, rules of thumb are decision rules designed for routine and recurrent problems.

7 See also Janis and Mann's (1977: ch. 3) analysis which is summarized in a later section.

8 For an annotated bibliography of this literature, see Agor (1986: 149–77).

9 The psychic readings of the late Edgar Cayce provide decision-making recommendations. According to the readings, after proceeding through the usual decision-making steps involving reasoning, logic, applying good judgment and analyzing implications, the decision maker should meditate for the purpose of attunement. Then the decision maker should ask the question and should listen for the answer from within. Cayce's readings provide assurance that "there is no question we can ask that cannot be answered from within" (Puryear 1982: 157).

10 For a discussion of the meaning of self-actualization, see Maslow (1971: ch. 3).

11 For a list of the cultural characteristics of a really effective decision-making group, see McGregor (1960: 232–4).

12 Amitai Etzioni (1988: 145) considers decision making using intuition to be subconscious and automatic, and therefore, not rational.

5 Strategy and structure in the human firm

1 Corporate strategy differs from the terms, competitive strategy or business strategy, in that the latter refer to the product market strategies of particular business units. The term "functional strategy" refers to the strategy of particular functional areas, for example, marketing strategy.

2 In *The Economic Institutions of Capitalism*, Williamson (1985: 395) apparently acknowledges for the first time the quasi-integration alternative. He refers to it as the "quasi-market" alternative.

3 According to Granovetter (1985: 502–3), the existence of opportunism has little to do with organizational form and much to do with the "nature of personal relations and networks of relations between and within firms." Granovetter also finds fault with Williamson's view of natural selection: in Williamson's work, "the operation of alleged selection pressures is neither an object of study nor even a falsifiable proposition but rather an article of faith" (1985: 503).

4 In *Tales of a New America*, Reich (1988) refers to his ideal as "collective entrepreneurialism." While differing in emphasis, it is similar in many ways to flexible-system production.

5 Organizational failure occurs when despite the sufficiency of market incentives, the social influences on firms cause firms to fail to adopt the most economically appropriate organizational features such as flexible and integrated strategies and structures. These failures, if widespread in an economy, could substantially impair the nation's competitiveness relative to that of other countries. For more on this, see Chapter 2.

6 Beyond the machine model of the firm

1 The other three elements of Hawley's (1993: 12) management model are head, heart and body.

2 The right balance, B*, will differ among organizations depending on what stage of their life cycle they are in. For example, a recently started firm's activity may be largely entrepreneurial. For this firm, the right balance will be relatively heavy on the leadership side. For a mature firm, B* would presumably involve a much heavier dose of management.

3 Although the diagnosis of the U.S. economic decline in this chapter differs from the diagnosis of Chapter 2, the two diagnoses are compatible. While Chapter 2 focuses on the failure to adopt world class management methods, this chapter focuses, among other things, on the failure to achieve the right balance between leadership and management. Presumably, Z-firms with the desired balance

between leadership and management will be the ones that choose to replace obsolescent, mal-adaptive management with world class management.

8 The human firm and the natural environment

1 For a rigorous, systematic analysis of five types of regulatory incentives and their ability to promote technological change in pollution control, see Milliman and Prince (1989).
2 For information on a course being offered at Boston University, see Post (1990).
3 Subscribers to the CERES (formerly Valdez) Principles pledge to reduce their pollution, make sustainable use of natural resources, minimize waste creation, use safe sustainable energy sources, market safe products, take responsibility for past harm, minimize employee risks, conduct an annual public environmental audit, and put an environmentalist on the board of directors.
4 In functional form, the socio-economic model is as follows:

$$EB = f(MK, RegIn, OPP, CAP, MSoc, EFI, OReg)$$

where EB is the firm's environmental behavior, MK represents the market incentives, RegIn represents the explicit regulatory incentives, OPP represents the firm's environmental opportunities, CAP represents the firm's internal organizational capabilities, MSoc represents the macro social forces, EFI represents the micro social forces of the extra-firm institutions and infrastructures, and OReg represents the other regulatory influences. Given MK and RegIn, the greater the OPP and CAP the better will be the environmental behavior (EB) of the firm. EB will also be better when MSoc, EFI and OReg encourage it, and EB will be worse when MSoc, EFI and OReg discourage it.

In contrast, the neoclassical model is

$$EB = f(MK, RegIn)$$

The neoclassical firm's environmental behavior is determined only by MK and RegIn.

9 Beyond transaction markets, toward relationship marketing in the human firm

1 For these points, I am indebted to Chuck Brunner of Manhattan College's Marketing Department.
2 According to Regis McKenna (1991: 72), "in a world of mass manufacturing, the counterpart was mass marketing. In a world of flexible manufacturing, the counterpart is flexible marketing."
3 The reader should note that the managerial beliefs and practices known as total quality management (TQM) are a crucial ingredient in both the CIF and relationship marketing (Evans and Laskin 1994: 440–2).
4 Paradoxically, given a customer's switching costs, a buyer with increased patience might be more likely to switch because the return in the form of increased satisfaction from the new provider would be weighted more heavily over a longer time horizon. Of course, the return to not switching (and investing in RM) would also be higher.
5 In functional form the socio-economic model is as follows:

MkO = f(EconI, CustO, CAP, MSoc, EFI, Prod, Tech)

where MkO is the firm's marketing orientation, EconI represents the economic incentives from its markets, CustO is the customer's orientation, CAP represents the internal organizational capabilities of the firm, MSoc represents the macro societal influence, EFI is the micro social influences of extra-firm institutions and infrastructures, Prod represents the special factors related to the nature of the product, and Tech represents the technological opportunities available to the firm. Given EconI and Prod, the greater the Tech, CAP and CustO the more likely the firm is to choose relationship marketing as its marketing orientation. RM is also more likely to be chosen when the external social influences from MSoc and EFI are encouraging.

10 A new rationale for industrial policy

1 Further theoretical support for governmental intervention on behalf of industry comes from the "strategic trade policy argument." This holds that given increasing returns in an industry, implying that there is only room for a small number of profitable firms, government protection and support of domestic firms can deter foreign entrants and preserve the ability of domestic firms to earn returns in excess of opportunity costs, thereby raising national welfare at another country's expense (Krugman 1987: 134–7).

2 If the social rate of discount is lower than the private rate of discount, implying that society places a higher value on future benefits than the market does, the government could justifiably intervene to prevent underinvestment in the infant industry. The government would be intervening on behalf of future generations or others whose preferences are not reflected in the market.

3 The distinction between adaptive and generative learning is closely related to "single-loop" and "double-loop" learning concepts developed by Argyris and Schon (1978).

Bibliography

Adler, Mortimer (1985) *Ten Philosophical Mistakes*, New York: Macmillan.
Agor, Weston H. (1984) *Intuitive Management: Integrating Left and Right Brain Management Skills*, Englewood Cliffs, NJ: Prentice-Hall.
—— (1986) *The Logic of Intuitive Decision Making: A Research-Based Approach for Top Management*, New York: Quorum Books.
Akerlof, George A. (1984) "Gift Exchange and Efficiency-Wage Theory: Four Views," *American Economic Review*, 74 (May), 79–83.
Andrews, Kenneth R. (1987) *The Concept of Corporate Strategy*, Homewood, IL: Irwin.
—— 1989. "Ethics in Practice," *Harvard Business Review*, 67 (September–October), 99–104.
Anonymous (1995) "Companies Hit the Road Less Traveled," *Business Week*, June 5, 82–4.
Ansoff, H. Igor (1988) *The New Corporate Strategy*, New York: Wiley.
Aoki, Masahiko (1986) "Horizontal vs. Vertical Information Structure of the Firm," *American Economic Review*, 76 (December), 971–83.
—— (1988) *Information, Incentives, and Bargaining in the Japanese Economy*, Cambridge: Cambridge University Press.
—— (1990) "Toward an Economic Model of the Japanese Firm," *Journal of Economic Literature*, 28 (March), 1–27.
Argyris, Chris (1960) *Understanding Organizational Behavior*, Homewood, IL: Dorsey Press.
Argyris, Chris and Schon, Donald A. (1978) *Organizational Learning: A Theory of Action Perspective*, Reading, MA: Addison-Wesley.
Armstrong, Ellen. (1985) "Bottom-Line Intuition," *New Age Journal*, December, 32–7.
Arrow, Kenneth J. (1973) "Social Responsibility and Economic Efficiency," *Public Policy*, Fall, 303–17.
Auerbach, Paul. (1988) *Competition: The Economics of Industrial Change*, New York: Blackwell.
Baldwin, R.E. (1969) "The Case against Infant-Industry Tariff Protection," *Journal of Political Economy*, 77 (May–June), 295–305.
Baumol, William J. (1974) "Business Responsibility and Economic Behavior," in Melvin Anshen (ed.), *Managing the Socially Responsible Corporation*, New York: Macmillan.

Baumol, William J. and Blinder, Alan S. (1988) *Economics: Principles and Policy*, 4th edn, New York: Harcourt Brace Jovanovich.

Baumol, William J. and Oates, Wallace E. (1979) *Economics, Environmental Policy, and the Quality of Life*, Englewood Cliffs, NJ: Prentice-Hall.

Baumol, William J. and Quandt, Richard E. (1964) "Rules of Thumb and Optimally Imperfect Decisions," *American Economic Review*, 54, 23–46.

Beach, Lee Roy and Mitchell, Terence R. (1978) "A Contingency Model for the Selection of Decision Strategies," *Academy of Management Review*, 3, 439–49.

Bennis, Warren (1993) "Learning Some Basic Truisms about Leadership," in Michael Ray and Alan Rinzler (eds) *The New Paradigm in Business: Emerging Strategies for Leadership and Organizational Change*, New York: Jeremy P. Tarcher/Perigee, 72–81.

Best, Michael H. (1982) "The Political Economy of Socially Irrational Products," *Cambridge Journal of Economics*, 6, 53–64.

—— (1986) "Strategic Planning and Industrial Policy," *Local Economy*, Spring, 65–77.

—— (1990) *The New Competition: Institutions of Industrial Restructuring*, Cambridge: Harvard University Press.

Blake, Robert R. and Mouton, Jane S. (1969) *Building a Dynamic Corporation Through Grid Organizational Development*, Reading, MA: Addison-Wesley.

—— (1985) *The Managerial Grid III*. Houston, TX: Gulf Publishing Co.

Blanchard, Kenneth H. and Peale, Norman V. (1988) *The Power of Ethical Management*, New York: Ballantine.

Blinder, Alan S. (1987) *Hard Heads, Soft Hearts: Tough-Minded Economics for a Just Society*, Reading, MA: Addison-Wesley.

Bollier, David. (1996) *Aiming Higher: 25 Stories of How Companies Prosper by Combining Sound Management and Social Vision*, New York: American Management Association.

Bowen, Howard R. (1953) *Social Responsibilities of the Businessman*, New York: Harper and Brothers.

Bowen, Howard R. (1978) "Social Responsibility of the Businessman—Twenty Years Later," In Edwin M. Epstein and Dow Votaw (eds), *Rationality, Legitimacy and Responsibility: The Search for New Directions in Business and Society*, Santa Monica, CA: Goodyear.

Bradshaw, Thornton and Vogel, David (eds) (1981) *Corporations and Their Critics: Issues and Answers to the Problems of Corporate Social Responsibility*, New York: McGraw-Hill.

Buchholz, Rogene A. (1982) *Business Environment and Public Policy: Implications for Management*, Englewood Cliffs, NJ: Prentice-Hall.

—— (1988) *Public Policy Issues for Management*, Englewood Cliffs, NJ: Prentice-Hall.

Business Ethics (1997) "Company Watch," March–April, 6.

Byron, William J. (1982) "In Defense of Social Responsibility," *Journal of Economics and Business*, 34, 189–92.

Cavanagh, Gerald F. (1990) *American Business Values*, 3rd edn, Englewood Cliffs, NJ: Prentice-Hall.

Caves, Richard E. (1980) "Industrial Organization, Corporate Strategy and Structure," *Journal of Economic Literature*, 18 (March), 64–92.

Chaiken, Sol C. (1982) "Trade, Investment, and Deindustrialization: Myth and Reality," *Foreign Affairs*, 4 (Spring), 836–51.

Chandler, Alfred D., Jr (1962) *Strategy and Structure: Chapters in the History of the American Industrial Enterprise*, Cambridge, MA: MIT Press.

Channon, Jim (1992) "Creating Esprit de Corps," in John Renesch (ed.), *New Traditions in Business: Spirit and Leadership in the 21st Century*, San Francisco: Berrett-Koehler, 52–66.

Chappell, Tom (1993) *The Soul of a Business: Managing for Profit and the Common Good*, New York: Bantam.

Chatman, Jennifer A. (1991) "Matching People and Organizations: Selection and Socialization in Public Accounting Firms," *Administrative Science Quarterly*, 36 (September), 459–84.

Clark, John M. (1957) *Economic Institutions and Human Welfare*, New York: Knopf.

Clarkson, Max B.E. (1990) "The Moral Dimension of Corporate Social Responsibility," paper presented at the Second Socio-Economic Conference, George Washington University.

Cole, William E. and Mogab, John W. (1995) *The Economics of Total Quality Management: Clashing Paradigms in the Global Market*, Cambridge, MA: Blackwell.

Coleman, James S. (1988) "Social Capital in the Creation of Human Capital," *American Journal of Sociology*, 94 (Supplement), 95–120.

Coser, Lewis A. (1984) "Introduction," in Emile Durkheim, *The Division of Labor in Society*, New York: Free Press, ix–xxx.

Cuomo Commission on Trade and Competitiveness (1988) *The Cuomo Commission Report: A New American Formula for a Strong Economy*, New York: Simon and Schuster.

Cyert, Richard M. and March, James G. (1963) *A Behavioral Theory of the Firm*, Englewood Cliffs, NJ: Prentice-Hall.

Datta-Chaudhuri, Mrinal (1990) "Market Failure and Government Failure," *Journal of Economic Perspectives*, 4 (Summer), 25–39.

Davidson, Paul (1989) "Achieving a Civilized Society," *Challenge*, 32 (September/October), 40–6.

Day, Richard H. and Pingle, Mark A. (1988) "Economizing Economizing," paper presented at the Society for the Advancement of Behavioral Economics Conference in San Diego, CA on June 16, 1988.

Dean, E.D. *et al.* (1974) *Executive ESP*, Englewood Cliffs, NJ: Prentice-Hall.

De Geus, A.P. (1988) "Planning as Learning," *Harvard Business Review*, 66 (March–April), 70–4.

Dosi, G., Tyson, L.D. and Zysman, J. (1989) "Trade, Technologies, and Development: A Framework for Discussing Japan," in C. Johnson *et al.* (eds) *Politics and Productivity: the Real Story of Why Japan Works*, New York: Ballinger.

Drucker, Peter F. (1988a) "The Coming of the New Organization," *Harvard Business Review*, 66 (January–February), 45–53.

—— (1988b) "Management and the World's Work," *Harvard Business Review*, 66 (September–October), 65–76.

ENR (1990) "Industry, Environment Harmonize through Pollution Prevention," 224 (July 12), 28–31.

Etzioni, Amitai (1988) *The Moral Dimension: Toward a New Economics*, New York: Free Press.

Evans, Joel R. and Berman, Barry (1995) *Principles of Marketing*, 3rd edn, Englewood Cliffs, NJ: Prentice-Hall.

Evans, Joel R. and Laskin, Richard L. (1994) "The Relationship Marketing Process: A Conceptualization and Application," *Industrial Marketing Management*, 23, 439–52.

Franko, L. (1983) *The Threat of Japanese Multinationals: How the West Can Respond*, New York: Wiley.

Frey, Bruno S. and Foppa, Klaus. (1986) "Human Behavior: Possibilities Explain Action," *Journal of Economic Psychology*, 7, June, 137–60.

Friedman, David (1988) "Beyond the Age of Ford: Features of Flexible-System Production," in Frank Hearn (ed.), *The Transformation of Industrial Organization: Management, Labor, and Society in the United States*, Belmont, CA: Wadsworth.

Friedman, Milton (1962) *Capitalism and Freedom*, Chicago: University of Chicago Press.

—— (1970) "The Social Responsibility of Business Is to Increase Its Profits," *New York Times Magazine*, September 13.

Fuller, C.B. (1983) "The Implications of the 'Learning Curve' for Firm Strategy and Public Policy," *Applied Economics* 5, 541–51.

Grandori, Anna (1984) "A Prescriptive Contingency View of Organizational Decision Making," *Administrative Science Quarterly*, 29, June, 192–209.

Granovetter, Mark (1985) "Economic Action and Social Structure: The Problem of Embeddedness," *American Journal of Sociology*, 91 (November), 481–510.

Grayson, C. Jackson, Jr. and O'Dell, Carla (1988) *American Business: A Two-Minute Warning*, New York: Free Press.

Grossbard-Shechtman, Amyra (1988) "Virtue, Work and Marriage," in Shlomo Maital (ed.) *Applied Behavioural Economics*, Brighton: Wheatsheaf Books, vol. 1, 199–211.

Gunn, Thomas G. (1987) *Manufacturing for Competitive Advantage: Becoming a World Class Manufacturer*, Cambridge, MA: Ballinger.

Haberler, G. von (1936) *The Theory of International Trade*, New York: Macmillan.

Hamel, Gary and Prahalad, C.K. (1989) "Strategic Intent," *Harvard Business Review*, 67 (May–June), 63–76.

—— (1994) *Competing for the Future*, Boston: Harvard Business School Press.

Hamilton, A. (1961) "Report on Manufactures," in W. Letwin (ed.) *American Economic Policy Since 1789*, Chicago: Aldine.

Hampden-Turner, Charles (1988) "Three Images of Government: The Referee, the Coach, and the Abolitionist," *New Management*, 6 (2), 43–9.

Hardin, Garrett (1968) "The Tragedy of the Commons," *Science*, 13 (December), 1243–8.

Harrison, Bennett and Bluestone, Barry (1987) "Managerial Capitalism and the Economic Crisis," in Frank Hearn (ed.), *The Transformation of Industrial Organization: Management, Labor, and Society in the United States*, Belmont, CA: Wadsworth.

—— (1988) *The Great U-Turn: Corporate Restructuring and the Polarizing of America*, New York: Basic Books.

Hattwick, Richard (1986) "The Behaviorial Economics of Business Ethics" *Journal of Behavioral Economics*, 15 (Spring–Summer) 87–101.

Hawley, Jack (1993) *Reawakening the Spirit in Work: The Power of Dharmic Management*, San Francisco: Berrett-Koehler.

Hayes, Robert H. and Abernathy, William J. (1980) "Managing Our Way to Economic Decline," *Harvard Business Review*, 58 (July–August), 67–77.

Hayes, Robert H. and Jaikumar, Ramchandran (1988) "Manufacturing's Crisis: New Technologies, Obsolete Organizations," *Harvard Business Review*, 66 (September–October), 77–85.

Hearn, Frank (ed.) (1988) *The Transformation of Industrial Organization: Management, Labor, and Society in the United States*, Belmont, CA: Wadsworth.

Hickman, Craig R. (1990) *Mind of a Manager, Soul of a Leader*, New York: John Wiley.

Hinden, Stan. (1990) "Joan Bavaria's Crusade for the Environment," *Washington Post*, December 23, H1.

Hirschhorn, Joel S. (1988) "Cutting Production of Hazardous Waste," *Technology Review*, 91 (April), 52–61.

Huber, George P. (1980) *Managerial Decision Making*, Glenview, IL: Scott, Foresman.

Institute for Local Self-Reliance (1986) *Toward Pollution-Free Manufacturing*, New York: American Management Association.

Irwin, D.A. (1991) "Challenges to Free Trade," *Journal of Economic Perspectives*, 5 (Spring), 201–8.

Jackson, Phil (1995) *Sacred Hoops: Spiritual Lessons of a Hardwood Warrior*, New York: Hyperion.

Jacquemin, Alexis (1987) *The New Industrial Organization: Market Forces and Strategic Behavior*, Cambridge, MA: MIT Press.

Janis, Irving L. and Mann, Leon (1977) *Decision Making: A Psychological Analysis of Conflict, Choice, and Commitment*, New York: Free Press.

Jensen, Michael C. and Meckling, William H. (1976) "Theory of the Firm: Managerial Behavior, Agency Costs and Ownership Structure," *Journal of Financial Economics*, 3 (October), 305–60.

Johnson, C. (ed.) (1984) *The Industrial Policy Debate*, San Francisco: Institute for Contemporary Studies.

Johnston, Russell and Lawrence, Paul R. (1988) "Beyond Vertical Integration—The Rise of the Value-Adding Partnership," *Harvard Business Review*, 66 (July–August), 94–101.

Jones, Thomas M. (1980) "Corporate Social Responsibility Revisited, Redefined," *California Management Review*, 22 (Spring), 59–67.

Kanter, Rosabeth Moss (1989) "The New Managerial Work," *Harvard Business Review*, 67 (November–December), 85–92.

Kay, Neil M. (1982) *The Evolving Firm: Strategy and Structure in Industrial Organization*, New York: St. Martin's Press.

Kelman, Steven (1981) "Economists and the Environmenatal Muddle," *Public Interest*, Summer, 106–23.

Kemp, M.C. (1960) "The Mill-Bastable Infant-Industry Dogma," *Journal of Political Economy*, 68 (February), 65–7.

Kiefer, Charles (1992) "Leadership in Metanoic Organizations," in John Renesch (ed.) *New Traditions in Business: Spirit and Leadership in the 21st Century*, San Francisco: Berrett- Koehler, 174–91.

Kinder, Peter D., Lydenberg, Steven D. and Domini, Amy L. (1993) *Investing for Good: Making Money While Being Socially Responsible*, New York: Harper Business.

Kindleberger, Charles P. (1974) "An American Economic Climacteric?," *Challenge*, January–February, 35–44.

—— (1980) "The Economic Aging of America," *Challenge*, January–February, 48–9.

Kochan, Thomas A. and Piore, Michael J. (1988) "Will the New Industrial Relations Last? Implications for the American Labor Movement," in Frank Hearn (ed.) *The Transformation of Industrial Organization: Management, Labor, and Society in the United States*, Belmont, CA: Wadsworth.

Kotler, Philip, and Armstrong, Gary (1993) *Marketing: An Introduction*, 3rd edn, Englewood Cliffs, NJ: Prentice-Hall.

Kotter, John P. (1973) "The Psychological Contract: Managing the Joining-Up Process," *California Management Review*, 15 (Spring), 91–9.

—— 1988. "How Leaders Grow Leaders," *Across the Board*, 25 (March), 38–42.

Krugman, P.R. (1987) "Is Free Trade Passé?," *Journal of Economic Perspectives*, 1 (Fall), 131–44.

Kuran, Timur (1988) "The Tenacious Past: Theories of Personal and Collective Conservatism," *Journal of Economic Behavior and Organization*, 10 (September), 143–71.

Kuttner, Robert L. (1988) "A Progressive Labor Agenda After Reagan," *Challenge*, September–October, 4–11.

Lazear, Edward P. (1981) "Agency Earnings Profiles, Productivity, and Hours Restrictions," *American Economic Review*, 71 (September), 606–20.

Leavitt, Harold J. (1975a). "Beyond the Analytic Manager," *California Management Review*, 17 (Spring), 5–12.

—— (1975b). "Beyond the Analytic Manager: Part II," *California Management Review*, 17 (Summer), 11–21.

Leibenstein, Harvey (1976) *Beyond Economic Man: A New Foundation for Microeconomics*, Cambridge, MA: Harvard University Press.

—— (1985) "On Relaxing the Maximization Postulate," *Journal of Behavioral Economics*, 14 (Winter), 5–20.

—— (1987) *Inside the Firm: The Inefficiencies of Hierarchy*, Cambridge, MA: Harvard University Press.

—— 1989. "The Kibbutz: Motivations, Hierarchy and Efficiency," in Kenneth Button (ed.), *The Collected Essays of Harvey Leibenstein*, New York: New York University Press, vol. 1, 231–43.

Levi, Yair and Pellegrin-Rescia, Marie Louise (1997) "A New Look at the Embeddedness/Disembeddedness Issue: Cooperatives as Terms of Reference," *Journal of Socio-Economics*, 26 (2), 159–79.

Lindblom, Charles E. (1959) "The Science of 'Muddling Through'," *Public Administration Review*, 19, 79–88.

Lublin, Joann S. (1991) "'Green' Executives Find Their Mission Isn't a Natural Part of Corporate Culture," *Wall Street Journal*, March 5, B1.

Lutz, Mark A. and Lux, Kenneth (1988) *Humanistic Economics: The New Challenge*, New York: Bootstrap Press.

Maccoby, Michael (1981) *The Leader: A New Face for American Management*, New York: Simon and Schuster.

MacDuffie, John P. (1988) "The Japanese Auto Transplants: Challenges to Conventional Wisdom," *ILR Report*, 26 (Fall), 12–18.

Machina, Mark J. (1987) "Choice Under Uncertainty: Problems Solved and Unsolved," *Journal of Economic Perspectives*, 1 (Summer), 121–54.

Magaziner, I.C. and Reich, R.B. (1982) *Minding America's Business: The Decline and Rise of the American Economy*, New York: Vintage Books.

Main, Brian G.M. (1990) "The New Economics of Personnel," *Journal of General Management*, 16 (Winter), 91–103.

Makower, Joel. (1993) *The E-Factor: The Bottom-Line Approach to Environmentally Responsible Business*, New York: Tilden Press.

Malerba, F. (1992) "Learning by Firms and Incremental Technical Change, *Economic Journal*, 102 (July), 845–59.

"Managing Innovation" (1989) *Business Week* Special Issue on "Innovation in America," 104–10.

Mandel, Terry (1993) "Giving Values a Voice: Marketing in the New Paradigm," in Michael Ray and Alan Rinzler (eds) *The New Paradigm in Business: Emerging Strategies for Leadership and Organizational Change*, New York: Tarcher/Perigee.

Manne, Henry G. and Wallich, Henry C. (1972) *The Modern Corporation and Social Responsibility*, Washington, DC: American Enterprise Institute.

March, James G. (1976) "The Technology of Foolishness," in James G. March and Johan P. Olsen, *Ambiguity and Choice in Organizations*, Oslo: Universitetsforlaget.

—— (1978) "Bounded Rationality, Ambiguity, and the Engineering of Choice," *Bell Journal of Economics*, 9 (Autumn), 587–608.

March, James G. and Simon, Herbert A. (1958) *Organizations*, New York: John Wiley.

Maslow, Abraham H. (1971) *The Farther Reaches of Human Nature*, New York: Penguin.

Matsushita, Konosuke (1984) *Not for Bread Alone: A Business Ethos, A Management Ethic*, Tokyo: PHP Institute.

McCain, Roger A. (1988) "Learning by Doing in Capitalist and Illyrian Firms: A Control Theoretic Exploration," *Economic Analysis and Workers' Management*, 22 (1/2), 35–52.

McGregor, Douglas (1960) *The Human Side of Enterprise*, New York: McGraw-Hill.

McKenna, Regis (1991) "Marketing is Everything," *Harvard Business Review*, 69 (January–February), 65–79.

Meade, James E. (1973) *The Theory of Externalities: The Control of Environmental Pollution and Similar Social Costs*, Geneva: Sijthoff.

Milgrom, Paul and Roberts, John. (1992) *Economics, Organization and Management*, Englewood Cliffs, NJ: Prentice-Hall.

Mill, J.S. (1965) *Principles of Political Economy*, New York: Augustus M. Kelley.

Miller, D. Patrick (1994) "Investing with Your Heart," *Yoga Journal*, January–February, 51–7.

Miller, William C. (1992) "How Do We Put Our Spiritual Values to Work?," in John Renesch (ed.), *New Traditions in Business: Spirit and Leadership in the 21st Century*, San Francisco: Berrett-Koehler, 69–77.

Milliman, Scott R. and Prince, Raymond (1989) "Firm Incentives to Promote Technological Change in Pollution Control," *Journal of Environmental Economics and Management*, 17 (November), 247–65.

Mintzberg, Henry (1976) "Planning on the Left Side and Managing on the Right," *Harvard Business Review*, 54 (July–August), 53–61.

—— (1987) "Crafting Strategy," *Harvard Business Review*, 65 (July–August), 66–75.

—— (1990) "The Design School: Reconsidering the Basic Premises of Strategic Management," *Strategic Management Journal*, 11 (March–April), 171–95.

Mintzberg, Henry, Raisinghani, Duru and Theoret, Andre (1976) "The Structure of 'Unstructured' Decision Processes," *Administrative Science Quarterly*, 21 (June), 246–75.

Naj, Amal Kumar (1990) "Some Companies Cut Pollution by Altering Production Methods," *Wall Street Journal*, December 24, A1.

National Research Council (1985) *Reducing Hazardous Waste Generation: An Evaluation and a Call for Action*, Washington, DC: National Academy Press.

Norton, R.D. (1986) "Industrial Policy and American Renewal," *Journal of Economic Literature*, 24 (March), 1–40.

Nota, Bruna (1988) "The Socialization Process at High-Commitment Organizations," *Personnel*, 65 (August), 20–3.

Nutt, Paul C. (1976) "Models for Decision Making in Organizations and Some Contextual Variables Which Stipulate Optimal Use," *Academy of Management Review*, 1, 84–98.

Oates, Wallace E. (1990) "Economics, Economists, and Environmental Policy," *Eastern Economic Journal*, 16 (October–December), 289–96.

Okun, Arthur M. (1980) "The Invisible Handshake and the Inflationary Process," *Challenge*, January–February, 5–12.

—— (1981) *Prices and Quantities: A Macroeconomic Analysis*, Washington, DC: Brookings.

Olson, Mancur (1982) *The Rise and Decline of Nations: Economic Growth, Stagflation and Social Rigidities*, New Haven, CT: Yale University Press.

O'Reilly, Charles (1989) "Corporations, Culture, and Commitment: Motivation and Social Control in Organizations," *California Management Review*, 31 (Summer), 9–28.

Organ, Dennis W. (1988) *Organizational Citizenship Behavior: The Good Soldier Syndrome*, Lexington, MA: Lexington.

Oster, Sharon M. (1990) *Modern Competitive Analysis*, New York: Oxford University Press.

Ouchi, William G. (1984) *The M-Form Society: How American Teamwork Can Recapture the Competitive Edge*, New York: Avon.

Ozaki, Robert S. (1991) *Human Capitalism: The Japanese Enterprise System as World Model*, New York: Kodansha International.

Pascale, Richard T. (1984) "Perspectives on Strategy: The Real Story Behind Honda's Success," *California Management Review*, 26 (Spring), 47–72.

—— (1985) "The Paradox of 'Corporate Culture': Reconciling Ourselves to Socialization," *California Management Review*, 27 (Winter), 26–41.

Pascale, Richard T. and Athos, Anthony G. (1981) *The Art of Japanese Management: Applications for American Executives*, New York: Simon and Schuster.

Peppers, Don and Rogers, Martha (1993) *The One to One Future: Building Relationships One Customer at a Time*, New York: Currency/Doubleday.

Peters, Thomas J. (1987) *Thriving on Chaos: Handbook for a Management Revolution*, New York: Harper & Row.

—— (1988) *Thriving on Chaos: Handbook for a Management Revolution*, New York: Perennial Library.

—— (1992) *Liberation Management: Necessary Disorganization for the Nanosecond Nineties*, New York: Alfred A. Knopf.

Peters, Thomas J. and Waterman, Robert H., Jr (1982) *In Search of Excellence: Lessons from America's Best-Run Companies*, New York: Harper & Row.

Piasecki, Bruce (ed.) (1984) *Beyond Dumping: New Strategies for Controlling Toxic Contamination*, Westport, CN: Quorum.

—— (1988) "Extinguishing Hazardous Waste Liabilities: New Strategies and Old Fallacies," *Houston Law Review*, 25 (July), 855–76.

Pine, B. Joseph, Peppers, Don and Rogers, Martha (1995) "Do You Want to Keep Your Customers Forever?," *Harvard Business Review*, 73 (March–April), 103–14.

Piore, Michael J. and Sabel, Charles F. (1984) *The Second Industrial Divide: Possibilities for Prosperity*, New York: Basic Books.

Polanyi, Karl (1957) *The Great Transformation*, Boston: Beacon Press.

Porter, Michael E. (1985) *Competitive Advantage: Creating and Sustaining Superior Performance*, New York: Free Press.

—— (1987) "From Competitive Advantage to Corporate Strategy," *Harvard Business Review*, 65 (May–June), 43–59.

—— (1990a) *The Competitive Advantage of Nations*, New York: Free Press.

—— (1990b) "The Competitive Advantage of Nations," *Harvard Business Review*, 68 (March–April), 73–93.

Post, James E. (1990) "Managing Environmental Issues," paper presented at the Second Annual International Conference on Socio-Economics, Washington, DC, March 16.

Prahalad, C.K. and Hamel, Gary (1990) "The Core Competence of the Corporation," *Harvard Business Review*, 68 (May–June), 79–91.

Puryear, Herbert B. (1982) *The Edgar Cayce Primer: Discovering the Path to Self-Transformation*, New York: Bantam Books.

Ray, Michael (1993) "Introduction: What Is the New Paradigm in Business?," in Michael Ray and Alan Rinzler (eds), *The New Paradigm in Business: Emerging Strategies for Leadership and Organizational Change*, New York: Tarcher/Perigee.

Reder, Alan (1995) *75 Best Business Practices for Socially Responsible Companies*, New York: G.P. Putnam's Sons.

Reich, R.B. (1983) *The Next American Frontier*, New York: New York Times Books.

—— (1988) *Tales of a New America: The Anxious Liberal's Guide to the Future*, New York: Vintage Books.

—— (1990) "Who Is Us," *Harvard Business Review*, 90 (January–February), 53–64.

Renesch, John (ed.) (1992) *New Traditions in Business: Spirit and Leadership in the 21st Century*, San Francisco: Berrett-Koehler.

Robey, Daniel (1986) *Designing Organizations*, 2nd edn, Homewood, IL: Irwin.

Roddick, Anita (1991) *Body and Soul*, New York: Crown.

Rowan, Roy (1987) *The Intuitive Manager*, New York: Berkeley Books.

Rumelt, Richard P. (1986) *Strategy, Structure, and Economic Performance*, Boston: Harvard Business School Press.

Schein, Edgar H. (1978) *Career Dynamics: Matching Individual and Organizational Needs*, Reading, MA: Addison-Wesley.

Schein, Edgar H. (1988) "Organizational Socialization and the Profession of Management," *Sloan Management Review*, 30 (Fall), 53–65.

Schorsch, Jonathan (1990) "Are Corporations Playing Clean with Green?" *Business and Society Review*, Fall, 6–9.

Sen, Amartya (1977) "Rational Fool: A Critique of the Behavioral Foundation of Economic Theory," *Philosophy and Public Affairs*, 6, 317–344.

—— (1987) *On Ethics and Economics*, New York: Basil Blackwell.

Senge, P.M. (1990a) *The Fifth Discipline: The Art and Practice of the Learning Organization*, New York: Doubleday/Currency.

—— (1990b) "The Leader's New Work: Building Learning Organizations," *Sloan Management Review*, 32 (Fall), 7–23.

—— (1993) "The Art and Practice of the Learning Organization," in Michael Ray and Alan Rinzler (eds), *The New Paradigm in Business: Emerging Strategies for Leadership and Organizational Change*, New York: Jeremy P. Tarcher/Perigee, 126–37.

Sethi, S. Prakash (1975) "Dimensions of Corporate Social Performance: An Analytical Framework," *California Management Review*, 17 (Spring), 58–64.

—— (1990) "Corporations and the Environment: Greening or Preening," *Business and Society Review*, Fall, 4–5.

Shapiro, Benson P. (1993) "Close Encounters of the Four Kinds: Managing Customers in a Rapidly Changing Environment," in B.P. Shapiro and J.J. Sviokla (eds) *Seeking Customers*, Boston: Harvard Business Review Books.

Silk, Leonard and Vogel, David (1976) *Ethics and Profits: The Crisis of Confidence in American Business*, New York: Simon and Schuster.

Simon, Herbert A. (1955) "A Behavioral Model of Rational Choice," *Quarterly Journal of Economics*, 69 (February), 99–118.

—— (1957) *Administrative Behavior: A Study of Decision-Making Process in Administrative Organization*, New York: Free Press.

—— (1959) "Theories of Decision-Making in Economics and Behavioral Science," *American Economic Review*, 49 (June), 253–83.

—— (1976) "From Substantive to Procedural Rationality," in Spiro J. Latsis (ed.) *Method and Appraisal in Economics*, Cambridge: Cambridge University Press, 129–48.

—— (1978) "Rationality as Process and as Product of Thought," *American Economic Review*, 68 (May), 1–16.

—— (1979) "Rational Decision Making in Business Organizations," *American Economic Review*, 69 (September), 493–513.

—— (1981) *The Sciences of the Artificial*, 2nd edn, Cambridge: MIT Press.

—— (1983) *Reason in Human Affairs*, Stanford, CA: Stanford University Press.

Skinner, Wickham (1988) "Wanted: Managers for the Factory of the Future," in Frank Hearn (ed.), *The Transformation of Industrial Organization: Management, Labor, and Society in the United States*, Belmont, CA: Wadsworth.

Smith, Randolph B. (1991) "A U.S. Report Spurs Community Action by Revealing Polluters," *Wall Street Journal*, January 2, A1.

Smith, Adam (1937) *An Inquiry into the Nature and Causes of the Wealth of Nations*, New York: The Modern Library.

Stata, R. (1989) "Organizational Learning: The Key to Management Innovation," *Sloan Management Review*, 30 (Spring), 63–74.

Steger, Ulrich (1990) "Corporations Capitalize on Environmentalism," *Business and Society Review*, Fall, 72–3.

Stokey, Edith and Zeckhauser, Richard (1978) *A Primer for Policy Analysis*, New York: W.W. Norton.

Succar, P. (1987) "The Need for Industrial Policy in LDCs—A Re-statement of the Infant Industry Argument," *International Economic Review*, 28 (June), 521–34.

Sutton, Francis X., Harris, Seymour E., Kaysen, Carl and Tobin, James (1956) *The American Business Creed*, New York: Schocken.

Taggart, William and Robey, Daniel (1981) "Minds and Managers: On the Dual Nature of Human Information Processing and Management," *Academy of Management Review*, 6 (E2), 187–95.

Technology Innovation and Economics Committee (Environmental Protection Agency) (1990) "Permitting and Compliance Policy: Barriers to U.S. Environmental Technology Innovation," draft report and recommendations, October.

Thompson, John W. (1992) "Corporate Leadership in the 21st Century," in John Renesch (ed.), *New Traditions in Business: Spirit and Leadership in the 21st Century*, San Francisco: Berrett-Koehler, 208–22.

Toffler, Alvin (1980) *The Third Wave*, New York: Bantam Books.

Tomer, John F. (1980) "Community Control and the Theory of the Firm," *Review of Social Economy*, 38 (October), 191–214.

—— (1984) "Mortgage Redlining Behavior and Anti-Redlining Policy," *Journal of Business* (Manhattan College), 12 (Spring), 10–20.

—— (1986) "On Relaxing the Maximization Postulate: A Comment," *Journal of Behavioral Economics*, 15 (Winter), 17.

—— (1987) *Organizational Capital: The Path to Higher Productivity and Well-being*, New York: Praeger.

Tomer, John F. (1992a) "The Human Firm in the Natural Environment: A Socio-Economic Analysis of its Behavior," *Ecological Economics*, 6, 119–38.

—— (1992b) "The Social Causes of Economic Decline: Organizational Failure and Redlining," *Review of Social Economy*, 50 (1), Spring, 61–81.

—— (1992c) "Rational Organizational Decision Making in the Human Firm: A Socio-Economic Model," *Journal of Socio-Economics*, 21 (2), Summer, 85–107.

—— (1994) "Social Responsibility in the Human Firm: Towards a New Theory of the Firm's External Relationships," in Alan Lewis and Karl-Erik Warneryd (eds), *Ethics and Economic Affairs*, New York: Routledge, 123–47.

Tosi, Henry L., Rizzo, John R. and Carroll, Stephen J. (1986) *Managing Organizational Behavior*, Marshfield, MA: Pitman.

Vaill, Peter B. (1990) *Managing as a Performing Art: New Ideas for a World of Chaotic Change*, San Francisco: Jossey-Bass.

Vaughan, Frances E. (1982) "What Is Intuition?" *New Realities*, Spring, 16–22.

Walters, Kenneth D. (1977) "Corporate Social Responsibility and Political Ideology," *California Management Review*, 19 (Spring), 40–51.

Walton, Richard E. (1985a) "From Control to Commitment in the Workplace," *Harvard Business Review*, 63 (March–April), 76–84.

—— (1985b) "Challenges in the Management of Technology and Labor Relations," in Richard E. Walton and Paul R. Lawrence (eds) *HRM Trends and Challenges*, Boston, MA: Harvard Business School Press.

Wheatley, Margaret J. (1994) *Leadership and the New Science: Learning about Organization from an Orderly Universe*, San Francisco: Berrett-Koehler.

Wiener, Yoash (1982) "Commitment in Organizations: A Normative View," *Academy of Management Review*, 7 (3), 418–28.

Williams, Larry J. and Anderson, Stella E. (1991) "Job Satisfaction and Organizational Commitment as Predictors of Organizational Citizenship and In-Role Behaviors," *Journal of Management*, 17 (3), 601–17.

Williamson, Oliver E. (1971) "Managerial Discretion, Organization Form, and the Multi-division Hypothesis," in R. Marris and A. Wood (eds), *The Corporate Economy*, London: Macmillan, 343–86.

—— (1981) "The Modern Corporation: Origins, Evolution, Attributes," *Journal of Economic Literature*, 19 (December), 1537–68.

Winter, Sidney G. (1987) "Knowledge and Competence as Strategic Assets," in David J. Teece, *The Competitive Challenge: Strategies for Industrial Innovation and Renewal*, Cambridge, MA: Ballinger.

Yellen, Janet L. (1984) "Efficiency Wage Models of Unemployment," *American Economic Review*, 74 (May), 200–5.

Yoshino, M.Y. and Lifson, Thomas B. (1986) *Invisible Link: Japan's Sogo Shosha and the Organization of Trade*, Cambridge, MA: MIT Press.

Zaleznik, Abraham (1989) *The Managerial Mystique: Restoring Leadership in Business*, New York: Harper & Row.

—— 1992. "Managers and Leaders: Are They Different," *Harvard Business Review*, 70 (March–April), 126–35.

Zuboff, Shoshana (1985) "Technologies that Informate: Implications for Human Resource Management in the Computerized Industrial Workplace," in Richard E. Walton and Paul R. Lawrence (eds), *HRM Trends and Challenges*, Boston, MA: Harvard Business School Press.

Index

Page numbers in *italics* denote references to figures